P9-CQY-787

Handbook of Planning in Religious Education

Handbook of Planning in Religious Education

edited by

Nancy T. Foltz

Religious Education Press
Birmingham, Alabama

Library of Congress Cataloging-in-Publication Data

Handbook of planning in religious education / edited by Nancy T. Foltz.
  Includes bibliographical references and index.
  ISBN 0-89135-102-7 (pbk.: alk. paper)
  1. Religious education—United States—Planning. I. Foltz, Nancy T.
BL42.5.U5H36 1998
291.7'5—dc21   97–52020
                                                   CIP

Religious Education Press
5316 Meadow Brook Road
Birmingham, Alabama 35242-3315
10 9 8 7 6 5 4 3 2

Religious Education Press publishes books exclusively in religious education and in areas closely related to religious education. It is committed to
enhancing and professionalizing religious education through the publication
of serious, significant, and scholarly works.

PUBLISHER TO THE PROFESSION

CONTENTS

PART THREE
IMPLEMENTING PLANNING

FIGURES

EDITOR'S INTRODUCTION

Nancy T. Foltz

It was the first class of the fall term at seminary. It was a course in adult religious education, and a student in the back of the room wanted a definition of adult religious education. He was a rabbi who led a large synagogue and he wanted a precise definition of adult religious education. His pen was poised to write. My response to him was a question: "When you plan in your synagogue, when you develop leaders, when you initiate new possibilities for teaching and learning, are you engaging in religious education?"

In a planning session, a bishop who was reviewing a new book on the future of the church opened her comments with the statement: "What stood out to me were the words 'if there is time for the church.'" Watching the planning team, I was aware that a very serious statement had just been made.

I do believe that planning in religious education is not an option; it is a necessity. Religious education is about the entire scope of teaching and learning for a congregation. The ministry of every congregation is positioned to offer religious education that fits the need, the context, and the vision of a particular people. There may be time for the church; but it will be time for fearless leaders to boldly initiate change.

The greatest roadblock to the future of planning in religious education may be the professionals: pastors, rabbis, priests, and religious educators. Those who have heavy investments in the past are often the people who cannot see beyond what they have created.

We stand on a plateau of planning in religious education. Much of what we are offering is irrelevant. Standing face-to-face with leaders, we hear that there is little impetus to participate in religious life as we know it. Guilt and routine do not hold people when the messages make little sense. It is time to rethink (1) who we are as a religious people, (2) what we can offer the world, and (3) how we can make our offering available. Planning occupies center stage in this endeavor.

A dry, repetitive, uninteresting, 1950s style of religious education is not enough. We cannot settle for what we have done. It is time to refashion, reimagine, redefine planning in religious education. We need to speak a language that makes sense in a world that is desperately searching for meaning in life.

What we rethink and plan today will serve for a limited time. The planning window was once able to project for a decade. Now we focus on a one- to two-year window. If we develop a five-year plan, we expect to revisit that plan each year to make the necessary adjustments, given new information that was not available when the plan was formed.

Planning in religious education is about resilience more than stability. Planners who can work in times of turbulence and ambiguity are desperately needed. The call is out for leaders who can create new pathways, planners who know there are no long-term securities in designing ways for congregations to be faithful to God.

*   *   *

This book is a resource for professionals who in one way or another are engaged in planning religious education. It is divided into three parts. Part 1 offers an overview of planning in religious education and considers the critical elements of values and beliefs, and especially as they underlie the work in times of conflict. Part 2 identifies the boundaries for planning. Part 3 addresses the more elusive elements of implementing a plan.

PART ONE: ESTABLISHING THE BASICS

Chapter 1, "Planning in Religious Education as Making Midrash," uses the Hebrew term *midrash* in the extended sense of encountering and challenging religious education with a new set of questions and answers. Midrash as activity is explored for its potential to reimagine why and how religious educators plan. Nancy T. Foltz discusses why planning in religious education is critical to the future and how change and chaos are part of the planning fabric. This chapter suggests that a congregation's history offers clues to its present and its future.

Chapter 2, "Understanding How Beliefs and Values Affect Planning Today," introduces, from the author's congregational experience, the challenge of hearing conversations in which values and beliefs are blocking or expediting the process of planning. In our multicultural society, with its special interest in subcultures, congregations are characterized by complex beliefs and values. Douglas Alan Walrath encourages religious education planners to be inclusive, respecting differences in beliefs and values. By honoring differences and identifying common values, a congregation can design effective and inclusive planning in religious education.

Chapter 3, "Transforming Moments of Conflict and Forgiveness throughout the Planning Process," introduces ways of transforming moments of conflict into occasions of remembering the true values that underlie the work of religious education. Bradley Shavit Artson and Mark N. Staitman begin with the assumption that "conflict is an inevitable corollary of human interaction." Conflict is a basic element of change. Planners of religious education must prepare the congregation for conflict. The authors show how congregations in the process of long-term planning can turn stresses and disappointments, which are inevitably produced in the process of planning, into spiritual growth and deepened wisdom. The writers bring the abstractness of forgiveness and repentance into concrete and approachable examples central to understanding planning in religious education. The chapter concludes with an invitation to transformation through planning.

PART TWO: DRAWING THE BOUNDARIES

Chapter 4, "Knowing the Difference between Operational and Strategic Planning," opens with the question, What is planning? The clarity and detail of Paul M. Dietterich's work offers planners an opportunity to distinguish between operational planning and strategic planning. Since religious education decisions are made in the context of total ministry concerns, the author examines the broader question of what kind of planning approach is appropriate for a congregation. The two approaches—operational planning and strategic planning—are discussed in detail, including a unique management system for each.

Chapter 5, "Assessing the Needs of a Congregation," examines congregational needs assessment. Approaches are offered to guide planners in this time of multiple expectations. Gilbert R. Rendle challenges planners of religious education to remember that unless needs are assessed, planners are liable to repeat old programs, continue established groups, and choose the familiar, often being oblivious to the needs of the people the congregation serves and hopes to serve. The author offers models and techniques for understanding how to identify new audiences. Building databases and knowing how to use the information gathered are discussed, as well as the impact of assessing needs based on congregational size and a complex, changing culture.

Chapter 6, "Engaging Effective Planning Teams," begins with a slice-of-life conversation about religious education in a congregation. The dialogue with a planning team reveals why some teams are ineffective. Estelle Rountree McCarthy inquires into the nature of teams and what makes high-performance teams. The author surveys theories and practices since the mid-forties that have influenced the way religious educators view teams. Specific implications, characteristics, and guiding principles for engaging effective teams in religious education are offered.

Chapter 7, "Evaluating the Planning Process," offers ways to evaluate the religious education planning process. Trenton R. Ferro addresses questions such as, What is evaluation? Why should evaluation be done? What should be evaluated? He also looks at ways to evaluate planning in religious education. Numerous tables and examples illustrate the evaluation of planning in religious education. Making decisions about program components, procedures, and results of religious education efforts necessitates a clearly defined process of evaluating the religious education planning process.

PART THREE: IMPLEMENTING PLANNING

Chapter 8, "Inviting Ownership beyond the Planning Team," describes ways to involve the congregation in the planning process. Elizabeth Francis Caldwell presents a case study of three congregations within a ten-mile radius of each other that worked together in a program of religious education. The writer explores three phases: implementing the plan, maintaining the plan, and visioning beyond the plan. This chapter explores practical and theoretical ownership.

Chapter 9, "Imagining Religious Education Planning Anew," suggests that planning in religious education is more about resilience and periods of chaos than about stability and maintaining a sense of calm. Invisible fields are identified as starting places for planners. Nancy T. Foltz delivers a comparison between leadership characteristics of planning using two models: the new sciences model and the Newtonian model. Issues of change and transition are discussed as part of the landscape of planning in religious education. Planners are encouraged to be bold and daring in their planning efforts. Ambiguity and flexibility are centerpieces for religious education planners.

Each chapter includes research, theory, and practice. Each author furnishes citations that can be used as additional resources. This book is a guide to planning in religious education. We offer it to inspire and encourage professionals who desire to shape the future.

The contributors are all involved in teaching and planning religious education. The illustrations and examples they offer provide more effective ways to shape our future.

This book presents the essentials of planning to professionals in religious education. As they read it, they bring to its pages the experience and wisdom to make the necessary adjustments for their particular parishes. This book encourages religious educators to reimagine and redefine planning in religious education. This book endeavors to provide a new sense of energy for creating and implementing religious education in fresh ways.

Remember that there is no "right way" being offered in these pages. The challenge is to reduce religious educators' fear of failure and to increase their sense of experimentation.

Believing God has called us to serve, our greatest hope is that all religious educators will be able to risk enough and have sufficient courage to try what has never been tried, to do what has not been done, and to live in ways we have only just imagined.

WHY A BOOK ON PLANNING
IN RELIGIOUS EDUCATION?

Why is it that good people in leadership positions trying to make changes feel exhausted and done in by the very organizations they are trying to energize? Why is it that the larger the religious organization the harder it is to make any change that produces a significant difference in anyone's life? Is there a religious organization that has a handle on getting a single direction, mission, and vision? Knowing that most people and congregations avoid imaginative, intentional, integrated planning, how in heaven's name can leadership begin to make a dent in the ministry-as-usual mentality that seems to prevail? The hope seems diminished, the vision seems limited, and the dollars lock the gates to anything that is new and different. Why is it that we are suspicious of one another, leery of working together, and generally stuck in the boring and the inconsequential?

In my work as a planning consultant, I plan with a variety of religious groups, large and small. My intent is to learn what moves a group from incremental maintenance planning to quantum imaginative planning. What is it that excites a group so that implementing a plan is a thrill rather than an ordeal? The questions Margaret J. Wheatley raises questions for organizations that congregations need to address:

> Why do so many organizations feel dead? . . . Why does change itself, that event we're all supposed to be 'managing,' keep drowning us, relentlessly reducing any sense of mastery we might possess? And why have our expectations for success diminished to the point that often the best we hope for is staying power and patience to endure the disruptive forces that appear unpredictably in the organizations where we work?[1]

It does not matter whether we call it reconfiguring, reimaging, reengineering. This is a time of struggle, confusion, ambiguity, discontinuity, and basic frustration for professional planners in religious education. What once worked can no longer be assumed.

WHAT IS PLANNING IN RELIGIOUS EDUCATION?

This handbook defines planning in religious education as intentional decisions to forecast, create, implement, and evaluate the teaching-learning environment in light of a congregations' mission and vision.[2]

The language we once used is inappropriate. Looking for leadership that can provide stability is outmoded in today's cultural chaos. In fact, we need leaders who understand the importance of flexiblity and resilience in a time of change.

---

1. Margaret J. Wheatley, *Leadership and the New Science* (San Francisco: Berrett-Koehler, 1992), p. 1.

2. For more information on the history of planning in religious education, see pp. 487–89 in *Encyclopedia of Religious Education*, ed. Iris V. Cully and Kendig Brubaker Cully (San Francisco: Harper & Row, 1990).

Long-range planning betrays us unless we reexamine the plan on an annual or a semi-annual basis. Conflict is not to be avoided; in fact, we need leaders who understand how to bring conflict issues to the planning table so that planning teams can move forward together. The historical posture of avoiding conflict has not served the field well.

The strong, independent solo leaders of the past are potential roadblocks to our future. We need leaders who can anticipate, innovate, and demonstrate excellence.

I worked on a denominational staff for fifteen years. There were five educators who consulted with congregations. Each request was initiated by the local leadership. Some days were devoted to long range-planning sessions, and others were spent in problem resolutions. Many days were given to examining ways to meet religious education needs in the congregation and in the community. We were not a program. We were planners in relgious education who listened first and then entered the conversation and proposed possible directions.

After years of working in religious communities, I began to plan in other nonprofit organizations as well as in corporate settings. For eight years I have worked with a creative planning company as a lead facilitator in planning sessions. I have found that planning, whether for corporate America or for our religious communities, has many commonalities. One of the basic commonalities is the desire to balance our lives with healthy relationships and meaningful work.

APPRECIATION AND DEDICATION

As editor, I am grateful for the writers' endurance and their willingness to rewrite and to continue after what seemed to be interminable delays. The story of getting this project to press is probably the real story of planning. It included confusion, conflict, loss, and numerous other complications.

Writing is hard work. Without family and friends it would be impossible. My husband, Bob, read more drafts than he ever expected to. Our sons Nelson and Drayton and our daughter-in-law Chuck E. gave encouragment and support through their own creative work and their solicitous inquiries about "the book." To my friends and colleagues, Bardarah McCandless, Sherry H. Blumberg, Gil Rendle, Kelley Sacco, Po Sacco, and Barry Jackson, who were kind enough to read the drafts and offer words of wisdom, I am grateful.

It is always a learning experience to work with James Michael Lee, a publisher who cares about the content and the process. Without the support of Nancy Vickers, vice president of Religious Education Press, I am not sure the book would have made it to press.

This book is dedicated to Mary Alice Dody Edwards, my mentor and professor from Wesley Theological Seminary. She is an imaginative, creative planner who continues to challenge me. Many individuals are fine teachers, planners, and religious educators; but excellent is she who knows the learner, the content, and the process. Mary Alice Dody Edwards is such a religious educator.

AN INVITATION

This book is designed to give you an opportunity to address the topics in planning that need to be reworked. This is a chance to reimagine designing environments that invite people to participate in life-changing experiences. I am reminded of a wise rabbi who suggests that there is no difficulty finding persons who agree that the problems are urgent. "The challenge is to persuade them to join in the struggle for answers."[3] This book presents the very best of what I believe is necessary to recreate our future in religious education. Welcome to an invitation to imagine anew!

---

3. Neil Gillman, *Sacred Fragments: Recovering Theology for the Modern Jew* (Philadelphia: Jewish Publication Society, 1990), p. xxvii.

PART ONE

ESTABLISHING THE FACTS

1

PLANNING IN RELIGIOUS EDUCATION AS MAKING MIDRASH

Nancy T. Foltz

We too have to carve out our own new set of tablets. But we also know that we can never discard the fragments of the old, however inadequate they may seem to us. . . . we must refashion our new tablets precisely out of the fragments of the old. The Hebrew term for the process we are describing is midrash.[1]

"It's good enough! My life, my family, my profession, how I do what I do . . . it's good enough. For years I lived with that thought. Then one day I decided that it was not good enough." These words from a devout rabbi began a journey that changed his life, his family, and his ministry. No longer would he tolerate the expected, the usual. No longer would he put up with just getting by, with stopping before the extras were added. He was now committed to reaching for the excellent, for the extra, for what he could create. He would no longer simply react to events; he would initiate, he would be proactive. He would begin to refashion a new life out of the fragments of his history. He would be a midrash maker.

---

1. Neil Gillman, *Sacred Fragments: Recovering Theology for the Modern Jew* (Philadelphia: Jewish Publication Society, 1990), p. xxv.

A TIME OF MAKING MIDRASH

If religious educators only knew where to reach for the magical switch that turns an average leader into a passionate, focused midrash planner, the landscape of congregational life would change. Religious education would be understood as the implicitly and explicitly intentional creating of a teaching and learning environment. What captured our interest in this rabbi's personal story was his awareness of "it's good enough." He was numb to life; in fact, planning only occurred *after* something happened. Personally and professionally, he was a reactive planner rather than a proactive planner. As an adult with experience in seminary and then in a synagogue, he began to challenge his "family-of-origin notion" that "it's good enough."

It is a time of making *midrash*. This Hebrew term is "usually understood to be a reading of a text, but in an extended sense, it can also be taken as a reading of the world, of human experience. In this extended sense, myth and *midrash* share many characteristics."[2] They are shaped by the culture, and they share continuities and discontinuities as they move through history. They depend on a vital community that refashions the new by discarding what is no longer viable and then reusing the old fragments.[3] Each religious community has a myth. When a portion of that myth dies, there is a time of making midrash, a "remythologizing".[4]

During a time of midrash, leaders enter the painful experience of abandoning and recreating mythic structures.[5] Midrash is a time of encountering and challenging a whole new set of questions and answers which are understood against a backdrop of rich history.[6] Making midrash in this sense is a process of activity rather than an outcome. Making midrash is the struggle of examination, integration, and proclamation of something new, of weaving the threads of history into a new fabric.

Fragments from the old tablets are valuable connecting links from humankind's history, through the present and into the future. Wisdom is required to discern which fragments to keep and which to discard. The work of careful selection is done by the community, not an individual.

---

2. Ibid., p. 31.
3. Ibid., p. 32.
4. Ibid., p. 88.
5. Ibid., p. 89.
6. Ibid., p. xxvi.

Courage and wisdom are needed to separate the old fragments and to celebrate the new.

The "it's good enough" mentality is unacceptable in religious education. Assuming that religious education as we know it is good enough suggests a lack of awareness of and an insulation from the powerful forces that impact people's lives. Job changes and relocations, divorces and family stresses are affecting lives and raising questions about who people are in relation to work, about how values and faith are influenced by ever changing conditions. Religious education leaders shape environments and can invite all persons to participate in God's redemptive and imaginative unfolding of community engagement in this global arena. The beginning point is beyond the doors of the congregation. People live outside the facility of the church or synagogue. The starting place for planners of religious education is the population that surrounds and includes the congregation and beyond. For too long we have been in ministry "to our own" and have cared little for the needs of those who live in the shadow of the church.

The process of changing and rethinking religious education begins with some basic questions. What is religious education? Why do we give attention and energy to religious education? What is included in a plan of religious education? Why plan? How does the history of planning shape our future? Where do religious educators begin? Regardless of what planning process is used, these basic questions deserve the attention of all religious education leaders.

What Is Planning in Religious Education?
It is impossible to understand planning in religious education until religious education itself is defined. The intent of this book is to suggest that educator, staff, and leaders begin by defining religious education.

There is no "one way" of planning, no template for any congregation. The uniqueness of religious education lies in the initial ground plan, which is rooted in a congregation's history and experience. Once a definition of religious education is agreed upon, leaders can begin to explore a process of planning. This book offers the basic touchstones of planning.

The religious education theory held by a congregation shapes the planning process. Theory and practice interact dynamically as decisions are made in the context of the history, tradition, and context of a congregation.[7] Plans for religious education must be consistent with the congregation's history, its theory and definition of religious education, and its experience of planning. Without a carefully conceived plan, the basics of religious education, including aim, content, teacher, learner, environment, and evaluation,[8] are empty words floating in air that the congregation can neither own nor live.

Planning in religious education is a faith community's engagement in and active response to God's leading. The basic continuities of faithfulness are evidenced in the historical, imaginative, intentional, contextual, congruent response of God's people. Realistic plans build the congregational pathways to that which, without God's guidance and support, would not be possible.

Why Is Planning Important?

Many religious education professionals are not sure that anyone needs to plan. They trust that the whole religious education of a congregation will emerge somehow and that all the details will be cared for and a livable future will result without intentional participation from planners. But the fact is that planning takes an incredible amount of time, patience, imagination, collaboration, energy, and risk.

Religious educators have experiences and information that are vital to healthy living and can impact the world in a significant way. Planning is necessary to create an education and an environment that is coherent and imaginative, an environment that offers stimulation and energy for a congregation to be fully responsive and proactive as God's faithful people.

Knowing that each planner lives with basic assumptions that often surface during the planning process and knowing that collectively we may have assumptions that clash with those held by others on the planning team, it is wise to begin by articulating our assumptions about planning in religious education. The intent is to start the planning process by finding common ground. Each person is participating on behalf of the congregation.

---

7. For a complete examination of theory and practice in religious education, see Harold W. Burgess, *Models of Religious Education: Theory and Practice in Historical and Contemporary Perspective*, (Wheaton, Ill.: BridgePoint, 1996).

8. Ibid. Burgess used these six basics as the outline for his models of religious education.

What Are Basic Assumptions about Planning in Religious Education?

Start the conversation with the question, What are your basic assumptions about planning in religious education? This effort determines both the common ground—the places we all agree on—and the difficult terrain—what some take for granted but others oppose. For example, if one assumption is that "our congregation can add two part-time positions for youth and children's ministry within the next nine months," and a second assumption is that "all leaders are requested to hold the line on every expenditure for the next year," clarity is needed on what can and be a part of this specific conversation and what cannot.

Planning in Religious Education Is a Statement of Faith: Planning is about God leading a congregation. Leaders participate in the activity of God. Where a congregation has been, how a congregation views and defines religious education, and where a congregation sees God leading is included in planning religious education.[9]

Planning in Religious Education Is an Intentional Communal Effort: The purpose of planning in religious education is to be highly intentional in offering experiences of a faith community to persons for whom God is known or unknown.

Planning in Religious Education Is a Dynamic Process: Planning is a dynamic rather than a static process. A dynamic religious education plan is in motion—being created or implemented—is not completely finished and motionless.

Planning in Religious Education Is Shaped by History: Each congregation has a planning history in which the religious educator can find clues to unlocking the future. The congregation's past experience with planning and its ability to implement a plan is important historical information.

Planning in Religious Education Must Have Contextual Integrity: New planning must have integrity within the context of the congregation and its history of planning.

Planning In Religious Education Is Designed Around Needs: Canned, prepackaged programs will probably not work, even if we follow the

---

9. For more information on planning Iris V. Cully and Kendig Brubaker Cully ed., see K. O. Gangel's section on planning in *Harper's Encyclopedia of Religious Education,* (San Francisco: Harper & Row, 1990, pp. 487–89. Gangel suggests that "goals are statements of faith. They suggest what people might be able to do at a certain point in the future if God makes it possible." I suggest that planning is a statement of faith.

directions. Knowing how to adapt, modify, and rework a program to fit specific needs is a basic principle of planning. This is the artistic, culinary dimension of planning. The finest religious education plan needs a well-designed presentation so that the plan is perceived as balanced and enticing by those sitting at the congregational table.

Planning in Religious Education Necessitates Trust and Risk Taking: Building trust is essential for a risk-taking leadership team. Risk taking is essential in planning. The status quo and the unappealing deaden rather than energize. Planning in religious education is about rethinking, about imagining possibilities that are impossible at present for a variety of reasons. It takes a level of trust and the ability to risk being "right" to start the planning conversation about the what could be. Imagining a church without walls, considering learning needs that link religious education with community services takes some discipline, takes suspending judgment on whether or not the idea is right. Hearing new ideas and suspending judgment takes trust within a planning team.

One model for a planning process uses the analogy of a diver.[10] This circular planning process suggests a nonlinear approach (see fig. 0). Each of the four phases describes a particular group activity which may occur in different sequential patterns. The intent of this model is to be aware of the complete act of diving. No planning process would be complete without the diver's getting wet. Conversely, few divers would spring from the diving board without being sure of their ability to dive, the height of the dive, the depth of the water, and their ability to swim. Some planning teams begin be describing the vision of their desired future. Although the team may have a clear vision, the team will probably need accurate information about the present state of their religious education plan. Vision in particular does not appear on demand, and the planning team may find that one phase of the process emerges and overlaps another phase. This four phase circular model is one of many possible planning processes that can be used to guide the religious educator.

Planning in Religious Education Encourages Imagination: Breathing new life into what religious educators do best in planning requires

---

10. The video, Taking Charge of Change, available from CRM Films in Carlsbad, California, uses a diver image to describe William Bridges's change cycle. Change model adapted form William Bridges, *Surviving Corporate Transition* (Mill Valley, Calif.: William Bridges and Associates, 1992).

Figure 1.0
Diving Into the Water:
A Planning Process

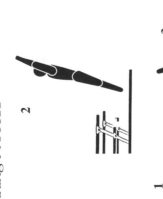

Phase 1: Climbing the Ladder

- Identifying the present state of what exists in environment, finances, structure, staff (internal and external)
- Stating the mission: who the organization is and why it exists
- Naming the core values: the central values that remain constant
- Selecting critical issues: statements supported by facts that need examination and possible change

Phase 2: Stepping to the Edge of the Diving Board and Looking into the Water, Describing What the Dive Would Be Like

- Describing the vision: the desirable future
- Recommending the changes needed to bring about the desired future: what action, by whom, at what cost, and when

Phase 3: Diving into the Water

- Implementing the desired future: actions, persons accountable, timeline, and costs in a sequence that brings the desired future into the present

Phase 4: Swimming Around

- Changing the plan: as the transition is made from a paper plan to a full implementation it is necessary to make changes which could not be foreseen when designing the plan imagination and creativity. One planning team began a Bible study series[11] showing a video on *The Lion King*, a metaphor of a relationship between a father and a son. Each section of the study included a segment of the video which was discussed along with the Bible. Visioning begins with immersing the planning group in imaginative experiences.

Planning in Religious Education Means Collaborative Leadership: Planning at its best is a shared, collaborative activity in which the religious educators who implement have opportunity to create and debrief what they have planned. Expediting the work of planning in religious education can mean working in small teams. Enlarging the conversation so that others in the congregation participate is often helpful.

Questions and assumptions that the congregation has about planning help religious educators get to know the lay of the land. Each congregation has a history of planning in religious education. Leaders bring their personal assumptions and experiences of religious education to the planning table. "Limiting Assumptions are things that we may be acting on as if they were true and that, as a result, may be limiting our possibilities."[12] Limiting assumptions identified by the Congregation Beth Am included: "The teachers we need to implement the kind of Jewish education we want are by and large not available."[13]

Uncovering a congregation's history of planning in religious education begins the identification of critical fragments necessary to make midrash. Questions can be used in sorting and sifting the precious fragments of experience and history out of which the new will emerge. Can you describe religious education in this congregation? What effect does religious education have in this congregation/community? What are the most memorable experiences of religious education? If one new idea could be introduced, which today does not exist in the plan of religious education, what would it be? If one element from the present plan of religious education could be eliminated, what would it be?

---

11. Vicki L. Gordy-Stith, "Mission Area Ministry Bible Study," The Peninsula-Delaware United Methodist conference transition team offered this Bible study as a part of their strategic plan. For information on the study, contact: The Peninsula-Delaware Conference, 139 N. State St., Dover, DE 19901.

12. Isa Aron, Sara Lee, Seymour Rossel, eds., *A Congregation of Learners: Transforming the Synagogue into a Learning Community* (New York: UAHC Press, 1995), p. 244.

13. Ibid., p. 245.

WAYS OF APPROACHING THE PLANNING
PROCESS IN RELIGIOUS EDUCATION

One synagogue begins by reviewing its history. Excellence in teaching has become a hallmark of the congregation. It is ready to expand an understanding of what it means to be a "learning congregation." The rabbi and staff are beginning to select a leadership team to examine the needs of the congregation and the community. The options at this stage of planning are multiple. The leadership team can select a particular approach that is consistent with the congregation's needs.

A congregation's history of planning may have a lock on its future. Picking the lock in order to open the gates of tomorrow remains a challenge for planners. This section explores five approaches to the planning process in religious education: (1) historic role of planning, (2) diagnostic questions about planning, (3) congregational profile, (4) arrogant assumptions and pregnant possibilities, and (5) imagining religious education planning anew—a holistic approach. These are just some of many ways planning teams can begin to plan—to make midrash.

The Historic Role of Planning in Religious Education

Planning incorporates the history of a congregation. It describes the present state of affairs and it anticipates the future in a proactive way. Planning in religious education therefore has three distinct roles to play. Each role is necessary for movement and change to occur. These roles are not invariantly sequential, meaning that once religious educators finish the first they may nevertheless go back to it.

The three roles are interactive, each intersecting with, impacting, and influencing the others at different times during the planning process. The three roles are "the was," "the is," and "the what can be."

Planning in religious education begins with a series of mental pictures. Imagine a photo album titled "Our Congregational Plan of Religious Education." The album is divided into three sections: what "was," what "is," and what "can be." Together these pictures reveal the congregation's historical pattern of planning in religious education, its present plan, and its hopes and dreams for the future.

The historical section of what "was" includes photos of leaders, study classes, changes in the building, outdoor picnics, curriculum, and minutes from the planning sessions. The pictures might be one

Figure 1.1
Three Roles of Planning

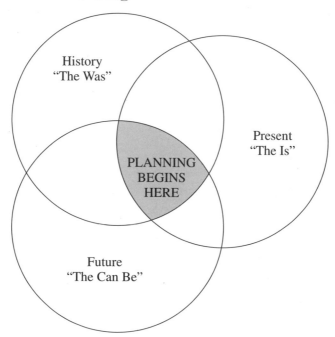

way of tracing the history of religious education planning. Another
approach might use personal interviews to gather accurate data about the
congregation's history of planning in religious education. Nevertheless,
planning begins at the "was" and the "is" picture. Accurate information
about the history of planning in religious education comes first and
establishes baseline factual data.

    The second section of the photo album includes the "is" pictures
for this congregation. The critical question is, What at present shows
the plan of religious education? These pictures reveal what is currently
included in the plan of religious education. There might be pictures
of bus trips to mission areas, cooperative soup kitchens, a thrift store
run by volunteers from the congregation, a literacy program, study
groups, worship settings, camping experiences, committee planning
sessions, and spiritual retreats. These pictures reveal an answer to the
question, What is the present plan of religious education? Interviews and

planning session minutes will also be useful in discerning the present reality.

The organization of the photo album reminds the viewer that there is a history behind the present pictures, a history that flows into the present picture of religious education. The final section of the photo album has some blank pages. Religious educators are challenged to make midrash, to bring some of the fragments of the past and present forward to form the new.

The planning team establishes where the three pictures intersect. Planning for the future begins at the point of intersection. How much history must be taken into the future? How does the present reality picture inform future directions? What current projections, studies, and trends will shape the future?

History and continuity are both vested in the human capacity to bring accuracy and clarity to the past and the present realities. Each of these three pictures provides baseline information on the history and the present plan of religious education. Momentum can be generated only when an agreed-on base is established.

Planning in religious education begins with establishing a common picture of the past and present plan of religious education. Disparate pictures or mental models of religious education undermine the creation of a future plan.

The intersecting circles (fig. 1) suggest three reasons for planning in religious education. First, information and experience from the past have potential to change the world. The historic role of planning in religious education is one of contributing to the future by honoring past tradition, history, and the integrity of a congregation.

The second reason for planning in religious education is that there are people who are looking for meaning in their lives. These individuals can be offered environments in which life-changing experiences are available to them. The role of naming the present reality gives a shared starting point. The "is" picture tells the facts of the present condition of religious education. An agreed-on present reality with historical roots can release energy to imagine, create, and design a plan of religious education for the future.

A third reason for planning in religious education is its prophetic role in the life of the church. "By prophetical in this context I mean hastening and advancing the future by introjecting what will be into

what now is . . . to make tomorrow's Incarnation occur today. Religious
instruction has as one of its main tasks the extension of the frontiers
of church, world and theology."[14] If plans of religious education use
outmoded approaches, leaders will be isolated and marginalized and
unable to offer meaningful contributions to congregations, communities,
and the world.

Diagnostic Questions about Planning in Religious Education

Another way to approach the need for planning in religious education
is to ask the following basic questions, encouraging the leadership to
reflect on the past year and to respond to each question with as much
information as possible:

1. Would the religious educator and/or pastor, priest, or rabbi want
   to participate in religious education events if that person were not
   in their leadership role? Reviewing the year's religious education
   plan, did the professional leadership long for, await with great
   expectation, and earnestly desire to implement at least half of the
   events?
2. Who encourages people to participate in upcoming religious education events, pointing out that participating makes a difference
   in people's lives? Describe changes in people's lives that can be
   encouraged, produced, or supported by religious education.
3. Does the pastor/religious educator regularly lead a religious education event? What are the ways a religious education leader models
   participation in religious education?
4. Describe specific differences that exist between this year's religious
   education plan and last year's. Five years ago? Explain why specific
   changes were made. Explain why some things have remained the
   same.
5. How does religious education fit into the overall ministry of a congregation? Think of the ministry of this parish as a drawing. What
   does the drawing look like? How is religious education depicted
   in it?

---

14. James Michael Lee, *The Shape of Religious Instruction* (Birmingham, Ala.:
Religious Education Press, 1971), pp. 309–10.

6. What is the mission and the vision of this congregation? Is religious education supporting the congregation's mission and vision? In what ways is the support evidenced?
7. How is leadership in religious education selected and supported? What is the plan to develop and enlarge the leadership base?
8. What will religious education look like in the absence of bold changes in the next five years?
9. What would the leadership like to see happen in the plan for religious education that is not happening at the present time? What is blocking change?
10. What characterizes a God-centered plan of religious education?

Questions such as these are annoyingly necessary. Asking these basic questions can clarify the definition of planning in religious education. Leaders have settled for too little for too long. If a number of persons ask these questions and record responses, the planning team can review the collective responses for insights.

Congregational Profile of Planning in Religious Education

Each congregation has an operational definition of religious education. Identifying the scope means gathering baseline information on what is offered as religious education (fig. 2a). Until this information is available it is impossible to know how the congregation has planned religious education. The profile that is drawn describes the existing work of planners in religious education.

A planning team clarifies what is included in religious education and what is needed for the future plan by identifying what a congregation has included in its planning of religious education. Gaps in religious education offerings are identified as the congregational profile is studied. These gaps offer valuable direction for planners.

Begin by defining religious education (fig. 2b). What is included and what is not included? Then proceed through the questions. This baseline information offers insight on existing gaps between what a congregation desires and what a congregation has.

Facts offer a reality that can be checked with a number of people. For example, using figure 3, write ten statements of fact about planning in religious education in this congregation. These would include statements

Figure 1.2a
Congregational Profile of Planning in Religious Education

Congregation's Name _____

Size of Membership _____

Avg. Worship Attendance _____

Religious Education Events	Age Range of Participants	Average Attendance	Length of Existence	Realistic Potential	Leader's Name	Length of Service	Purpose of Group	Hopes/Dreams for Future

Figure 1.2b
Congregational Profile of Religious Education
(A Description of Religious Education Events)

1. Define religious education. What is included and what is excluded?
2. Religious education events: Using the congregational profile (fig. 2a), begin in the left hand column marked "Religious Education Events" and list each event in the course of a year which this congregation makes available and considers religious education.
   You may want to separate congregation-wide events from those offered for specific age groupings: adults, youth and children. Be certain to include community wide events and the congregation's participation in judicatory and/or global events.
3. Age range: Beside each event indicate the age range of participants.
4. Average attendance: Indicate the average attendance of each event.
5. Length of existence: Write down the number of months or years this group has been in existence.
6. Realistic potential: If the group has been in existence for a year or more, it may be closed to new members. Be realistic in your assessment of the number of persons who can participate in this specific group.
7. Leader's name: Name the leader(s) who gives direct leadership to this group.
8. Length of service: Indicate how long the leader(s) has given direction to this group.
9. Purpose of group: Why does this group exist? What purpose does this group serve in relation to religious education?
10. Hopes/dreams for the future: What does the group itself hope to accomplish? What hopes do you have for this group?

such as "the last planning session in religious education was held five years ago." Use the information as a departure point for conversation about how planning is done and what changes are desired.

Arrogant Assumptions and Pregnant Possibilities
"The process of creating a new midrash almost invariably causes anxiety. First, it takes time. Second, it shakes up our familiar world of discourse and points to a new, as—yet—unknown."[15]

---

15. Gillman, *Sacred Fragments,* p. 105.

Figure 1.2c
Questions for Leaders of Religious Education
(A Diagnosis of Religious Education)

1. What insights or observations can we make about religious education
    given this congregational profile?
2. Does information in the events column give us any clues to the needs
    in religious education? How do present religious education offerings
    fit in light of the congregation/community and their needs?
3. What gaps are in ministry opportunities in the events column?
4. Does the age range column indicate that the needs of the variety of
    ages represented in the congregation/community are being met?
5. Does the attendance column indicate any changes (loss or gain of
    participants)? Are the reasons for these changes understood?
6. Into which events are new people coming? Are there cycles that tell
    why new people stay or why particular people leave?
7. Does the leader(s) column indicate that particular leaders are over-
    worked? How are leaders supported? Is there an intentional leader-
    ship support system?
8. How long has the average leader held that position?
9. How are new people finding places to serve and to be served?
10. How was the last new group started? Who was involved and what
    supports were offered?

"My congregation has no vision. I have tried to plan with my people,
but we end up doing the same thing year after year." It is impossible
to plan from the pew. If planners do not visit other congregations, do
not find out the needs of the people who live in the community, do not
experience other ways of planning religious education, how can the plan
change? Ask members of the congregation to visit other congregations
and inquire about how they do religious education planning. Generate
three basic questions that members who visit other congregations can
ask and bring back to the planning team. Imagining something new from
the pew in the absence of other people's experiences is difficult.

Changes need to be made in how religious education is planned. Planners may not be able to see the future clearly. They may not know how
to plan during chaotic times or how to work with leaders who have little
practice in collaboration. But planners know that what has been offered
as planning in religious education in the past is no longer sufficient.

Figure 1.3
Factual Statements of Present Reality:
Our "Is" Picture

The present reality of a congregation includes the most important information needed to understand life in this congregation. Reflect on your congregation/community and answer the question below:

What statements reflect a clear picture of the religious education in this congregation? Write eight to ten statements of fact about your size, location and members, and forces that shape planning in religious education for your congregation. If you were talking with someone who knew nothing about your congregation, where would you begin this conversation? Focus on statements about planning in religious education.

Statements of Fact About Planning in Religious Education: (Information about the congregation and community.)

1.
2.
3.
4.
5.
6.
7.
8.
9.
10.

Planning in religious education means that planners must read the future in Braille, navigate in constant whitewater, teach the elephants to dance, eliminate paradigms that paralyze. Whatever the image, the metaphor, the example, now is the time for new and imaginative planning.

Rich histories sometimes carry arrogant assumptions about the way life in a congregation has been, is how, and forever will be. Frequently pregnant possibilities never see the light of day because arrogant assumptions squeeze them out.

Arrogant practices need to be replaced. Religious education planners are doomed to repeating history instead of creating a pathway to the future if these arrogant assumptions are not challenged.[16]

---

16. Edward DeBono has written several books on creativity and unlocking the creative powers of the mind. *New Think* (New York: Avon, 1968), includes a chapter on arrogance and its powerful ability to keep the old in place: (chap. 6, pp. 113–26).

Nancy T. Foltz

What future does a congregation wish to live into? What changes
does a congregation intend to make? These questions make no sense
until planners ask, "What is making planning in religious education so
difficult? Why is the congregation unable to create the new? What is
blocking pathways to the future?"

Begin with planners and planning teams examining congregational
life and identifying arrogant practices and considering how these practices may be replaced with new, imaginative possibilities. Each congregation has a history that is told to the next generation. It can be instructive
to list descriptive information about planning over the past fifteen years.
Ask members about their participation in planning and note information
such as how was planning initiated, what kind of planning was done,
and what resulted from the planning effort.

Arrogant practices keep a congregation stuck in antiquated paradigms
of planning in religious education: Worship can only be meaningful at

Figure 1.4
History of Congregational Event Planning

Interval	Critical Events (name the event)	Notes on Planning (record what is remembered about the event include names and planning information)	Insights (gather the observations and insights)
15 years			
10 years			
5 years			

Insights and Observations:

11 A.M. on Sunday; all religious education learning takes place inside the synagogue; if the people around our parish wanted to come, they would; and we know the needs of our congregation and we don't need to study them. Each overbearing practice is touted as the way planning is done in this congregation. Arrogant ideas keep planners knee-deep in the mud of history, in old ways of planning in religious education. Planning is limited to minor changes, if any, in what a congregation did last year. Past memories hold the religious educators hostage. It is time to be bold, to be daring enough to know what to keep and what to release.

Three arrogant practices and corresponding pregnant possibilities are identified as examples for beginning the conversation about planning in religious education. Congregational planners may want to identify the arrogant practices that exist in their parishes prior to reading the ones listed below.

Arrogant Practice 1: We are locked into a patchwork mentality of planning: Planners in religious education focus on "children, youth, and adults" in formal teaching settings. Most religious educators plan in professional isolation, locked into a parts mentality and having decision-making authority over a segment of the full ministry.

Pregnant Possibility 1: We long for a seamless planning garment: Planners are responsible for the entire learning environment of the congregation—its inreach and its outreach. One congregation devoted 80 percent of their dollars, energy, and resources to their membership. The community surrounding the congregation was in transition and received little to nothing from this congregation. The building, which was large, old, and costly, consumed the congregation's attention.

The entire scope of religious education must be identified. What is and is not included in the definition of religious education for this congregation? When a religious educator's ministry is segmented to include only one age-group and when the educator is not included in the full planning for religious education needs of the congregation and community, the ministry becomes isolated, and age segmented. It is reduced to perpetuating a parts mentality religious education rather than a ministry of the whole. Buildings rather than religious education ministry needs can become the focus of attention.

Arrogant Practice 2: We are hearing impaired. Religious leaders are hearing impaired. Either planners have not heard the messages about planning in religious education or they have chosen selected pieces of information to use for the planning process. For example, many congregations are located in neighborhoods that are in transition. The needs of the people who surround the parish property are often overlooked. Religious education planners with a skilled listening ear are sorting and sifting through such difficult, complex, overlooked needs. Most persons are either speaking or preparing to speak; few truly hear.[17]

Pregnant Possibility 2: The art of dialogue leads to a path of discovery. Planning in religious education is more about listening than it is about talking. There is a cycle in dialogue that begins with silence. Silence is preparation for the experience of deep listening. Persons who assume such a posture become vulnerable. It is strangely true that "to have influence, you have to be influenced. That means you have to really understand."[18]

Some planners ask questions, wait for the other person to take a breath, and then enter by stating what can and cannot be done. Such low-level listening is not what is intended here. Dialogue necessitates the suspension of "telling" or "responding." This form of dialogue is about "understanding."

The depth of listening depends on the authenticity of the listener and the teller. Herein lies the challenge. Imagine in the planning session extra chairs where members of the congregation and/or unchurched people who live in the shadow of the church, and people who live in another part of the country or world would be seated. From time to time a planning session can probe the question, If these people in the empty chairs where speaking to us about our work this day, what would they would say?

Since planning in religious education is a collective process, knowing how to listen and participate in dialogue is at the heart of recovering and renewing a congregation's identity and its reason for existing.

One way of recovering the lost art of dialogue begins with each person's experiences, biographies, stories. Planners must be vulnerable enough to speak their own words and to hear stories that point to the needs of a congregation and world. What would religious education look like if planners included the skill of dialogue as a way of hearing the needs of congregation, community, and world? Surely there would be both delights of disclosure and discovery for those involved.[19]

---

17. Stephen R. Covey, *The Seven Habits of Highly Effective People* (New York: Simon & Schuster), p. 239.

18. Ibid., p. 243.

19. Thomas H. Groome, *Christian Religious Education: Sharing Our Story and Vision* (San Francisco: Harper & Row, 1980), p. 189.

Religious education planners work with one ear to the world of need and one ear to the congregation's living space. Knowing how the resources of these people in the faith community can respond to the needs in the world becomes one listening space. Congregations do not need more discussions. Religious educators need to develop their skills in the lost art of dialogue.

The properties of dialogue include an encounter for reflection and action, and a desire to transform and humanize the world. A dialogue is not one person "depositing" ideas in another, nor is it a simple exchange of ideas. "Nor yet is it a hostile, polemical argument between *persons* who are committed neither to the naming of the world, nor to the search for truth, but rather to the imposition of their own truth."[20]

Dialogue is a form of discovery. Planning in religious education can renew our capacity to listen and engage in dialogue. Paulo Freire suggests four basic requirements for this participative activity: (1) a profound love for the world and persons; (2) humility since reimaging the world cannot be an act of arrogance; (3) a faith that persons can reimage the world and a refusal to accept failure as the final verdict; (4) hope. Dialogue includes an awareness of being incomplete along with a determination not to settle for the absence of understanding and not to escape from the reality that must be faced. The last requirement assumes that participating in dialogue presupposes critical thinking.[21]

Religious education planners can initiate the art of dialogue as a form of discovering the needs of the congregation and the world. Dialogue necessitates a collaborative style of leading. Without the ability to hear religious educators cannot know why or what needs to be included in a plan.

One clergy group on a leadership retreat agreed to a dialogue on an issue that the group chose. Fifteen minutes was allotted for the full dialogue of five clergy. The group of five had ten minutes to hear the basic guidelines of a dialogue and to clarify their critical "issue" without actually having the dialogue. Once in the dialogue it was clear that few clergy had the skill of listening. Points were made, arguments were presented, few clergy were able to build on another person's idea. When the dialogue time ended, the reflection responses indicated that the clergy were

---

20. Ibid. p. 190. The italics represents a change from the original. This quote originally was found in Paulo Freire, *Pedagogy of the Oppressed* (New York: Seabury, 1970), p. 77. Groome, *Christian Religious Education,* p. 190.

21. Ibid., p. 190. Freire, *Pedagogy of the Oppressed,* pp. 77–81.

aware of how it was to listen, to give up trying to be right, to resist making a point. The second dialogue group greatly improved its listening skills and was able to hear one another and thus better understand an issue.

Arrogant Practice 3: We can use clever programs to combat our spiritual deprivation and suffering. Looking around congregational living rooms and watching people's traffic patterns reveals people who are worn out and meetings that accomplish little or nothing. Meeting preparation that is more frantic than thoughful, leads to stress and bewilderment as fruitless planning sessions continue.

Figure 1.5
Dialogue Is . . . Not[22]

DIALOGUE is for . . .
understanding
streams of meaning
revealing assumptions
discovering
participating
loving people and the world
humility
faith
hope
critical thinking
reflection and action
naming personal truth
a desire to transform and humanize the world

DIALOGUE is NOT for . . .
depositing ideas in others
persuading
convincing
positioning
defending
analyzing
arguing
telling

---

22. I drew information to create this figure from the following work on dialogue: Groome, *Christian Religious Education,* p. 189; Paulo Freire, *Pedagogy of the Oppressed*, pp. 77–81; and David Bohm, *On Dialogue,* pp. 1, 14–15, 33.

Who is tending to the spiritual life of leaders in the congregation? If spiritual life is not the centerpiece of religious education, what is? How can the spiritual leaders find support, care and restoration?

Where can people meet for prayer, Bible study, conversation, and reflection on their spiritual lives? How does attention to the spiritual discipline of Scripture study and prayer fit with programs, events, and overall planning in religious education? Knowing the health of and attending to the spiritual life of the congregation is critical in religious education planning.

Pregnant Possibility 3: We must address our spiritual poverty: What if religious educators were asking questions such as, How is your spiritual life? and What are the supports you need to keep your spiritual life healthy? Few religious educators deny that spiritual suffering and searching surrounds us. People hunger for ways to find meaning in their lives.

Planning in religious education must first be about congruity between the mission and vision of a congregation and the spiritual life of the congregation. Religious leaders are hollow without a strong spiritual discipline.

Books on male and female spirituality, caring for the soul, and creating spiritual workspaces are evidence of a thirst for the spiritual. Books such as *Iron John, Women Who Run with the Wolves, Care of the Soul, The Fifth Discipline,* and *The Celestine Prophecy* all demonstrate the insatiable desire for conversation about the soul. It is no accident that books such as *Five Challenges for the Once and Future Church* and *Discerning Your Congregation's Future* address the spiritual needs of a congregation.[23]

What are the ways to be attentive to the soul work of planning? The goal of planning in religious education needs to be discussed in each congregation. If, the goal is to nurture and develop faithful people, our faithfulness is lived out in the world becomes a congregational and individual response. Each congregation is challenged to care for the soul of its people.

If a camcorder were taken into the parish to record the ways leaders are attentive to developing the spiritual life of a congregation, what

---

23. Loren B. Mead, *Five Challenges for the Once and Future Church* (New York: The Alban Institute, 1996), pp. 32–42. Mead suggests that congregations have a "cool" spirituality and that one of the skills for congregational leaders is managing the polarities of spirituality between the needs of traditional spirituality and charismatic spirituality. See pages 36–42. Roy M. Oswald and Robert E. Friedrich Jr., *Discerning Your Congregation's Future: A Strategic and Spiritual Approach* (New York: The Alban Institute, 1996). See appendix B for a congregational health inventory.

pictures would be on the tape? If twenty people were interviewed from a congregation at random, how would each person interviewed describe this congregation's efforts in developing their spiritual life?

Perhaps it is time for congregations to take the miner's canary test. Coal miners, early in the twentieth century, would check the underground environment with canaries. If the canaries stopped singing, the miners knew that the environment was too toxic to breathe.[24] The early warning system of environments that are far from healthy need to be changed. For example, how are people encouraged to share their prayer needs? After Sara was hospitalized for depression, it was difficult for her to come back to church. Phone calls to let her know she was missed and that people were praying for her helped. Often, people encounter the depth of despair and sorrow alone because those who might respond are doing "other tasks" which might in the long run be much less important than caring for the spiritual life of people. Early warning signs that a person is in spiritual danger often go unnoticed.

A pregnant possibility is a seamless garment of planning in religious education. This garment includes staff and structure questions. Planners often want to discuss staffing issues: How many persons, paid or volunteer, will be needed? What does the organizational chart include? These questions need to be answered after a congregation defines religious education. A planning trap occurs when religious educators begin with a structure before anyone knows why that specific structure is desirable. The conversation on structure must be resisted until needs have been clarified. Religious education requires structures that support new visions and missions.[25]

When arrogant ideas are challenged and pregnant possibilities bring forth change, there is unrest, a time of chaos, a need for religious education planners to be resilient leaders. Effective planning can accommodate these changes when leaders are comfortable with the ambiguities and new variables that necessitate reworking, rethinking and redesigning.

---

24. Pat Barrentine, ed. *When the Canary Stops Singing: Women's Perspectives on Transforming Business*, jacket cover.

25. Mead, *Five Challenges for the Once and Future Church*, chap. 2, pp. 16–31. This chapter speaks specifically to denominational structures. Mead is stating what many already know, that the old structures broke years ago. Most congregations care little if denominational headquarters exist or not. Imagine the possibilities if denominational structures recognized their role of support for congregations in offering religious education to communities and congregations.

Using figures 6a and 6b, consider how the congregation has experienced change and transformation over the past five years. Fill in the columns, listing how each change was initiated and who participated and/or led the change. Take time to think about insights leaders have on the history of change as well as information on the outcome of the change.

When the pastor asked how the congregation decided to have "listening postsessions" in the community to hear persons identify their spiritual needs, she was told that Bernice and Edgar Hunting had a similar idea when the community was going through some difficult problems at the public school. An issue over the location of elementary schools divided the community. In an effort to bring people together, Bernice and Edgar suggested "listening postsessions," which were held in several locations of the community. Each session began and ended with prayer. Leaders were skilled in keeping the conversation open rather than closed. It has been seven years since the first "listening postsessions." Bernice and Edgar have been asked to explore ways "listening postsessions" could be used in the congregation and community to discern spiritual needs.

Religious education planners can learn from the history of change in a congregation and community. Planning is contextual to a people, to their history, needs, fears, and visions. Planning is fluid and dynamic. A new model of planning in religious education envisions planners who live trust and hope rather than fear and suspicion—planners who know the change history as well as the spiritual needs of the people.

Imagining Religious Education Planning Anew

Much has been written about the reengineering work of organizations which addresses outmoded systems and processes. This notion has value for are the motivating force for planning in religious education. What if planners considered starting over in religious education? What would reimagining or reframing planning in religious education mean?

Reengineering is about beginning again with a clean sheet of paper. It is about rejecting conventional wisdom and assumptions accepted in the past. When religious education planners search for new models of organizing work and invent new approaches that have little resemblance to those previously used, reengineering is at work.[26]

---

26. Michael Hammer and James Champy, *Reengineering the Corporation: A Manifesto for Business Revolution* (New York: HarperCollins, 1993), p. 49.

Figure 1.6a
Congregational History of Change and Transformation

Every congregation and congregational leader has experience with change. The world demands participation in change. Knowing how to participate is critical. Identify the congregation's patterns of participation and history of change over the past five years.

Reflections on Congregational Changes over the Past Five Years		
The change (identify what changed)	What prompted the change (how change was initiated)	Who participated (individuals and/or groups)

Insights on Changes That Have Occurred in the Past Five Years

Record insights on how this congregation participates in change. Are there specific groups or individuals who are involved in each change? Note how participation assists or impedes change. Is change initiated by outside influences or by internal factors?

Figure 1.6b
What Is the Outcome or Result of Change in the Congregation?

Change is sometimes painful and destructive and sometimes change challenges our faith. How is life of the congregation different because of these changes?

There are four critical terms that apply to reengineering: *fundamental*, *radical*, *dramatic*, and *processes*. The first word *fundamental* means asking the most basic questions such as, Why do we do what we do? And why do we do it the way we do?

The second word *radical* means uncovering brand-new ways of accomplishing the work of religious education, not incremental changes or adjustments: creating new procedures and structures that address the root of what needs to be accomplished. Making minor changes here and there in a planning process does not constitute a radical approach.[27]

Dramatic is the third word. Reframing planning in religious education calls forth the bold, risk-taking decisions that result in quantum rather an incremental improvements.

The fourth word is *processes*. What are the activities that relate to evaluating the effectiveness of religious education? What are the multiple ways our congregation identifies, recruits, develops, and supports new leaders? How will the needs of the congregation and community be identified?

Processes "are a collection of activities".[28] Generally, planners of religious education focus on tasks, on particular people, including their roles and responsibilities of ministry, as well as the structures. But they do not focus on the processes. What if planners in religious education used the reengineering model suggested by figures 7a and 7b? Note the sequence change of the four critical words.

Until a congregation knows what future it desires to live out, a conversation about structures is not helpful; in fact, it is an unnecessary energy trap. Premature conversation on structure does not give energy, it saps it. A congregation's mission and vision must be clear first. Structure supports this mission and vision.

Redefining planning in religious education involves a fundamental rethinking and a radical redesigning of assumptions and processes. Our intent in planning is to achieve dramatic improvements in our capacity to know why a congregation does religious education in a particular way. Congregations can be learning organizations. Planners can be passionately attentive to the needs of congregation, community, and world.

Our central intent is to be diligent in our desire to improve the way religious education planning in a congregation is reviewed, reconsidered, and reimagined. There are valuable pieces of congregational history that show pathways to the future. The essential work is to uncover the precious historical fragments of planning in religious education.

---

27. Ibid, p. 33.
28. Ibid, pp. 32–35.

Figure 1.7a
Imagining Religious Education Planning Anew

1. *Fundamental*: Why do we do what we do? Why do we do it the way we do?

2. *Radical*: What are new ways of accomplishing our work (our mission and vision)?

3. *Dramatic*: What bold, risk-taking decisions are needed? What three quantum leaps or fundamental changes could we make? If we created a new tomorrow, what would it include?

4. *Processes: What does it take to deliver what we offer?*

Figure 1.7b
The Present and Future Church

The Present Church		
People (name the current leaders)	Roles (identify each leader's position or role in the congregation)	Responsibilities (delineate each leader's two or three most crucial responsibilities)
The Future Church		
People (how many leaders will there be)	Roles (what the leaders will be doing)	Responsibilities (what results will be expected from the leaders)

What resistance will there be to changing present structures?

What structures will be needed to support what we want to create?

What present structures are no longer needed?

REWORKING THE FRAGMENTS OF OUR HISTORY

> The Passover Haggadah is both script and textbook: the *seder* table
> is both theater set and classroom; the rituals of drinking the wine,
> dipping the herbs, and eating, lifting, and lowering the *matzah*
> are both stage directions and experiential learning devices. The
> whole forms an elaborate pageant designed to teach the founding,
> or "master," story of this community to a new generation.[29]

Congregational identity is attached to the congregation's myth, its raison
d'être.[30] When the congregational myth is no longer accepted by the
faithful, there comes an invitation to examine the historical fragments.
Holding, touching and remembering the old gives insight, strength, and
courage to fashion the new. Planning becomes a time of holding and
examining the fragments.

Faith communities review and reformulate their stories—their historical myth. To work the fragments of congregational history is to
"remythologize," or to make *midrash*. Beginning this process of midrash
means visiting our historical record of planning in religious education.
Three ways of examining the precious historical fragments of congregational life include (1) root congregational stories, (2) congregational
event planning, and (3) congregational faith histories. Determining
which precious historical fragments to keep and which ones to discard
is part of this sometimes painful and confusing and at other times
exhilarating and refreshing historical search.

Root Congregational Stories

Each congregation has a core religious education planning story. "Our
congregation began as a German-speaking church. The stained-glass
windows in our sanctuary carry the story of our history. About fifty
years ago our congregation was on the corner of Smithfield Street about
four blocks from our present location. Actually, we own the land under
some of the major businesses in the city. Our ministry is to the people
in the city." From this root story emerge the central themes of history,
continuity, diversity in ethnic background, and an inseparable link with
the city. Knowing, respecting and working from a congregation's root

---

29. Gillman, *Sacred Fragments*, p. 230.
30. Ibid., p. 88.

story is another way to stitch the history of a congregation to the future.

A root planning story is the story told when religious educators are asked the question, How does this congregation plan and how does it live out its plan?[31] The process of planning is like the mortar, that which holds bricks together to create a solid foundation. But before one brick is placed next to another, those who will live in the structure need to design the space, imagining life in the space and creating it in such a way that it will not be outgrown prematurely or become boring. Imagination is needed to create the space that will provide "home" for the people of God. Invitational space is needed where new people are welcomed, but there needs to be confidence that the space being built will serve its purpose. What confidence do this congregation's leaders have in the brick-and-mortar work of planning?

Religious education has a historical role of relating stories.[32] Studying biblical stories can remind a congregation of God's participation in leading followers through complicated plans. Thus a major task of religious education planning is to integrate, remind, and connect stories that help a faith community remain mindful of God's full participation and activity in planning.

In Exodus 32–33, which describes the golden calf incident, Yahweh gives the "next steps" to Israel under Moses leadership. Israel's existence is viable only on the condition of God's presence.[33] The real crisis in this story is the absence of God's presence. God's presence is *similarly central* to planning in religious education.

Every congregation has a root religious education planning story. Hearing the root story helps planners understand how God's presence

---

31. This use of the word "root" was stimulated by reading Clarissa Pinkola Estes's work on root story. "A root story is one that contains a truth so fundamental to human development that without integration of this fact further progression is shaky, and one cannot entirely prosper psychologically until this point is realized." *Women Who Run with the Wolves: Myths and Stories of the Wild Woman Archetype* (New York: Ballantine Books, 1992), p. 167. This is not unlike Peter Senge's use of "core story" or James Fowler's use of "master story.' I think that congregations have a root congregational story that has many of the characteristics of core, master, and root story. The definitions of root are modified from the *Webster's Third New International Dictionary* (Chicago: Lakeside, 1966), pp. 1972–73.

32. Jerry H. Stone, "Narrative Theology and Religious Education" in *Theologies of Religious Education,* ed. Randolph Crump Miller, (Birmingham, Ala.: Religious Education Press, 1995), p. 272.

33. *The New Interpreter's Bible*, volume l, (Nashville: Abingdon, 1994), pp. 936–37.

is part of the planning. Each congregational root story shares certain characteristics (see fig. 8).

When religious educators ask congregational leaders how the plan of religious education is developed and lived out? leaders are requesting a walk down the lane of history. What is remembered and told often varies from leader to leader. There are some similar threads that planners can use to guide them in knowing how and where to begin.

When Noah began ordering the lumber and materials to build the ark, it was not raining. When Moses led the Israelites to the banks of the Red Sea, it had not yet parted. When Queen Esther requested that the lives of her people be saved, she had no guarantee that the king would grant her petition. These persons were planners. However, their approaches differed as much as the implementation they required. Once

---

Figure 1.8[34]
Characteristics of a Congregational Root Story

1. Roots are usually below the ground.
Root stories are usually below the surface of usual conversation.
This suggests that the planner must work to uncover this story.

2. Roots store food
Root stories contain substance to describe what
makes this congregation strong or weak in planning.

3. Roots are embedded.
It is not just the root story which gives planners
insight into the health of congregational planning;
but it is important to listen for what surrounds the root.
What is this root story attached to?

4. Roots are the source, origin, or cause of an action.
Life grows from the root.
What a congregation has planted underground needs to be uncovered.
The congregational root story informs us of a history.
A root story helps us to understand the present
and gives us ways of approaching the future.

---

34. This chart was developed out of the readings on root story, master story, and purpose story referred to in footnote 31.

you know about Noah's building of the ark, Moses's parting of the Red Sea, and the standard set by Queen Esther, you sense a different energy around these leaders. Why? Each leader implemented a plan. Effective implementation of a plan creates a story that people never forget. The story itself becomes the blood and tissue of the people. It becomes a root story—one that is told and retold.

Each new planning effort is started out of the last planning effort. Each religious education leader speaks on behalf of a people who are attached to a history. Participation in God's direction is the central dynamic in religious education planning.

Congregational leaders know their comfort zone when planning religious education. For some congregations, their language about their history makes the planner's work easier because there is clarity on the congregational definition of religious education. The planner knows what is and what is not included. Others speak more about their inability to follow through on the implementation of plans. In one congregation, a leader reflected that "maybe one of the reasons we have been ineffective in carrying out our plans is that we had no one designated to follow up on what had been decided. We come to meet and generate a lot of ideas; but we never designate any one person to take charge or carry them out." Many times leaders tell the story of their sadness about having participated in a great, uplifting planning session only to find that nothing was done after the planning day ended. *Each false start in planning makes the next effort more difficult.* Every time there is a disappointment in implementing a plan, people have a difficult time believing that things will be different next time.

Conversely, in congregations where religious education leaders plan and then fully implement the plan, there is high energy to engage in the next planning effort. Success breeds enthusiasm because there is stored confidence that time in planning is well spent. "Something of significance will happen in implementation" is the attitude brought to subsequent planning session.

Congregational Event Planning

Critical events such as annual gatherings, homecomings, and community-wide celebrations are some of the indicators of why and how congregations plan. When leaders discuss life together these events are usually the ones described. Planning may be designed around events, around the calendar year, or around some of both.

The history of congregational event planning information (see fig. 4) gathers basic historical information such as who in the congregation has carried the new ideas forward, how this congregation participates in the community and beyond, how is planning done by individuals or groups, what length of time can be planned, and what risks has this congregation taken? This information offers clues to the needs, interests, and experiences a congregation has had in religious education planning.

Congregational Faith Histories

There are many ways to observe the planning history of a congregation. Three specific stories of planning in religious education shed some light on faith histories. Referring to fig. 9, engage six or seven leaders in a conversation about the faith history of this congregation. For example, What was the faith taught in the congregation, community, family where you were raised? What was people's attitude toward persons of different

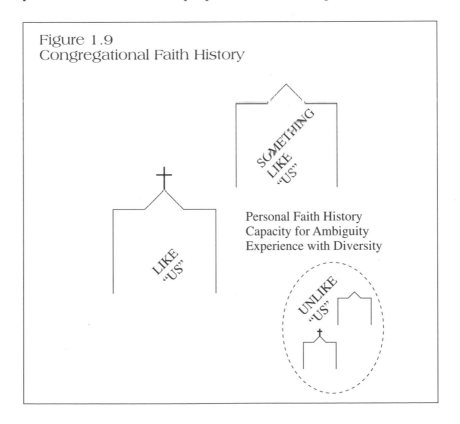

Figure 1.9
Congregational Faith History

Personal Faith History
Capacity for Ambiguity
Experience with Diversity

faiths? Were there conversations in your home, school, or congregation about persons with diverse expressions of faith?

Questions such as these can stimulate persons who hold different understandings of faith to share early experiences. These conversations may also hint at experiences with ambiguity and diversity.

"Like Us": The first congregation represents the root story of "like us." This suggests a homogeneous congregation characterized by harmonious values, beliefs, and lifestyles. People probably share similar personal faith histories thus limiting exposure to individuals of other traditions and faiths.

Outreach in planning will probably target people just like themselves. This congregation may be more interested in internal planning for the needs of their members. Outreach in this parish may mean sending dollars and support to mission areas beyond their geographical boundaries.

Planning in religious education encourages mind-expanding ideas and experiences. Dialogue and shared worship and/or work sessions will be most comfortable when conducted with faith communities something like their own. The capacity for ambiguity in planning and tolerance for diversity in faith histories and/or experience will probably be low.

"Something Like Us": This congregation plans for experiences with parishes that differ from it. The membership probably includes a range of persons who have faith experiences marked by some commonality, but it is more expansive than the "Like Us" group. Planning in religious education includes some ecumenical worship and service project experiences in the community and perhaps some projects outside the community. Dialogue with persons of other traditions and faiths is certainly a possibility.

Planning in religious education may also include short-term sessions on Eastern religions or other such studies for the purpose of expanding the information base. This congregational model suggests a moderate capacity for ambiguity and some experience with diversity.

Planning in religious education should be able to push the edges by introducing new opportunities for the congregation to experience both ambiguity and diversity and to have religious education experiences that include persons who have a faith that different from that held by most members of the congregation.

"Unlike Us": This congregation includes persons with a variety of faith histories who anticipate, await, gravitate to, and thrive on new opportunities in religious education. The possibilities range from taking

a large group to a mission enterprise somewhere out of the country to engaging in a long-term ecumenical project. The congregation's capacity for ambiguity and experience with diversity is probably high. New ideas can be implemented and the risk factor is not a major concern. The potential for return is not vested in proving that the event or effort is without risk.

Immersion experiences in religious education can provide new ways of viewing how a congregation is responsible for more than its own membership. Exchange weekends or weeks in the summer allow participants to experience different ministries across the community, country, and world.

In working with the continuing education leaders of the Jewish Theological Seminary of America, some of their rabbis have spoken of institutes that might include Protestant, and Catholic, and Jewish clergy; gathered for scripture study, professional development, and conversation on life stories. Such possibilities are encouraging because they would change the very way professionals might be open to planning in their own congregations. The richness of a diversity, once experienced, would create a thirst for more than a bland, homogeneous religious education plan.

One congregation is known for their work with community agencies. They have an area ministry that includes mentally challenged youth involved in renovation projects and "Green Thumb" workers (senior citizens helping in soup kitchens, retired people repairing equipment and lending medical equipment such as walkers, wheelchairs, and hospital beds). They have participated in swimming programs and adult education programs that benefit the community.[35] These ministries are expressions of faith—clear, concrete examples of actions that follow declarations of beliefs and values as a people of God. Planning of religious education includes a faith response.

A congregation that has rich experience with diversity probably has an equally positive capacity for ambiguity. A leader who is aware of this has a head start in planning religious education. There is no "better" or "best way" to do planning, there is, however, a way to plan that has contextual integrity. Study the history. Listen into stories that reveal the life of a congregation. Learn about a congregation's interest in, experience

---

35. "Connellsville, Still Caring" in *The United Methodist Review*, Western Pennsylvania Conference edition 13, no. 7, (March 1996): 1–2.

with, and probable capacity for planning in religious education. It is wise for planners to learn history before beginning to offer guidance in planning.

These three ways of examining congregational history are only some of the many avenues planners can take to gather the clues to the planning history of a congregation. Each clue is a fragment of the historical record of a congregation's planning life.

A COVENANT UNDER THE CANOPY

> There is no more central theme in Jewish self-perception than that of covenant. . . . it is the linchpin of the Jewish myth, that structure that Jews use to lend meaning to their experience in the world and to locate their place in the flow of nature and history.[36]

Covenants have been made between congregations and planners. Religious educators want to be responsible to the history and tradition of their respective congregations. Each congregation has a place in the flow of history; each congregation also has a desired future, a new space to live into. No longer can religious education ignore communities that live in the shadow of the church. Making midrash includes examining our historical covenant and our visionary covenant with God and our congregations.

Planning in religious education can create a new tomorrow. First steps toward the new plan must be taken. The skills, resources, imagination, and leadership necessary are vested in priests, pastors, and rabbis who are energized by creating the new and facing the unknown. Congregations that are ready to change will emerge, resurrecting and reimagining planning in religious education. Congregations that resist change will be left to live old forms of ministry, not responding to or attracting new people. Old leaders, old styles, old missions will soon be relegated to the past.

The Power of Making Midrash

The power in creating midrash is not "power over" but "power to."[37] It takes energy to uncover the layers of new meaning of religious

---

36. Gillman, *Sacred Fragments,* p. 41.
37. Barrentine, *When the Canary Stops Singing,* p. 33.

education planning. We can keep our covenant as a faithful community by recovering what is needed, and by creating new religious education environments. Layers and layers of possibilities exist. For example, some congregations have time-out houses for troubled teens and job clubs that support those who are unemployed. Some congregations have afterschool community tutoring ministries and "fix-it-up" resource people who provide assistance with small household repairs.

Finding vitality for planning in religious education means scanning the leadership for new configurations, images, glimpses of being mission and vision. Congregations in one area, are planning for "mission areas" that include several congregations in ministry to the population. Leveraging collective resources can offer people, buildings, and ministry efforts that would be impossible for a single congregation to duplicate. Every congregation may not be able to have a singles ministry or a food pantry; but six congregations working together can. Collaboration among leadership teams extends ministry strength into the community and the world in a way that does not exist otherwise.

The invitation for planning in religious education begins with the spiritual life—disciplined prayer and a commitment to read the Scriptures as if for the first time. New meaning frequently surfaces in the reading. In archaeological digs the earth is gently sifted and scratched for pieces of pottery, maybe a dish or a bowl with links to the past. This same spirit applied to Scripture uncovers new connections that can guide planners to create what is needed but does not yet exist. "Thus an ancient tradition retains its vitality in multiple new cultural contexts."[38]

Planning in religious education takes an enormous effort. Knowing congregational history and tradition sets the context for authenticity and continuity. The reality of the present time must be acknowledged.

A congregation's mission and vision clarify a congregation is and who a congregation called to be. Mission is the present ministry. Vision is the desired future. (figs. 10–12.) The old view of vision was that it created a destination. Vision was something that pulled the present into the future. Wheatley compares this notion with the old view of gravity. Instead of vision "pulling" what if vision were viewed as a field. Not a linear destination; but a field of vision that permeated congregational space.[39] If we are not called to be any different from this moment, has God's purpose been fulfilled?

---

38. Gillman, *Sacred Fragments*, p. 258.
39. Wheatley, *Leadership and the New Science*, p. 53.

There is a scene in *Fiddler on the Roof* when Tevye's middle daughter tells him that she is leaving to follow her beloved to Siberia. She and her father are waiting for the train to come when she acknowledges that she will probably never see her father again. The sadness of the moment is broken when she promises her father that she will be married under the canopy. This promise she gives as a gift to her father. The Jewish wedding canopy represents both the home that is created by the marriage and the whole household of Israel.[40]

The canopy metaphor supports a rich traditional heritage. The promise of planning in religious education may be to plan under the historical canopy. Since the canopy may have frayed edges, perhaps planning is a time of reweaving it, remembering its significance, and repairing the tattered parts.

---

40. Sharon Parks, *The Critical Years: The Young Adult Search for a Faith to Live By* (San Francisco: Harper & Row, 1985), p. 22.

Figure 1.10
Mission Statement

OUR MISSION

A mission discloses a congregation's identity and calling. For a congregation this means examining life together in this faith community, in this geographical area, in this part of the world. Determine if you are writing the congregation's mission statement or the mission statement of religious education. Either statement can guide a planning team in knowing what priorities and efforts are consistent with the mission. Complete the statements below.

When we describe our congregation we say that:

We are _____

The reason we exist is _____

Take these two statements and write ONE sentence in the space below. Remember that a mission statement tells who we are and why we exist. Make certain that each word is needed and that your words describe your uniqueness. If a mission statement is to be used and remembered it needs to be short, clear, distinct, and unique in describing your congregation.

OUR MISSION STATEMENT

Figure 1.11
Vision Statement

OUR VISION

A vision is the desired future. In five years this congregation will be different from what it is today. Changes can be made to create the future our congregation desires. A mission statement discloses a congregation's identity and calling, then a vision statement pictures what the congregation will be. A vision is what God calls a congregation to be in three to five years.

Each congregation has a reality picture of who it is as a congregation. Each congregation has insights and facts about what is changing in the world around the church. Congregations are called into the world to express their faith. Creating a vision statement is imagining the desired future and writing plans to live into it.

1. What does God call our congregation to?

2. What one fundamental change does this congregation desire?

3. What is one major improvement that could be made?

4. What do you personally and passionately want to make happen in the next three years?

OUR VISION STATEMENT

Using the most descriptive phrases from the responses above, create a one- or two-sentence vision statement defining the desired future.

Figure 1.12
Living the Vision

What does it mean to live in our mission and into our vision? What would it take for us as a congregation to create this picture of the future in the next three years? List ways of living into the vision. Each item you list is a potential objective for your congregation. You are answering the question, What would it take for us as a congregation to bring about the future we desire? (Be certain to use the vision statement on figure 10.)

1.

2.

3.

Creating our future is not easy. There is resistance to change and transformation. Fortunately there are supports and networks that can help as a congregation progresses. Review figure 3 for factual statements, figure 10 for mission statement, figure 11 for vision statement, and figure 12 for living the vision. Then generate the resources and supports needed to begin.

Resources needed:

Supports needed:

Getting started:

Change can overwhelm leaders. Be sure that you manage change so that it does not immobilize you. Take the first three steps. List those three first steps below:

	Describe the action	Name who does it	State when
STEP ONE			
STEP TWO			
STEP THREE			

What if planning in religious education were seen as both honoring the past and energizing the present? Instead of being viewed in linear ways, what if planning in religious education permeated congregational space into the community and the world? Instead of living into a vision, congregations would be surrounded, engulfed, and embraced by a vision.[41] Planning religious education under the canopy honors both the historical and the visionary. Making midrash under the canopy honors a remembering of the congregation's history and promises a refashioning of a desired future.

---

41. Wheatley, *Leadership and the New Science*, pp. 53–54.

2

UNDERSTANDING HOW BELIEFS AND VALUES AFFECT PLANNING TODAY

Douglas Alan Walrath

During the late 1960s I unexpectedly discovered how beliefs and values can affect planning in religious education. I found myself in the middle of an enormous argument. I had just become the senior minister of a large suburban congregation. Religious education was very important to the members of this church. Coordinating education had been the full-time job of one staff member with whom the congregation had become increasingly dissatisfied in the years prior to my arrival. The staff member left just before I came, and the religious education committee told me they wanted to move quickly to seek a replacement. Sensing a lack of consensus, I urged the group to slow down—to consider what they wanted the new director of religious education to do and what goals they wanted education to serve before they began to search for a new director. Many, but not all, members of the committee had been happy to see the previous religious education staff person leave. A minority was very unhappy with the majority who had "forced" a termination. I suggested that they identify and negotiate their differences before trying to choose another director.

As a first step, I proposed that the committee engage a local high school teacher as a consultant to help them set goals. I was able to assure the group that this person was very competent, since I had observed his work for many years. Though he was not a church member and had never worked with volunteers in a church, I was sure he could help. He was an excellent educational planner.

One month later I introduced Ralph, the consultant, to the committee. I then left the meeting, confident that Ralph would work his wonders. He stopped at my house over two hours later—about an hour later than I expected. The evening had not been a success. Ralph had begun the meeting by asking the committee, "What is your curriculum?"

The committee stared blankly in response. Then one committee member replied, "We use the Faith and Life curriculum" and held up a couple of books.

"Those are materials, resources, not your curriculum," Ralph responded. More blank stares. Obviously they had no understanding of a curriculum in general or of a religious curriculum in particular. So, Ralph continued, "I tried to help the group by offering some leading questions, such as, 'If everything works as you want it to work, what will happen to those who go through the church school? What will the learners learn? What will they be equipped to do? The answer to those questions is your curriculum.' "[1] "Did your suggestion help to resolve the dilemma?" I asked. "No," Ralph said, "it launched a terrible conflict! They argued for almost two hours, and didn't resolve anything. We finally just quit because everybody was too tired to go on. I can see why the previous staff person was frustrated; the members of that committee are miles apart. The older members want the church school to teach children 'what the Bible says' so that they will have 'sound moral values.' It's obvious that they are very troubled by the questioning nature of contemporary children. They think the core problem is that 'kids today need more discipline.' As one of them put it, 'Children won't learn what they need to learn until they are made to sit still and listen.' At this point it was clear that when this group spoke of learners they meant children. Their view of religious education included children only; adults and youth were not a part of their conversation.

"Their comments really set off some other members of the committee. Members of that faction wanted those who participated in the religious education program, which they refer to as 'the church school,' 'to learn

---

1. For an examination of the classic expressions of religious education, see Mary C. Boys, *Educating in Faith: Maps and Visions* (San Francisco: Harper & Row, 1989), pp. 9–10. The matrix analysis offers classic expressions of religious education and foundational questions for planners.

how to think critically about what they believe.' They thought children should be encouraged to question. They would even give students a role in defining the curriculum, basing the curriculum on questions students are asking. As one of them put it, 'There's no sense in answering a lot of question no one's asking.' "

"That statement moved one of the traditionalists to begin a long speech about the need 'to protect our children from growing secularism until they are mature enough to protect themselves.' "

"A younger woman, obviously a social activist, proposed that church school should 'equip us to stand up for our faith; it should prepare us to join with others to protest against injustice.' Frankly, it's hard for me to believe these people all belong to the same church," Ralph concluded.

It had been a very difficult evening for my friend. But he agreed to meet with the committee once more in two weeks to try to help them set goals. That meeting produced agreement on one point: the differences that separated the factions were not negotiable. They never did resolve their disagreements. The committee was able to set goals and write a job description after two more meetings because the younger and more liberal members gave up and withdrew.

FROM THE RIGHT WAY TO MANY WAYS

Experiences such as the one with the religious education committee set me on a quest for understanding the complexities of planning in religious education. That quest is described in the book *Frameworks: Patterns of Living and Believing Today*.[2] Within a decade the multicultural encounters came to dominate our society.[3]

In those first years of the "social revolution," few of us anticipated the difficult exchanges between different social, generational, ethnic,

---

2. Douglas Alan Walrath, *Frameworks: Pattern of Living and Believing Today* (New York: Pilgrim, 1987). This book includes a thorough discussion of the three different cohorts: Strivers, Challengers and Calculators. Planning in religious education is more able to meet the faith needs for these cohorts when planners are aware of specific distinctions.

3. In *Harper's Encyclopedia of Religious Education,* ed. Iris V. Cully and Kendig Brubaker Cully (San Francisco: Harper & Row, 1990), pp. 431–34, multicultural religious education is defined as "the infusion of the traditions of ethnically diverse people into religious curricula and educational settings." The charts on pages 432–433 describe age-groups, their level of understanding, and teaching activities that are appropriate in multicultural religious education.

and religious groups that are now a fact of daily life. What distinguished those young adults on that religious education committee from the young adults of previous generations was their refusal to abandon their own perspectives and adopt those of their elders. When the older members who dominated the committee refused to grant validity to the young adults' alternative perspectives, they left. That was different. A host of books written during the 1970s, 1980s and 1990s seek to clarify that difference.[4] Basic principles of planning in religious education were emerging. Those young adults made one principle abundantly clear: they would "vote with their feet" when their beliefs and values were not taken into account.[5] When the committee was unable to resolve the differences they left.

As a child I assumed I would learn how the world worked from adults who already knew how it worked. I was not always a willing learner. I challenged and I questioned, especially when I was an adolescent. But deep down I always believed that the adults around me were probably right. The majority of my peers rebelled similarly. But it was just a phase. Once we passed through it we "came around." We adopted most of the beliefs and lifeways of our elders. We became adults who went to work, got married, joined churches, and had children, whom we then brought to churches or synagogues. We had every reason to believe that they would someday adopt the same beliefs and values that we had received from our parents.

In the context of this chapter the word "belief" refers to a common "framework" of perspectives through which an individual views and approaches living and believing.[6] An individual or group's belief provides a perspective on seeing the world.

Viewing the world in a particular way from a specific vantage point creates choices. "Value" as used in this chapter refers to personal or group preferences. "Values" are the activities, and experiences, that a

---

4. Some of the major works are summarized in *Frameworks*. Important works published since that book appeared include Wade Clark Roof and William McKinney, *American Mainline Religion: Its Changing Shape and Future* (New Brunswick, N.J.: Rutgers University Press, 1987), which appeared in the same year as *Frameworks*, and more recently Wade Clark Roof, *A Generation of Seekers* (San Francisco: Harper San Francisco, 1993).

5. Leon McKenzie, *The Religious Education of Adults* (Birmingham, Ala.: Religious Education Press, 1982), p. 220.

6. The use of the term "belief" in religious education has changed significantly. For a summary of the changes, see *Harper's Encyclopedia of Religious Education*, pp. 58–59.

person or group deems desirable, worthwhile, preferred.[7] People make these choices consistent with their beliefs. If beliefs are the framework, then values are the preferences.

The connection between "framework" and "preference" is based on a value system that influences participation in religious education. Each person carries both a "framework," a perspective on religious education, and a preference or a "value" attached to the options, say, the options a congregation offers in religious education. Planning in religious education challenges us to understand and anticipate differences based on these various beliefs and values.

Once my peers and I agree to fit in, few of us examined or questioned the basic validity of our beliefs and values. Our beliefs formed our framework and our values were our preferences. For us doubt was a "problem" to be resolved. The few among us who doubted sought help to believe again. Our religion, like our culture, was singular, dominant, cohesive, and normative.

When the baby boomers brought their basic challenge to everything that culture stood on and stood for—church, faith, marriage, work— everything at the core of "our way of life," the rest of us, my peers and I, were understandably shaken. Perhaps our greatest surprise was in the refusal to back down and fit in. Baby boomers are the most educated generation in history. As adults, they change jobs more frequently then preceding generations.[8] Baby Boomers believe that they have the right to examine everything critically, to make their own evaluations, even to redefine basic beliefs and values (what God is like, what purposes religious education in churches or synagogues should serve, what marriage is supposed to be). The baby boom generation brought about a fundamental transition in American society.[9] American society became multicultural. What began as a counterculture became

---

7. The term "values" has multiple uses in religious education. For a discussion of values and values in education, see *Harper's Encyclopedia of Religious Education*, pp. 678–79.

8. For a discussion on the new directions for the 1990s, see John Naisbitt and Patricia Aburdene, *Megatrends 2000: Ten New Directions For the 1990s* (New York: William Morrow, 1990), pp. 63, 221.

9. Tex Sample in *U.S. Lifestyles and Mainline Churches*, (Louisville: Westminster/John Knox, 1990) discusses the cultural map of America. Sample addresses social diversity and offers imaginative ways of approaching the diversity. He also discusses baby boomers and their economic struggles. See pages 19, 50.

established as an alternate culture and then proliferated into a variety of subcultures.[10]

Members of the baby boom generation became what sociologists call a "cohort." They are seventy million people who were born between 1946 and 1964.[11] Members of a cohort not only "see things differently" during a rebellious phase in their lives; they believe in their different vision *and persist in it*. They believe in the reality of their experience and order their lives accordingly. They trust mostly, or, often, only the accuracy of their vision and the perspective of those who share it. They put little trust in the perspectives of those who are not members of their cohort. They are a culture in time.

Members of a cohort reject the notion that their experiences at various stages of life are similar to the experiences of those who have preceded them. Margaret Mead captures the rationale for this rejection when she writes that older persons with a traditional perspective have long cautioned members of "the younger generation" with words like "You know, I have been young, but you have never been old." But members of the baby boom cohort challenge their elders: "You never have been young in the world I am young in, and you never can be."[12] Their response is worth pondering.

"When the world changes radically, human beings encounter radically different experiences as they pass through the same developmental stages of life."[13] As a result they experience a solidarity with one another that they do not experience with others. Slang that arose during the 1960s expresses this reality. Questions like Are you with it? and Do you read me? help members of a cohort identify those who understand and those who do not. Those who are not "with it" are "out of it." As members of the new cohort continue to encounter qualitatively different experiences at successive stages of life, their feelings of alienation from the general society are confirmed.

Contemporary comic strips that speak to members of different cohorts reflect the multicultural reality of our present society. Blondie and

---

10. For a discussion on the self-fulfillment ethic associated with baby boomers, see Sample, *Lifestyles and Mainline Churches,* pp. 14–19. See Kirk McNeill and Robert Paul, *Reaching for the Baby Boomers Workbook* (Nashville: General Board of Discipleship, 1989), pp. 7–10, for information on demographics.

11. Sharan B. Merriam and Rosemary S. Caffarella, *Learning in Adulthood* (San Francisco: Jossey-Bass, 1991), pp. 7–18. The authors discuss the baby boom cohort in its sociocultural context.

12. Margaret Mead, *Culture and Commitment* (New York: Doubleday, 1970), p. 63.

13. Walrath, *Frameworks,* p. 35. Italics in the original.

Dagwood still reflect the 1920s—Great Depression perspectives of a generation shaped profoundly by the years between two world wars that dominated the first half of the twentieth century. That worldview differs radically from the sixties and seventies perspectives of baby boomers who identify with Zonker and the other characters in *Doonesbury*.

The solidarity that early baby boomers formed within their cohort encouraged a cohort consciousness in American society. Even in their preteen years baby boomers began to see themselves as not only a distinct generation but as a *unique* generation. Their self-consciousness encouraged a similar self-consciousness among their parents. Members of that previous cohort, often called the Depression generation, became aware of unique experiences that shaped their distinctive framework. I call them, the strivers, to emphasize their core conviction, honed in a catastrophic depression and war, that adversity and adversaries can be overcome by dedicated, hard work. After thirty years of living next to challengers, most, but by no means all, strivers now recognize (perhaps begrudgingly) that their experiences and perspectives are unique rather than normative. An often vocal minority among strivers continue to see their way of life as normative and sincerely believe challengers will someday come around to see the light. Actually, the opposite appears to be occurring. For example, strivers who worked in the factories of industrial America did not find work to be fun; they worked to earn a living. Many strivers were determined to make available to their children what they themselves did not have. Therefore, their children, the challengers, are not more educated; they carry the notion that "work should be fun."[14] While some challengers have revised some of their original perspectives in the light of maturity, most challengers maintain their unique framework. They remain a distinctive culture in time.

Challengers changed the nature of American society. Most people now believe that they have the right to formulate and live by their own beliefs and values. The lack of assumed and pervasive social and religious norms encourages new groups to forge their own worldviews. While they were still teenagers, later baby boomers (sometimes referred to as baby busters) identified themselves as a distinctive cohort.[15] I call them the calculators. Calculators never embraced the radical optimism

---

14. John Naisbitt and Patricia Aburdene, *Re-Inventing the Corporation* (New York: Warner, 1985), p. 92.

15. For information on the work patterns of baby busters, see Naisbitt and Aburdene, *Re-Inventing the Corporation*, pp. 18–20.

that shaped the challengers in their early years. Calculators entered the
adult world when the reverses that caused disillusionment among so
many challengers were already in full swing. Their initial experiences
were sobering: energy shortages, Three-Mile Island, crowded schools,
a shrinking economy, competition on every side, the explosion of the
space shuttle *Challenger*, the negative aspects of the sexual revolution
and the drug culture, and so on.[16] As a result of these difficult orienting
experiences, calculators have always approached life more cautiously
than challengers did in their early years. But it is a mistake to assume
that calculator's beliefs and values represent a return to more traditional
views. Their pragmatic approaches to education and sexual relationships, as well as their lack of firm loyalty to churches and corporations,
demonstrate that they are a distinctive cohort.[17]

A MULTICULTURAL SOCIETY

During the 1980s the multicultural composition of American society
became more and more evident. It is obvious that many people now
function within what I call "special interest subcultures" designed to
protect and advance their primary commitment(s). The comprehensive nature of these primary commitments became evident to me at
a conference for leaders of small churches that I was leading once.
At the supper table on the last day of the gathering, a woman on
the staff of the conference center told me she would drop by that
evening to speak to our group about peacemaking. While I think that
peacemaking is very important, I suggested that this concern was not
what brought the leaders of small churches to the conference center.
But she persisted. She asserted that peacemaking was an "overriding"
issue and that the set agenda should be put aside to consider what
we can do as peacemakers. I held my ground—and alienated her as
a result.

As our society becomes more fragmented and conflicted, people
increasingly identify themselves by their commitment to overriding
concerns and align themselves with those who share their priority

16. Walrath, *Frameworks*, see the chart on p. 45.
17. Ibid., pp. 34–49, 69–87.

commitment.[18] In the absence of accepted, overarching beliefs and values, special interest groups will continue to develop subcultures that shape their identity and call for a high degree of loyalty from group members.

The intensity of these priority commitments emerges when members of opposing special interest subcultures are confronted with each other's views. A white, middle-aged clergy friend of mine led a service of worship on Martin Luther King Jr.'s birthday. He spoke with great feeling about the persecution he suffers as a homosexual. He suggested that this persecution gives him some appreciation of the stress and injustice experienced by members of racial and ethnic minorities. As I listened to his moving statement, I recalled the somewhat angry comments of another middle-aged clergyperson I recently heard speak on public radio. This African-American male described the resentment he feels when homosexuals compare their persecution to the persecution that African Americans have endured. "They can choose whether to be homosexual or straight," he said. "I have no choice about my color."

The beliefs and values of these two faithful people are in clear conflict. While my homosexual colleague and his friends can argue (supported by a significant body of research) that sexual orientation may be as genetically determined as race, no amount of research evidence will easily shake the conviction or change the perspective of those whose framework is dominated by the conviction that homosexuals are bad by definition.

Special interest subcultures abound in our society: militant gays and militant straights; right-to-life advocates and pro-choice advocates; environmentalists and industrialists; fundamentalist Christians and fundamentalist Muslims; women who blame working mothers for the breakdown of the family and women who work to assert their identity as persons; traditional fathers who see themselves primarily as breadwinners and fathers who provide childcare; charismatic Christians and New Age believers; those who advocate freely available contraception and those who advocate chastity, and so on and so on. Each of these special interest subcultures functions as a defining subculture for its core devotees.[19]

---

18. Naisbitt and Aburdene, *Ten New Directions For the 1990s*, p. 300, suggest that individuals seek community. Those who wish to avoid responsibility hide in the collective.

19. For an interesting examination of cohort through the life cycle, see Gail Sheehy, *New Passages: Mapping Your Life across Time* (New York: Random House, 1995),

Strong convictions elicit powerful feelings that may move members of some special-interest subcultures to forceful action. Members of a special-interest subculture may view people whose behavior and beliefs are contrary to their core convictions as threatening, even as evil. Defining others as dangerous or evil may justify taking strong measures against them. Thus peace activists sabotage U.S. Department of Defense installations, and right-to-life activists bomb abortion clinics.

The American religious and cultural landscape is more complex now that it was on that spring evening when my friend Ralph tried to help the religious education committee set goals. Belonging to the same congregation or even the same faith group does not mean that people share common beliefs and values, even on the most essential points. Thus any group assembled to plan religious education will include persons committed to special interest subcultures with conflicting beliefs and values.

LEARNING TO RESPECT THOSE WHO ARE DIFFERENT

Accepting the diversity of our present society tends to be difficult for those of us who became adults forty years ago, especially those among us who would like to recover the lifeways of that more homogeneous society. Most adults who grew to maturity in the first half of the twentieth century did not have to be aware of the human limits that shape believing and valuing. In those days radio and movies were the sole electronic media, and they tended to reflect a largely homogeneous cultural perspective. Though society included a variety of ethnic and social groups, most people "knew their place" in the social order and kept to their own kind. Few people had experiences that challenged their basic beliefs and values. In such a world it was not necessary to know *how* to believe and *how* to value.

Diversity within a society with a dominant, cohesive culture is quite different from diversity in a society that is multicultural. When President Eisenhower said, "Our government makes no sense unless it is founded in a deeply felt religious faith—and I don't care what it is,"[20] he reflected

---

pp. 5, 25. The chart on page 5 compares life stages in the 1950s with life in the 1990s. The chart on page 25 offers a key to understanding cohorts.

20. *The New York Times*, December 23, 1952; quoted in Wil Herberg, *Protestant-Catholic-Jew: An Essay in American Religious Sociology* (New York: Doubleday, Anchor Books, 1960), p. 84.

the pervasive belief of 1950s America that "we all worship the same God." In that more cohesive culture people commonly assented to statements like, We may approach God from different perspectives, but when it comes to core aspects or qualities of God, we all agree. In that former time most people assumed that everyone honored similar beliefs and values: We all live by the Ten Commandments and the Golden Rule.

The contemporary social pattern is much different. Beliefs shaped within different special interest subcultures *are based on different worldviews*. People rooted in different special interest subcultures see core realities differently.[21] They know their beliefs and values are in conflict with those whose worldviews reflect commitments to other special interest cultures. Many feminist believers, for example, see feminine as well as masculine qualities *inherent in the core reality of God*. When they pray to God as "our Father and Mother" and avoid using masculine terms like "Kingdom" in connection with God, these shifts in language to reflect *core convictions*.[22] The shift in beliefs is reflected in language that other subcultures may find offensive. For example, Christian fundamentalists represent what another subculture may believe is a theologically inaccurate picture of God. Feminist and fundamentalist subcultures affirm different and opposing worldviews.[23]

The intensive interaction among members of many special-interest subcultures reinforces the distinctive perspectives and commitments that each subculture represents. Contacts with other subcultures then clarify how "we" are different from "them." A friend of mine has severed her ties with the church because she thinks the "patriarchal theology" she hears many Christians affirm justifies and encourages the abuse of women. She believes that "patriarchal scriptures," which suggest that the "husband is the head of the wife" are cultural products that reflect dangerous cultural biases. She and her husband are actively engaged in

---

21. Gail Sheehy's review by decades suggests that religion once provided answers in how one is to live and relate; however, since the Vietnam generation the challenge to authority, including religion, has produced a time when there is no solid spiritual grounding on which to construct a worldview or philosophy for life. See Sheehy, *New Passages,* p. 88.

22. In the chapter "To Hell with Sexism: Women in Religion" there is a discussion of shifts that have taken place in language that clearly reflect core convictions. See Patricia Aburdene and John Naisbitt, *Megatrends for Women* (London: Century, 1993), pp. 133–56. Also see Susan Faludi, *Backlash* (New York: Crown, 1991), pp. 237–39.

23. For a discussion on the origins of these two subcultures and their clash, see Susan Faludi, *Backlash*, pp. 229–300.

groups that support abused women and oppose the beliefs and practices
of those who accept patriarchal perspectives in the Bible as inspired by
God. They are appalled that so many devout believers are unwilling to
admit that they are using Scripture to justify beliefs that may lead to
abusive behavior.

Many Americans assume that the beliefs and values of their particular
tradition are the best available. These persons would prefer that no
religious group, formal or informal, establish their particular beliefs
and values as normative. Even those of us who do not view our beliefs
and values as theologically relative recognize that they are culturally
relative—one cultural perspective among many. Beliefs and/or values
are personally owned and are shaped by particular traditions and experiences.

The human capacity to believe is a reality. Accepting this aspect of
human nature is the first step in learning to respect those who believe
differently and hold values that differ from one's own. When I am
teaching, I often represent the human character of believing in a diagram:

Figure 2.1
The Character of Believing

God ⟶ revelation ⟶ shared faith ⟵ believing ⟵ persons

Most religious traditions (represented as "shared faith" in the diagram)
are based on the conviction that God has been and is revealed to all or
some members of their group. Their shared faith reflects the revelation
they have received from God. Figure 2.1 suggests that shared faith not
only stems from the revelation a group receives from God but also
reflects the humanity of those who receive the revelation. Our shared
faith reflects the human limits of believing in each of us and in our
subculture.[24] The simple fact that disagreements about the nature and
requirements of God continue between and within religious groups
suggests that none of us receive the revelation of God with absolute
clarity. God may reveal with absolute clarity, but human beings do not

---

24. Randolph Crump Miller, ed., *Theologies of Religious Education* (Birmingham,
Ala.: Religious Education Press, 1995), pp. 283–85. Miller presents church, philosophical, and special theologies and the relation to the field of religious education.

perceive that revelation with absolute clarity. Humans are both inspired and fallible. The human nature that conditions one's believing shapes one's faith.[25] Our faith is never above what we believe God is like and wants a person to be like.

Core values that stem from core convictions are similarly conditioned. Like faith, values are based on one's perception of what God wants people to be and to do. What people value, what they seek to protect or strive toward is shaped by the picture they and those who are members of their tradition and/or group hold of God and God's requirements.[26] They have a picture of God and what God requires from individuals. That picture is shaped by tradition and groups.

Humility comes with the recognition that people's capacity to believe is subject to limits. Some beliefs are simply not believable. Yet we may appreciate the capacity to believe that others may have.

Many of my neighbors can locate water by dowsing. Sherry, my wife, also has this gift. For many years I have watched her locate water sources and water lines with great accuracy. One day a leak developed in the old water line that serves our barn. We need water in the barn for our animals, so Sherry went out early the next morning and dowsed the line. She marked the spot on the ground above the leak and went off to work. I began to dig where I thought she had marked the leak. After several fruitless hours I gave up and telephoned her. I was tired and frustrated. "This time it didn't work," I told her. "I'm sure the break is where I put those two sticks," she said. "What sticks? I've been digging where you put that rock." To which she replied, "What rock?" I had been digging in the wrong place.

After lunch a friend stopped by with a backhoe. I found the sticks that marked the spot above the break. "Sherry says the break is at a T right below here." My friend carefully placed the blade of the backhoe next to the sticks and began to dig straight down. At a depth of six feet he dug up the line which was broken at the T, just as Sherry had described it. He stared at the water running into the hole and then at the sticks Sherry

---

25. For a historic perspective of religious education in North America, see Mary C. Boys, *Educating in Faith* (San Francisco: Harper & Row, 1989), pp. 8 -12.

26. Dorothy C. Bass, ed., *Practicing Our Faith* (San Francisco: Jossey-Bass, 1997), pp. 1–12. Isa Aron, Sara Lee and Seymour Rossel, eds., *A Congregation of Learners: Transforming Synagogue into a Learning Community* (New York: UAHC, 1995), pp. 33–38.

had used to mark the location of the leak. "That's mighty impressive," he said.

It is. I cannot understand how the sticks or wires move when dowsers work. My limitation in this regard presents me with a choice: I can either doubt the reality of what dowsers perceive, or I can accept my own human limits, admit there must be some basis to what is not accessible to me personally, and benefit from their faith.

When cultural barriers separate persons from one another, what others believe may not sound sensible. The variety of special interest cultures in contemporary society represent divergent frameworks. What constitutes reality or common sense to members of a subculture stems from a common worldview based on shared assumptions and experiences. Members of different subcultures often develop different theologies and different pictures of God based on their different cultural experiences.[27] They may find justification for different values. They may hold theologies that differ.

Challenges to a subculture's core beliefs and values are not easy to take. Thus many religious educators are not skilled in dealing with challenges to their subculture. Most persons go along without questioning the way things are. If someone confronts their views or commitments, suggesting that they may be flawed, the people become understandably anxious. But rejecting these challenges out of hand may result in the loss of a learning opportunity. When people believe that their group's tradition and experience of God is or should be normative (even if only at the assumed "critical points"), they show that they have access only to their own and their group's tradition and experience as a foundation for beliefs and values. The dilemma of diverse beliefs and values is not easy to resolve.[28] But embracing some key attitudes helps religious education planners to address this dilemma.

To recognize that personal and congregational beliefs and values are culturally conditioned is not to assert that all beliefs and values are relative. All people need to be clear about the boundaries that mark their own core beliefs and values. But being certain of personal commitments

---

27. Randolph Crump Miller, ed., *Theologies of Religious Education*, p. 161. Miller discusses genetic inheritance and cultural information and the relationship that exists between the two. Values, morality, and religion are developed within this framework.

28. Larry Rasmussen defines the phrase "shaping communities" as the practice "by which we agree to be reliable personally and organizationally." For further discussion on ways religious educators are shaping communities, see Bass, *Practicing Our Faith*, pp. 119–23.

is not the same as being rigid. Individuals and congregations can hold
on to core beliefs and values without being close-minded. But such
commitments need not lead the individual to reject out of hand the
perspectives of those who differ. To accept the reality of human limits
is to permit the beliefs and values of those who are different to impinge
critically on our own. God will not be culturally contained. Even the
Bible, which holds authority for many of us, insists that God inspires,
speaks, and works through members of different cultures.[29] Exposure to
diverse beliefs and values may provide a complement, even a needed
corrective, to our own.

When an individual or a congregation becomes alienated from those
who represent perspectives other than their own there is little or no appreciation for the beliefs and values of those whose culture differs. Effort
is needed to understand and appreciate the cultural context that shaped
them.[30] For example, members of small and large churches commonly
misunderstand each other, since they view each other through culturally
shaped perspectives. Carl Dudley clarifies the difference between small
and large church perspectives in a small book with a formidable title:
Affectional and Directional Orientations to Faith.[31]

Members of small congregations usually reflect an affectional orientation. They experience faith relationally. They think that a church is
what it needs to be when everyone feels included and cared for. They are
relatively unconcerned about schedules and agendas. They are people
centered.[32]

29. Isaiah refers to Cyrus as "messiah" (Is 44:28 RSV), Jonah struggles to accept
God's work with the Ninevites (Jon 3:1–4:11); Jesus holds up a Samaritan, a member
of a cultural minority the Jews looked down on, as an example of godliness, in part
to challenge the egocentric and ethnocentric perspectives of his hearers (Jn 4:1 42;
Kg. 17:24–34 RSV).

30. "A Guide to Revisioning Local Church Education" offers several claims for the
future of religious education, for example, "building communities of faith capable of
helping people make religious sense of their encounters between their traditions of faith
and the explosion of new knowledge that surrounds them, the changing circumstances of
their lives, and the decisions they must make for living into a changing world" pp. 136–
37. See Charles R. Foster, *Educating Congregations* (Nashville: Abingdon, 1994). See
also chapter 1, "Flaws in the Church Education Vessel", pages 17–36. One particular
flaw, "the Cultural captivity of church education," describes a challenge to break from
the cultural status quo and embrace a transformational message.

31. Carl S. Dudley, *Affectional and Directional Orientations to Faith* (Washington,
D.C.: The Alban Institute, 1982.) Also see Carl S. Dudley and Douglas Alan Walrath,
Developing Your Small Church's Potential (Valley Forge, Pa.: Judson, 1988), pp. 66–68.

32. A basic tenet of the small congregation is that people know one another. Carl S.
Dudley discusses the caring cell and the primary group and how they are lived out in the

Members of large congregations usually take what Dudley calls a "rigorous" approach to faith.[33] The congregation feels the church is what it needs to be only when it is doing something significant. The church's top priority is mission. Members of large congregations are often very concerned about religious education programs, schedules, and agendas.[34]

Dudley believes the contrasting orientations that typify members of small and large congregations are rooted in their different cultures.[35] This cultural shaping may bias and even blind members of large and small churches to each other's needs. Members of one kind of congregation not only fail to understand members of the other kind, but they also commonly misunderstand them. Members of large congregations often view members of small congregations as self-centered and unconcerned about expressing their faith in "responsible" action. Members of small congregations often experience members of large congregations as cold people who become so caught up in activities that they have no time to care for one another. One friend summed up the contrast succinctly. Large-church people say, "Don't just sit there, do something!" Small-church people respond, "Don't just do something, sit there!"

The misunderstanding that often occurs between members of large and small churches is rooted in their common tendency to view the church solely in their own cultural norms. They view the other kind of church as less than adequate, which it would be in their culture. Small churches do not address the needs of most people who choose to participate in large churches, and vice versa. Large churches do not fail to nurture the faith of their own members adequately, but they would fail to nurture the faith of most members of small churches. One kind of congregational life is

---

small congregation in chapter 2, "The Caring Cell," in *Making the Small Church Effective* (Nashville: Abingdon, 1986), pp. 32–45. The relational lifestyle is also discussed in *Developing Your Small Church's Potential,* by Carl S. Dudley and Douglas Alan Walrath, (Valley Forge, Pa.: Judson, 1989), pp. 70–71.

33. Carl S. Dudley and Douglas Alan Walrath, *Developing Your Small Church's Potential*, p. 68.

34. Warren J. Harman and Robert L. Wilson, *The Large Membership Church* (Nashville: Discipleship Resources, 1989), p. 79. In this study of large congregations, the authors state that programs are built around: "preaching, singing, and intercessory prayer." Service programs in religious education and social ministries are seen as expressions of a congregation's personal encounter with God.

35. Carl Dudley identifies the different roles for community change based on congregation size. See Dudley and Walrath, *Developing Your Small Church's Potential*, pp. 90–91.

not inherently better than the other, although members of each do tend to see their own kind as better. The different lifeways and shapes taken by small and large institutions reflect the different needs and experiences of those who compose each culture. Planning in religious education grows out of such different perspectives and cultural backgrounds.

It is hard for people to appreciate those who challenge their core values. Several years ago I was delighted to meet Robert Gribbon at a conference. I had long admired his careful theoretical and practical study of contemporary young adults.[36] In a long conversation we talked about the difficulty that members of the older, more traditional generation (strivers) often have appreciating the lifeways of young adults (calculators) and middle-aged adults (challengers).[37] The sexual attitudes and behavior of the other cohorts are especially difficult for many strivers to accept. It is quite common, for example, for unmarried members of the challenger and calculator cohorts to live together without marrying. These relationships may (though not always) include sexual intimacy. This common practice seems immoral and is very difficult for many strivers to accept.[38]

During their young adult years strivers followed different patterns of relating to the opposite sex. In their time young people dated and, if they fell in love, might have decided to go steady. If the relationship continued for several months, they usually became engaged and after several more months married. They lived together only after they married. While the famous (and widely criticized) Kinsey research suggests that many strivers did become sexually intimate before marriage, religiously based cultural norms nevertheless permitted sexual intimacy only after and within marriage.

Most strivers continue to see their sexual norms as representing the right way, the moral way. During our conversation at the conference Gribbon suggested another perspective that would be helpful for strivers to consider. The strivers' approach seemed moral to them and it worked for them. But in certain ways the strivers' perspective does not work for young adults today. Strivers followed their patterns of sexual and

---

36. For a comprehensive study of the faith life in 18–35-year-old adults, see Robert T. Gribbon, *Developing Faith in Young Adults* (New York: The Alban Institute, 1990).

37. For specific examples of religious education planning with 18–35-year-old adults, see Gribbon, *Developing Faith in Young Adults*, pp. 85–90.

38. Douglas Alan Walrath, *Frameworks*, pp. 46–49. This particular section describes how frameworks are shaped.

marriage practices for practical as well as moral reasons. They could do so partly because the constraints of the world in which they lived as young adults were significantly different from the circumstances that face members of the younger cohorts.[39]

In fact, Gribbon went on to point out, close examination reveals that members of all three cohorts strive within their different circumstances to achieve the same goal: a stable, abiding relationship. Planning in religious education needs to include the notion that one-third of these young adults have had some kind of religious experience.[40] Continuing their faith explorations through continuing relationships in a congregation is critical. They proceed differently in their different times because they are constrained by different social contexts, "worlds," to use Margaret Meads term. Each cohort can say to the other, "You have never been young *in the world* I am young in."[41]

In the different world that existed during the strivers' formative years, those who married each other usually shared a common culture and geography. Those who grow up in the same culture and locale usually share the same values and life—expectations, especially in essential areas like work, sex roles (husband/father, wife/mother), the particular form marriage is to take, the way children are to be raised, the religious practices they will follow, and so forth.

Contemporary life is marked by widespread social and geographical mobility.[42] Many, if not[43] most, young people do not marry a girl or boy from the same locale. Many young people are uprooted from their families and communities in their late teenage years and move both geographically and culturally several times before they are ready to marry. The marriage partner often has different cultural, geographical, and ethnic roots. Unlike their parents, contemporary young adults cannot assume that their prospective marriage partners hold compatible values and expectations. They have to find out. And that need to find out,

---

39. For a summary of the significant cultural changes in cohorts see Gail Sheehy, *New Passages* (New York: Random House, 1995), pp. 27–48.

40. Gribbon, *Developing Faith in Young Adults,* p. 90.

41. Mead, *Culture and Commitment,* p. 63. Italics mine.

42. Not only are Americans living longer and having fewer children, they are also marrying later. See Sheehy, *New Passages*, pp. 4–5.

43. "The U.S. Census Bureau reports that adults in the age range from twenty-two to twenty-four change address more frequently than any others. . . . (In contrast, older adults are apt to become involved more slowly and make commitments on a more limited, but long-term basis.)" Robert T. Gribbon, *Developing Faith In Young Adults,* p. 21.

Gribbon suggests, is what prompts young adults to live together rather than marry.[44] Contemporary young adults function differently from their parents and grandparents in order to cope with the constraints of a different social context.[45]

When members of one subculture evaluate the practices of another subculture entirely through "their own" framework, they attain little or no appreciation for the beliefs and values the others hold. The same can be stated for planners in religious education. When planners in religious education evaluate the practices of a subculture through the planners' framework, they obtain little or no appreciation and insight into why particular beliefs and values are held. A willingness to step back and appreciate a subculture before judging the worth or morality of its members' beliefs or way of life is essential in a multicultural society. If planners of religious education consider just one set of beliefs and values to be correct they may need to guard against their dominant cultural faction attitude. Planning then becomes a competitive enterprise. The outcome is often a religious education program that reflects only the winners' values and addresses only the winners' needs and interests. That was precisely the outcome in the planning group with which my friend Ralph worked. Strivers won and challengers lost. Sadly, the challengers were also lost to the church. When it became apparent that their perspective would not be respected, the challengers withdrew.

INCLUSIVE PLANNING

Inclusive planning in religious education takes into consideration persons who hold different perspectives. Those who plan inclusively assume that multiple perspectives enrich religious education and strive to respect the beliefs, values, and unique needs of all groups represented. We will consider three congregations that were able to plan inclusively: the first from a small, rural church, the second from a large, metropolitan church, and the third from a medium-sized inner-city church.

---

44. Gribbon describes the difficult congregational issue of sexuality. Some congregations prohibit any form of ministry with young adults who have chosen to live with their partners instead of marrying them. See Gribbon, *Developing Faith in Young Adults,* p. 80.

45. Gribbon, *Developing Faith in Young Adults,* p. 20. Gribbon notes the career, family, and geographic changes experienced by young adults were not part of life for their parents.

When Paul Ferenczy became pastor of rural, 120-member Reformed Church of Middleburgh, New York, he faced an immediate crisis: the Sunday school had collapsed. The church was without a religious education program. The people responsible for religious education urged him to take immediate steps to rebuild the Sunday school. Paul suggested a different approach. He recommended that the education committee survey the congregation to discover what values and goals church members wanted religious education to serve. They did so by inviting the entire congregation to breakfast following a Sunday morning worship service. After breakfast the assembled group broke up into small discussion groups, each facilitated by a member of the education committee. When the groups reassembled to report their values and goals in religious education, the gathered congregation discovered they had a variety of goals for religious education.

Some members were concerned that children gain essential knowledge of the Bible. Others were concerned that the religious education program build loyalty to the church. Still others were concerned that Sunday school serve as a vehicle to reach unchurched persons in the community. The breakthrough to common ground came when nearly all of those present realized they wanted a religious education program that addressed families, not just children. The planning committee was encouraged to design religious education events that brought families together.

The planning committee met with a religious education consultant and shared both the common goal and the different concerns that were identified in their survey. The consultant suggested they consider a family cluster approach in their religious education program.[46] With his help they developed a program that brought church members of all ages together as families. Each group met in the early evening one day each week for a meal, worship, and Bible study. The religious education planning committee shared this proposal with the congre-

---

46. Margaret M. Sawin developed the first family cluster model in 1970 at the First Baptist Church, Rochester, New York. The definition is "a family cluster is a group of four or five family units that contract to meet together periodically for shared educational experiences related to their living in relationship within their families." This model includes the dynamic of intermingling many subgroups. See *Harper's Encyclopedia of Religious Education,* p. 254. For further reference on family clusters, see Margaret M. Sawin, *Family Enrichment with Family Clusters* (Valley Forge, Pa.: Judson, 1979) and Margaret M. Sawin, ed., *Hope for Families* (New York: Sadlier, 1982).

gation. Enough members responded to form several family clusters. The extended families they assembled included single-parent and two-parent households, single young adults, older adults, and children whose parents did not participate in the church. In the early stages of the family cluster experience, curriculum materials were developed by the religious education committee. But as the family clusters became more confident, most wrote their own curricula. When some clusters began to include those from households not connected with any church, the congregation discovered their new approach to religious education could also be a means of evangelism. By honoring their differences and identifying the values they hold in common, this congregation designed an effective and inclusive religious education program.

Some years ago while I was leading a planning retreat at the Warwick Conference Center, I ate lunch with members of a group from the Community Church of Glen Rock, New Jersey, who were also making a retreat at the same center. Their retreat, led by Morton Kelsey, focused on the interrelationship of theology and psychology in the task of spiritual formation. I was impressed that a group of three dozen adults from one congregation were engaged in this kind of spiritual quest. I asked them to tell me about their church's religious education program.

My lunch companions responded that religious education leaders in their church tended to assume that a large and diverse congregation needs to provide a variety of education programs. Church members are encouraged to propose education alternatives that address their varied interests, concerns, and priorities. Religious education planners listen carefully to proposals and help those committed to each to plan their own program. This retreat represented the concrete culmination of one group's planning. Many other proposals were in the planning and implementation stage. Leaders in this metropolitan congregation assumed that a church in a heterogeneous culture needs to provide a heterogeneous religious education program and that the members themselves are capable of planning their own program.

At the time I was working as a strategic planning consultant with leaders of a Presbyterian church located in the southeast quadrant of Washington, D.C. As I became acquainted with this congregation, I became more and more impressed by their ability to embrace cultural diversity. The church leaders with whom I worked included homosexual and heterosexual men, black and white women and men, residents of the immediate neighborhood and residents of the surrounding suburbs, persons with graduate degrees and persons with modest schooling, long-standing members and those who had joined in the past year. This congregation's religious education offerings included Bible study groups, issue-focused groups, a preschool for children, and an outreach group to neighborhood youth. What enabled this group to include such diverse approaches to education? The congregational culture that their pastor, Jean MacKenzie, encourages. "She insists that we respect and listen to one another."

A SUMMARY OF SUGGESTIONS FOR PLANNING

My experience with these three churches and as well as many others convinces me that congregations can include representatives of a variety of subcultures in their religious education planning. It is not easy to plan inclusively, but it is possible. Let me offer a few suggestions.

Begin By Describing Rather Than Judging
I was newly ordained and convinced that my vision of what faithful people needed to believe and do was almost entirely accurate. Then I participated in a conference led by Thomas Bennett, executive director of the national YMCA training center. During the conference Bennett taught the difference between what he calls "normative thinking" and "descriptive thinking." The discovery changed my self-image and my approach to ministry.

Normative thinking encourages evaluation—listening to others to determine whether their beliefs and values are right or wrong judged solely according to a specific set of norms. Beliefs and values that are affirmed may or may not be the ones held by the evaluating individual. People have a tendency to align themselves with beliefs and values that are most like what is known. The converse may also be true. This is not to suggest that affirmation is given only to beliefs and values that both parties hold in common but only to suggest that the first response may be evaluation against a personal set of norms.

While normative thinking at certain points is appropriate and essential, Bennett suggested that applying normative thinking first to unfamiliar ideas or experiences may possibly block valuable discoveries. He suggested engaging unfamiliar ideas or experiences by trying to describe them. Descriptive thinking moves the listener to ask questions such as,

What are they saying? What do they mean? Why are they doing that? Such questions encourages individuals to probe the rationale for others' thoughts or behavior and serves as a basis for evaluating what the other person believes and does with criteria drawn from personal experience. Descriptive thinking encourages people to find common ground with others.

When Disagreements Emerge, Focus on Issues, Not Personalities

It is not always easy for individuals to separate the beliefs and values people espouse from their personalities. Several years ago I found myself becoming increasingly annoyed during a conversation with a young woman who was deeply drawn to Native American spirituality. After the conversation I recognized how much my annoyance at her had blocked me from appreciating and learning from her. A friend helped me to recognize that the source of the annoyance was in me, not in the young woman. That recognition helped me to appreciate much more what the young woman has gained from Native Americans in a subsequent conversation.

When an individual reacts negatively to everything someone or some group is advocating, chances are the individual is focused on personalities rather than on issues. Simply recognizing what is happening may enable the person refocus on issues. If not the conversation may need to break off and resume at another time, when it becomes possible to appreciate the person and the issues without getting consumed by personality conflicts. Once the issue of personality is resolved, an appreciation of the individual is possible as well as an understanding of the issue.

Look Actively for Points of Agreement

Often the best way to identify points of agreement is to focus on ends rather than means. Recognizing that challengers and strivers seek the same end in marriage—a stable, lasting relationship—may help members of each subculture recognize that their differences are more a matter of means than ends. Sex outside of marriage remains a significant moral issue that divides cohorts such as strivers and challengers. But if the conversation begins by focusing on the goal that the cohorts have in common, members of each cohort are better able to appreciate members of the other cohort. Strivers are then often able to understand the cultural complexity that younger adults must now face. When they listen more openly to strivers, challengers and calculators begin to understand that for the older generation sex almost always occurred after marriage. Strivers see sex outside of marriage as a threat to marriage.

Design and Implement a Plan That Will Help Diverse Groups Work Together

Years of experience helping churches to manage conflict taught me the importance of defining a plan and following it. People can come to terms with theological and moral divisions when they all agree to follow procedures that commit them to be respectful with one another. For example, a planning group in religious education may agree to linger on issues that are uncomfortable. The purpose is to encourage persons holding one position to describe the opposite position. It is important that those who disagree be able to describe the beliefs and rationale *to the satisfaction of those who hold that opposite position.* A diverse group inevitably will need direction in protecting the interest of each subgroup. Members of subcultures who hold opposing, conflicting viewpoints bring those conflicts to church. Procedural suggestions in books like Speed Leas's *Moving Your Church through Conflict* and Hugh F. Halverstadt's *Managing Church Conflict* can help members of subcultures find common ground and reconciliation.

Planning with those who hold diverse and sometimes opposing beliefs and values can be very difficult. But diversity is and likely will remain a reality in our society for many years to come. With care religious educators can plan religious educational activities in our churches and synagogues that speak to the varied commitments and concerns of all their members.

3

TRANSFORMING MOMENTS OF CONFLICT AND FORGIVENESS THROUGHOUT THE PLANNING PROCESS

Bradley Shavit Artson and Mark N. Staitman

"FORGIVE THE INIQUITY OF THIS PEOPLE."[1]

"IF YOU ASK PARDON FOR YOUR SINS, DO YOU ALSO FORGIVE THOSE WHO HAVE TRESPASSED AGAINST YOU? FOR REMISSION IS GRANTED FOR REMISSION."

PHILO[2]

THE ISSUE

Judaism and Christianity hope for and await a messianic age. The time in which "every person shall sit under vine and fig tree, and none shall make them afraid"[3] is an ideal. Conflict is an inevitable corollary of human interaction. From the time of the tower of Babel, human endeavor has produced at least as much heat as light. As the task at hand takes on

---

1. Numbers 14:19
2. Edition by Mangey, vol. 2, 1742, p. 670, cited by Alan Unterman, "Forgiveness," in *Encyclopedia Judaica,* vol. 6 (Jerusalem: Keter, 1972), p. 1437.
3. Micah 4:4

a life of its own, its own value can become overwhelming,[4] making it difficult for participants to see the true values that underlie the work. Depth psychology suggests that the presence of a subconscious (the talmudic rabbis would have called it *a yetzer ha-ra*, evil inclination) results in latent goals that often frustrate and preclude the overt purpose of the human gathering in the first place. This conflict is an inevitable component in the planning of religious education.

Planning in religious education acknowledges that change will happen. All planning endeavors demand an evaluation of the present (an environmental scan), a statement of hope for the future (a vision), and a plan for getting there (implementation). Conflict is a basic element of change. Differing understandings of the present, hopes for the future, and methods for accomplishing the desired plan inevitably lead to conflict. Diverse understandings of religious education—its content, its locus and its method—inevitably lead to conflict. Fear of loss, discomfort with instability, and concern about the future all help to engender an environment in which conflict can grow. Consequently, religious education planning, by its very nature, is conflict inducing.

In a society where people are taught to see conflict as bad many individuals assume that conflict is to be avoided. This is not unique to this society or to this age. The rabbis praise Aaron and hold him up as an exemplar. "Be like the disciples of Aaron, loving peace and pursuing peace. When Aaron would see two men fighting, he would intervene to bring peace between them."[5] This understanding of conflict may well underlie much of the seeming reluctance to do serious and sustained planning in religious education. Religious educators want to be like the disciples of Aaron, not like those who were fighting. Perhaps more is to be learned from the rabbis about transforming moments of conflict and forgiveness. The difficulty in conflict-inducing endeavors lies in the way religious leaders deal with conflict. "Every controversy conducted for the sake of Heaven will in the end prove fruitful; every controversy

---

4. "Many, many years were passed in building the tower. It reached so great a height that it took a year to mount to the top. A brick was, therefore, more precious in the sight of the builders than a human being. If a man fell down, and met his death, none took notice of it, but if a brick dropped, they wept, because it would take a year to replace it. So intent were they upon accomplishing their purpose, that they would not permit a woman to interrupt herself in her work of brick-making when the hour of travail came upon her. Moulding bricks she gave birth to her child, and, tying it round her body in a sheet, she went on moulding bricks." Louis Ginzberg, *Legends of the Bible* (Philadelphia: Jewish Publication Society of America, 1968), p. 84.

5. *Pirke Avot* 1:12

not conducted for the sake of Heaven will in the end prove fruitless."[6]
Controversy, conflict, and disagreement—all lead can to growth. In and
of themselves bad they are not bad. It is the way in which religious
leaders deal with them that engenders hurt, sadness, and pain. Conflict
can be a positive force in the process of planning in religious education.[7]
Gregory E. Huszczo points out that conflict has certain advantages and
disadvantages. Conflict has advantages in that (1) it may indicate caring,
(2) it is a prerequisite to change, (3) external conflict usually results in
internal cohesion, and (4) the expression of conflict can be cathartic and
can reduce tension.[8]

The role of planners (and especially those who do planning in religious
education) is to manage conflict in constructive ways—to be like the
disciples of Aaron.[9]

A RATIONALE: CONFLICT AND FORGIVENESS ARE
CRITICAL TO PLANNING IN RELIGIOUS EDUCATION

Religious education is not merely the formal opportunities for learning
that occur in all religious institutions. Almost everything that a religious institution does is an opportunity for and very often an act of
religious education. To be cognizant of this opportunity is to recognize
that the values and beliefs of religious institutions must be present in
everything that institutions does. What is taught in the day to day life
of the institution is as important as what is taught in the classroom
in the intentional planning process of religious education. Where the
inevitability of conflict is anticipated, the constructive use of conflict
should be equally planned and intentional.[10]

------

6. Ibid., 5:20.
7. Donald E. Bossart, *Creative Conflict in Religious Education and Church Administration* (Birmingham, Ala.: Religious Education Press, 1980), pp. 9–25. Carl S. Dudley
and Earle Hilgert, *New Testament Tensions and the Contemporary Church* (Philadelphia:
Fortress, 1987), pp. 104–66.
8. Gregory E. Huszczo, *Tools for Team Excellence: Getting Your Team into High
Gear and Keeping It There* (Palo Alto, Calif.: Davies-Black, 1996), p. 152.
9. A process that uses conflict productively is discussed by Peter M. Senge in *The Fifth
Discipline: The Art and Practice of the Learning Organization* (New York: Doubleday
Currency, 1990), pp. 249–57.
10. Though the scenarios are taken from the lives of congregations, they are sufficiently grounded in common experience that generalizations can be drawn for all
planners of religious education.

A Scenario: The Core Religious Education Planning Committee Recognizes the Need to Develop a Task Force to Test out Its ideas about Informal Adolescent Religious Education

The task force will need to be representative of the broad range of communities that make up the congregation; young and old, married and single, liberal and traditional. For the task force to work well together, it needs to be made up of people who are reliable, generally positive in outlook, and willing to give of their time to the future of the congregation. Each core committee member brings a list of proposed candidates. Each name is discussed, and any core committee member can veto a candidate. Personal information about individuals is a part of the conversation.

The rabbi recognizes the danger of someone's proposing a conflict involving a close friend or relative about which someone on the core committee might say something perceived as hurtful. Confidentiality must be preserved as honest discussion takes place. In preparing for the meeting, the rabbi has gathered texts from the Talmud and the Midrash on the issue of slander and gossip. A full half hour is devoted to study of these texts. The committee recites a *bracha* (prayer), thanking God for the opportunity to study and expressing the hope that study of Torah will bring people closer to God and to God's purposes.[11] The Core Committee explores the difference between criticism and slander as found in the Torah. The group looks at the nature of gossip and the damage which gossip can do.

Studying Talmud and Midrash texts has a number of effects on the planning process. While one goal for the core committee is to select members of the task force, equally important is the religious education nature of the planning process itself. The values that the core committee wants the congregation to embrace must be modeled by the committee. The religiously based texts that inform the work of the congregation, being rooted in Torah, are values of the core committee and, it is to be hoped, of the congregation. Through the process of study, the committee participants were made wiser, godlier, and better able to share

---

11. "Blessed is the Eternal our God, Ruler of the universe, who hallows us with Divine Commandments and commands us to engage in the study of Torah. Eternal our God, make the words of Your Torah sweet to us and to the House of Israel, Your people, that we and our children may be lovers of Your name and students of your Torah. May the study of Torah bring us closer to all that is High and Holy. Blessed is the Eternal, the Teacher of Torah to the people of Israel." *Gates of Prayer: The New Union Prayerbook* (New York: Central Conference of American Rabbis, 1975), p. 52 (trans. by Mark N. Staitman.)

a perspective on the work of the committee. The nature of the religious education planning process is as visibly important as the final result of the plan itself. Members of the core committee came to understand that relaying any of the discussion which would take place in the room would risk engaging in gossip. Studying Talmud and Midrash texts allowed the participants to hear criticism of friends without imputing to the critics motives that were malicious or malevolent. Anticipating conflict, and using a value-based method to deal with it made the planning process as important as the outcome, and it ennobled the participants. If a method of forgiveness is not built into the planning process, the religious education planning process may well be undermined by mistrust among the participants.

MOVING TOWARD FORGIVENESS
IN THE PLANNING PROCESS

Planning in religious education is planning with a particular worldview. A religious worldview properly utilizes the process of planning for its own ends—moral and spiritual character formation—as well as for the fiscal and organizational well-being of the congregation as an institution. What congregational planning does for its participants is as important as the ultimate plan itself. The planning process itself in religious education expects to meet the goals of religious education. Those who participate in the planning process should recognize that they themselves are going to behave in ways that require them to seek forgiveness. As persons develop insight into their own behavior, they come to understand that others too need to seek forgiveness.

Toward that end, it is crucial to recognize that those who participate in religious education planning—like the congregation itself—are very much works in progress. Each person is always on the way to human becoming, without ever attaining a completed state of human being. Rather than construing our identity as monolithic—a single element that simply ages and passes through time—it is more accurate to recognize that each of us blends many different aspects of selfhood, for example, "I am a Jew, a man, an American, a husband, a father, a son, a jogger, and many other people who live together in a shifting combination that I call myself and trace across time." These different aspects of personhood interact dynamically and constantly create a new composite, integrating new experiences, moods, and realities. The philosopher Robert Nozick refers to this as "self-reflexive awareness" and "reflexive synthesizing of the self."[12] Each person is constantly constructing the self from the different contemporary aspects of identity, integrating earlier stages, and projecting who each is yet to become: "The self synthesizes itself not only transversely, among things existing only at that time, but also longitudinally so as to include past entities, including past selves which were synthesized."[13]

Creation, for religious souls, is never completed. It is an open-ended process, as are we who are ourselves works of creation. We are God's partners in that sacred journey. As works in progress, we will take positions we later repudiate; we will speak and act in ways we will later regret; we will hurt those we love, those whose faith we share. As a sage of the Dead Sea sect stated so well, "I know that righteousness is not of humankind, and perfection of the way is not of an individual."[14] Perfection is a final condition, one that is asymptotically approached yet never reached. The very hallmark of humanity is that although perfection is never reached seeking pilgrims continue striving for the goal. Each of us being on the way, we can exercise forbearance toward those with whom we disagree realizing that they may yet outgrow a posture, a position, a philosophy, or even a particular brand of theology. We may once have held such notions ourselves. Remembering the possibility that religious souls change at the very least cultivates the virtue of religious humility, which is itself an asset in spiritual formation.

Not only are we works in progress but we are imperfect works at that. No matter how long the progression continues, we remain imperfect. According to rabbinic tradition, no less a personage than the *kohen gadol* (the high priest) was called each year on Yom Kippur to admit his imperfections: "O LORD, I have committed iniquity, transgressed, and sinned before You, I and my house. O LORD, forgive the iniquities, transgressions, and sins which I have committed and transgressed and sinned before You, I and my house."[15] If even the *kohen gadol* was

---

12. Robert Nozick, *Philosophical Explanations* (Cambridge, Mass.: Harvard University Press, Belknap Press, 1981), chap. 1, esp. pp. 71–114.

13. Ibid. p. 91.

14. 1 QH 4:30. Cited by James H. Charlesworth in "Forgiveness, Early Judaism," in *The Anchor Bible Dictionary*, ed. David Noel Freedman, vol. 11 (New York: Doubleday, 1992), p. 834.

15. Mishnah Yoma 3:8

personally flawed, how much more so every other child of God? At
the most public moment of biblical Israel's most sacred ritual, at the
very core of temple worship, was the expression of human fallibility
and the resultant expectation of divine (and human) forgiveness. Thus
the recognition of weakness, willfulness, and fallibility prepares the
way for pardon. Just as it is helpful for a parent to recognize that a
child is acting out of uncontrollable impulse or ignorance, so too it is
helpful to remember that adults have more in common with little children
than adults may care to admit. Disagreement does not necessarily entail
disrespect. But the vituperation and passion that is injected into disagreements requires some explanation. Hurtful words, deeds, and views
often emerge from weaknesses, fears, and embarrassments rather than a
position of strength or deliberate cruelty. Understanding those responses
as concealed admissions of weakness invites forgiveness rather than
revenge, compassion rather than bitterness.

Forgiveness as a Biblical Art

The notion of forgiveness is no stranger to the heirs of biblical[16] traditions. The very premise of the biblical faiths[17] is that fallible humanity
can attain forgiveness from a loving God. The core biblical message is
that God is no less forgiving than any loving human parent who forgives

---

16. References in this chapter to "biblical" or to "the Bible" are to the canonized
books of the Hebrew Scripture, called the "*Tanakh*" by Jews (an abbreviation of
its three principal divisions: *Torah* (Pentateuch), *Nevi'im* (Prophets), and *Ketuvim*
(Writings). Within a specifically Christian context, this collection is referred to as the
"Old Testament," a term inappropriate for a readership that includes Jews. "*Talmud*"
refers to the Babylonian Talmud, a text of legal (*halachic*) and folkloritic (*aggadic*)
materials dating from the first to the sixth centuries. "*Midrash*" refers to the various texts
of biblical interpretation and explication from the same rabbis who authored the Talmud.
It uses a fixed set of hermeneutic principles, and is the method by which rabbis formally
addressed theological issues prior to Judiasm responding to systematic theology.

17. I use the term "biblical faith" to signify the three primary Abrahamic faiths:
Judaism, Christianity, and Islam. All three faiths have supplemented the Hebrew Bible
with (and have interpreted it through) their own particular texts—rabbinic writings for
Judaism, the Gospels and Epistles for Christianity, and the Quran for Islam. Each faith
sees itself as bearing faithful witness to traditions that began with the patriarchs and
matriarchs and were expounded through the revelation at Sinai. For a similar usage in
a brilliant book, see Will Herberg, *Judaism and Modern Man* (New York: Atheneum,
1977), p. viii. In no way do I mean to imply that other faiths lack the cultivation of
forgiveness. My lack of expertise suggests the wisdom of silence in regard to those
other rich religious traditions.

an erring and repentant offspring. In the words of the Midrash,[18] "My children, if you return/repent will you not be returning to your Father?"[19] All of us—in need forgiveness, and the prevalence of this need testifies to the presence of the One who would forgive. Here, as elsewhere, each person is called to acts of *imitatio Dei*, of making self in the image of God by performing the deeds of a loving God.

The Bible portrays forgiveness as a divine prerogative (indeed, a divine attribute[20]). Forgiveness is what God bestows and humans receive. Christianity developed a notion of unmerited forgiveness, or "grace," and the Bible itself speaks of forgiveness as following upon sincere repentance.

Before examining the nature of repentance, however linked it may be to the notion of forgiveness, it is worth dwelling for a moment on forgiveness itself. The multiple and overlapping terms the Bible develops to articulate this central idea testifies to its many nuances and to its complexity.[21]

The primary biblical term for forgiveness is the Hebrew root *salaḥ*. This term denotes something that God provides to humans when they show signs of repentance and regret. A second and related term is *nasa'* (to bear away or to remove). In this term, which is linked to words for guilt or sin, God postpones or transfers retribution, the consequence of sin. Yet another verb used in this context is *rapei* (to heal). Thus God "forgives all your iniquities and heals all your diseases."[22] God also can forget sins *al zakhar* as in ("I will forgive their iniquities and their sins I will no longer remember)."[23] *Rehem* ("mercy") is a divine attribute closely related to forgiveness, as with the prophet Micah's poignant "God will again have mercy on us, covering our iniquities. You will hurl all

---

18. *Midrash* is rabbinic exposition of biblical verses, either of law (*halakhah*) or narrative (*aggadah*). The classical period of Midrash lasted from 100–700 C.E.

19. *Deuteronomy Rabbah* 2:24, trans. J. Rabinowitz (London: Soncino, 1983), p. 53.

20. Exodus 34:6–7. See especially Leviticus 23:27–20. Rabbi Abraham ibn Ezra (twelfth century North African biblical exegete) interprets this to mean "this atones for those who repent (return to God's way), but it does not atone for the insincere."

21. Helpful, brief discussions of the biblical notions of forgiveness may be found in John S. Kselman, "Forgiveness (OT)," in *The Anchor Bible Dictionary*, 2: 831 33; Jacob Milgrom, "Forgiveness," in *Encyclopedia Judaica*, 6:1433–435, and Jacob Milgrom, "Repentance in the OT," in *The Interpreters Dictionary of the Bible: An Illustrated Encyclopedia, Supplementary Volume*, ed. Keith Crim (Nashville: Abingdon, 1962), pp. 736–38.

22. Psalm 103:3

23. Jeremiah 31:34

our sins into the depths of the sea."[24] Central to priestly understandings is the role of purification (*taher.*) Jeremiah shares God's commitment to "purify them of all their iniquities . . . I will forgive all their sins."[25] God can *moheh* ("erase")[26] or *kaper* ("atone")[27] for sin, and God can *ha'avir* ("make sin pass by").[28] Finally, God can *s'tar panim* (hide the divine face[29] so as not to see the sin). Surely there is no better role model than God for gracious forgiveness. God's procedures for forgiving sin and God's various strategies for coping with human offense can serve as exemplars for planners in religious education.

It is a meeting of the religious education committee. The chairperson is upset. He has received a telephone call from a member of the finance committee berating the work of the religious education committee for what he termed its "irresponsible, stupid request to waste money giving children an opportunity to play!" The committee has recommended that children be given scholarships to attend the summer Bible camp run by the local council of churches. The committee studied this religious education opportunity and felt that it fit well with the values of the church. Integrating religious studies into the daily life of children would reinforce the integral nature of religious education with identity formation. After hearing about the phone call, some on the committee want to confront the individual and "set him right." Others want to bring the matter to the minister to have her chastise this person. The committee takes time for a Scripture study at its meeting and looks at the Israelites' trek through the wilderness. Despite being frustrated with the complaining Israelites, God does not abandon them. God continues the relationship with Israel, but often, simply ignores their complaints. The committee then chooses to ignore the complaint. Budget constraints, coupled with balancing increasing demands on church resources made by committees put the finance committee under pressure, which the committee representative expressed.

Sometimes God forgives outright, frankly acknowledging that wrongdoing has occurred but choosing to remove the act as a factor that could disrupt the harmonious relationship linking God and the individual. Such

24. Micah 7:19
25. Jeremiah 33:8. See also Leviticus 16:30 and Ezekiel 36:25, 33
26. Psalm 51:3, Isaiah 43:25
27. Isaiah 27:9; Jeremiah 18:23; Ezekiel 16:63; Psalm 65:4; 78:38; 79:9
28. 2 Samuel 12:13; Zechariah 3:4; Job 7:21
29. Psalm 51:11

a gracious willingness to acknowledge what has happened and to move on is one effective way of dealing with what might otherwise constitute a serious disruption of cordiality and community.

The adult education committee is charged with the responsibility of planning an annual lecture, which has been endowed by a generous gift from the estate of the former president of the congregation. The committee has appointed a respected educator to chair the project, but now, three months before the lecture is to take place, nothing has happened. The lecturer has not been chosen, the publicity has not been prepared, and the family of the former president is furious. The committee meets to discuss the dilemma. A member of the committee explains that the religious educator chosen to chair the project has been very busy at work and has never gotten around to the task. Telling the family that the educator is at fault will do nothing to resolve the problem. The committee itself was ultimately responsible for the lecture and must accept that responsibility. Though embarrassed and angry, the committee quickly engages a lecturer, prepares the publicity, and meets with the family. The committee apologizes to the family and explains the plans for the lecture.

On other occasions, the offense may be so severe that moving past it is not possible. In some such instances, God bears the human iniquity. This is not outright forgiveness but a willingness to negotiate, as it were, with the legitimate anger that a wrongful act has elicited. Not quite able (or willing) to simply let go, the anger is put aside, perhaps to diminish with time, perhaps to require some action in the future. Postponing a response is itself a response.

The rabbi of the congregation wants to institute a curriculum in the Jewish religious school that addresses the issue of homosexuality. She has discussed this with the chair of the religious school committee and the youth committee. Committee members are split regarding the issue, and when the issue comes to the board of trustees of the synagogue, the tension is palpable. Voices rise as angry accusations are made. The entire board is upset following the meeting. The issue was divisive, but even so the behavior of trustees was hurtful. The rabbi, the president of the congregation and the cantor meet to discuss how to deal with this problem. The cantor suggests that healing is needed more than contrition. He suggests that "the subtle approach" may work. As it is his turn to lead the study at the next meeting, he decides to teach the music for the section of the *Yom Kippur* service that deals with confession of sin.[30] Healing can occur as people study this section together.

Like a wound, conflict requires healing, not justice. Planning in religious education can produce a pressure-cooker atmosphere that exacerbates tensions and weakens inner restraints. In such instances, the ability to rise above the moment and recognize an outburst or disruption as an illness—something that the individual regrets and cannot contain—can empower the unfortunate recipient to respond helpfully as healer rather than defensively as victim.

Four years ago a local diocese and synagogue began a joint Bible study group. The group met three times and then broke up. The rabbi who had led the congregation for nine years resigned last year and was so contentious that members of the study group were embarrassed. Now the new rabbi has a wonderful idea: an interfaith Bible study group. He brings the idea to the religious education committee, which meets to discuss the idea. Everyone remembers that a study was attempted once before, but "no one can remember why it failed." They encourage the new rabbi to try it again.

Forgetfulness is often a result of forgiveness. "Who can discern my errors?"[31] the psalmist asks, and one senses a palpable relief that no one can be completely free of hidden sins or mistakes.[32] Surely forgiveness would be hollow if we are not willing to forget. Without forgiveness and a willingness to forget, the memory of past hurts would intrude on all of congregational life. Cultivating of a charitable amnesia is a religious virtue of the first order. If the Omniscient can forget sins, who are we to do otherwise?

---

30. In this section of the Jewish liturgy, the *Viddui*, the individual first confesses sins of the past year. Then, the following is read by the cantor or the rabbi: "Our God and God of our ancestors, pardon our transgressions on this Day of Atonement. Blot out and cause to away our transgressions and sins from before Your eyes, as you have promised, I, even I, blot out your iniquities and I have made your transgressions to vanish like a mist, your sins like a cloud. Return to Me for I have redeemed you, as it is written, For on this day shall you be forgiven and purified of all your sinfulness. Before God be whole." *The Union Prayer Book for Jewish Worship,* rev. ed. (New York: Central Conference of American Rabbis, 1955), pp. 147–49 (trans. Mark N. Staitman). The intent of this liturgy is to depict the repentant sinner as one who has been purified, like the leper, and now stands healed and whole before God.
31. Psalm 19:12
32. Psalm 19:13

Joan is an active member of the church. She is known to be a devout and good woman, though a tough business person. She owns a travel agency and serves as a member of the Christian education committee. She advocates strongly for a congregational trip to the Holy Land. Many on the committee see no reason for members to spend so much money on travel when the church needs to support missions. They believe that Joan is just "drumming up business." The pastor knows that Joan was once a "lost soul." In the 1960s she was a hippie. In those days she traveled throughout Europe. When she arrived in Israel, she "found herself." The experience of "walking in the footsteps of Jesus" transformed her life.

The quality of mercy speaks not to a particular act, but to a special willingness to contextualize experience. "Judge every person favorably."[33] This dictum bids us to assume the best of intentions in others, not the worst. The planning process in religious education, by its very nature, engenders conflict. Uncertainty about the future and fear of change lead some persons to try to keep things as they are. For this fundamental reason, conflict often results from ascribing intentions to the positions of others, even when true motivations are unknown. The ability to step back and judge on the merits, not on ascribed or imputed intention is a must for all situations in which conflict is to be mediated. This ability produces honest discussion and avoids misrepresenting others.

The long-range planning committee has discussed the need to meet better the religious education needs of the church. The church has only one minister (who is nearing retirement), and some members are not being served. Few adult education classes are scheduled and little thought or effort is being put into the Sunday school. Two members of the committee, relatively new to the church, suggest that it retire the minister. A younger, more dynamic minister might devote the attention necessary to the religious education process. It will increase membership, and thus, help us to balance the budget, they say. It will be good for the business aspect of the Church. These members are seen as brash "outsiders," and their suggestion is attacked vigorously. The pastor has served the church well for thirty years. He attends to the needs of members who are shut-ins and visits every member in the hospital. His preaching is good, and he truly makes an impact on the members. Retiring this beloved pastor

---

33. Mishnah *Avot* 1:6. The saying is that of the sage Joshua ben Perahyah, understood by the Talmud to be the teacher of Jesus.

is out of the question. "You just don't understand our church. You are too business oriented, not people oriented" the chairperson tells them.

Sometimes forgiveness requires direct confrontation. The confrontation, the conflict, is cleansing in itself. It can serve as a fulfillment of the biblical commands to "reprove your kinsman" and to "love your fellow as yourself."[34] Sometimes the supreme act of commitment and love is a willingness to say what others are thinking (and saying to each other). Testing the reality includes bringing the truth back to the one who needs to hear it. Obviously there are constructive ways to carry such difficult truths and there are destructive ways.[35] When religious education planning committee members become aware of, and members begin to control, harmful or distancing behavior they offer a good deed and an act of *hesed* steadfast, loving kindness.

THE COMPLEXITIES OF FORGIVENESS

Forgiveness is a divine attribute.
Sometimes God forgives outright.
Sometimes forgiveness requires direct confrontation.
Sometimes God bears the iniquity . . . the anger is put aside.
Postponing a response is itself a response.
Some action is required in the future.
Rising above the moment and recognizing
the outburst or disruption
as a kind of illness
empowers the recipient to respond
as healer rather than as victim.
Often forgetfulness is a result of forgiveness.

Repentance: The Prerequisite to Forgiveness

As forcefully as the Bible presents God's eagerness to forgive the sinner, no less clearly does Scripture assert that a prior condition is our

---

34. Both of these two mitzvot (commandments) are found in the same paragraph of *Kedoshim* (the holiness code). The first is Leviticus 19:17 and the second is Leviticus 19:18.

35. See Bradley Shavit Artson, "*Sh'mirat ha-Lashon: Guard your Tongue*," *Jewish Spectator*, 55, no.1, (Summer 1990) and "The Mitzvah of Civilized Speech," *Outlook*, 60, no. 4, (Summer 1990).

own acknowledgment that our deeds or words were wrong.[36] Only by recognizing our sin, by resolving not to repeat it, and by attempting to redress it somehow do we make ourselves capable of receiving pardon from God and from each other.[37] Until we dissociate ourselves from our sin, it is as though we continue to perform it. Contrition and confession constitute a clean break, separating the sin from the person and opening the possibility to repair and to renewal. The ancient liturgy of the land of Israel explicitly links forgiveness to prior confession: "Forgive us, our Father, for we have sinned against You. Erase and blot out our transgressions from before Your eyes, for you are abundantly compassionate. Blessed are You, Adonai, Redeemer of Israel."[38]

Since planning in religious education can produce conflict among members of the planning team, *teshuvah* (repentance) is essential. Guiding persons toward proper ownership of their own hurtful words or harmful deeds requires balance, gentility, and strength. It must not rest continuously with one particular person. Rather, each member of the group must be willing to shoulder that responsibility when best able to persuade another to acknowledge wrongdoing. Often it will devolve to the clergy to take on that role, but the involvement of clergy will also frequently require careful words of rebuke from pastor, priest, or rabbi. Occasionally someone else may be more effective in convincing an irate congregant that a sincere apology is in order.

Jewish tradition has a long history of guiding its practitioners along the path of *teshuvah* (repentance).[39] Repentance constitutes *turning away* from sin, solipsism, and conflict, and *turning toward* God, community, and harmony. In an age that exalts the self, repentance in a religious

36. Leviticus 5: 14–26; 1 Kings 8:30, 34, 36; Mark 11:25

37. See, for example, b. Yoma 85a and *Shulchan Arukh Hayyim 606*. Here, the Talmud and its elucidation in the legal code makes clear that forgiveness depends on this "system" of repentance.

38. This version of the sixth benediction of the Amidah was found in the *Geniza*, a medieval synagogue repository of worn prayerbooks, poems, and documents located in Cairo. Cited by Charlesworth, "Forgiveness," p. 834.

39. For a masterful sampling of rabbinic material on repentance, one can do no better than Solomon Schechter, *Aspects of Rabbinic Theology: Major Concepts of the Talmud* (New York: Macmillan, 1909), chap. 18, "Repentance: Means of Reconciliation." This book as been reprinted several times, most recently by Jewish Lights Publishing Company. Also see Chaim Nussbaum, *The Essence of Teshuvah: A Path to Repentance* (Northvale, N.J.: Jason Aronson, 1993).

context offers an opportunity to embrace a more encompassing standard and a more exalted belonging. As Robert Coles explains of a prominent psychoanalyst whose deep insight brought her face-to-face with the realm of the spiritual, "She had been given pause by a particular instance of human turmoil, hurt, suffering, and yes, deviousness and cruelty—and had found herself, unwittingly almost, transported from one world to another, from (as she indicated) the world of the mind to the world of the soul. When will some of us learn that not rarely such a moment is not without important, redemptive consequences— that on our knees, in prayer, we might at last find His forgiving smile, at last accept His reminder that we are but part of something (someone) much larger, rather than (through our minds) the be-all and end-all of this life?"[40]

Repentance as a Biblical Art

Like forgiveness, repentance is as old as Torah and as sacred as the prophets of Israel. Forgiveness and repentance were blended in a later notion of repentance as a powerful way to secure forgiveness.

In the Torah forgiveness comes from the priests who ministered in the tabernacle in the wilderness. Offering sacrifices was the final step in expiating sin. The first steps, contrition and public admission of wrongdoing (*hitvaddah*, or "confession"),[41] were essential components of repentance in the priestly order. Even the name of the appropriate offering, *Asham*, signifies "feeling guilt."[42] For the priests, the notion of atonement was one that required an inner remorse demonstrated by a physical deed: "P insists that sacrificial expiation (k-p-r) is mandatory for the complete annulment of sin."[43]

---

40. Robert Coles, "On Forgiveness," in *Harvard Diary: Reflections on the Sacred and the Secular* (New York: Crossroad, 1990), p. 180.

41. Leviticus 5:5; Numbers 5:7. For extensive discussion and citation, see Jacob Milgrom, *Cult and Conscience: The Asham and the Priestly Doctrine of Repentance* (Leiden: Brill, 1976). See also Joseph P. Healey, "Repentance, Old Testament," in *Anchor Bible Dictionary*, 5:671–72.

42. Jacob Milgrom, *The JPS Torah Commentary: Numbers* (Philadelphia: Jewish Publication Society, 1990), excursus 33, "Repentance in the Torah and the Prophets," pp. 396–98.

43. *P* is the term used by higher bibilical critics for the priestly texts in the Bible. Milgrom, *Numbers*, p. 398.

The idea of human repentance, while not explicitly developed, lurks behind the narratives about Pharaoh and his hard heart[44] as well as the tragic fall of the sons of Eli[45] and several of Israel's early heroes: David,[46] Ahab,[47] and Josiah.[48]

The prophets of Israel, then, had a rich legacy on which to build. Yet their vision of repentance went well beyond any previous notions of human contrition, such as repentance as a human virtue. Neither God nor Moses ever needed to tell the people to repent nor did the sacrificial cult need to assert the mandatory nature of repentance. It was sufficient to explain what to do when remorse led the individual to seek atonement. That earlier version of repentance was not fully sufficient to reconcile the penitent to God. A sacrifice had the power to reduce a deliberate sin to an unintentional sin, but even in such cases, a sacrifice was necessary to complete the annulment of the sin.

The great biblical prophets expanded on that priestly pre-exilic base and insisted that repentance itself sufficed to nullify sin. The Hebrew term *shuv* (related to *teshuvah*,) means to turn away from sin and turn toward God. The very language the prophets use suggests that humanity is on a spiritual journey. As with any great turning, there are wrong turns, dead ends, impassable obstructions, and many monotonously level miles. Walking in the way of the Lord[49] is never easy, never final, and never without mishap. Yet that is the way, and the determined hiker is indeed a pilgrim—one who is always on the way. Perhaps that is why the three primary biblical festivals, *Pesaḥ* (Passover), *Shavuot* (Weeks), and *Sukkot* (Tabernacles) are known as the *shalosh regalim* (the three pilgrimage feasts). To walk on the way is to partake in the feast of life.

Prophetic ideas of *teshuvah* pertain to the nation as a whole,[50] to the national and the individual, as in Hosea's faithless wife and his plea to his neighbors, "Come, let us return to the Lord,"[51] and to the creation of a new inner life, as in Jeremiah's "new heart."[52] While the prophets

44. Exodus 7:3–4; 10:1; 11:10
45. 1 Samuel 2:25
46. 2 Samuel 12:13–14; 24:10–14
47. 1 Kings 21:27–29
48. 2 Kings 22:18–20
49. Psalm 1:1
50. Amos 4:6–13
51. Hosea 5:15—6:5
52. Jeremiah 31:33; see also Deuteronomy 30:6; Ezekiel 36:26–27

shared the priestly notion that *teshuvah* should inspire liturgical acts of contrition, they also insisted that *teshuvah*, by itself, could effect atonement between God and God's children.[53]

Repentance is reparation between human beings as well as healing between an individual person and the Holy One. This is not some abstract concept; it involves a concrete climb up the ladder of return. According to Samuel Rosenblatt, "Saadia, Bahya, and Maimonides agree that the essential constituents of repentance are regret and remorse for the sin committed, renunciation of the sin, confession and a request for forgiveness, and a pledge not to repeat the offense."[54]

Repentance includes (1) recognition with verbal confession and responsible ownership (regret and remorse as well as renunciation) (2) reconciliation to restore lost harmony (confession and a request for forgiveness and restitution), and (3) resolution the final phase of repentance (pledge not to repeat). These components constitute the core requirement for contemporary *teshuvah*.

Recognition: The essential first step in righting any wrong is to recognize it as such. Particularly in our own self-centered culture in which personal gratification claims pride of place, it takes real effort and determination to examine how our deeds affect other people. Our conscience and our community can provide essential support in this proces of introspection and insight. Recognition can be divided into two stages: (1) regret and remorse and (2) renunciation. While regret can emerge in response to pangs of guilt[55] or through the caring rebuke of friend or clergy, renunciation must emerge from oneself.

Reconciliation: The second step in repentance requires active, concrete measures to restore a lost harmony between the planning team members or in the congregation at large. The first requirement is verbal confession—a candid and public acknowledgment that what happened should not have—and a responsible ownership of improper behavior during the religious education planning process. The second stage of reconciliation is a request for forgiveness, that is made directly to the one who was wronged. Accompanying or preceding that request must be restitution, finding some way to right the wrong or to provide

---

53. See Isaiah 63:7–64:12; Hosea 6:1–3; 7:14; 14:1–3; Joel 2:15–18

54. Samuel Rosenblatt, "Repentance in Jewish Philosophy," in *Encyclopedia Judaica*, 14:76.

55. See Harlan J. Wechsler, *What's So Bad about Guilt?* (New York: Simon & Schuster, 1990).

balm for the hurt also so that the planning process can be enhanced. Reconciliation is at the heart of repentance, moving beyond the realm of inner thoughts and resolve to the public world of word and deed. Community is strengthened and developed precisely here, in the world of practice.

Resolve: The final phase of repentance turns the individual back to the personal realm of intention. The person resolves never to commit that same wrong again, hoping that the extensive steps of *teshuvah* provided a framework, both physical and mental, to strengthen that worthy resolve. Additionally, the process of repentance makes it easier to admit error in the future, since the participant has now walked through each step and has experienced the relief and the healing that repentance can bring.

Only if we are willing to consider our own actions and convictions in the light of possible error can we be open to the healing process of repentance. All participants in the religious education planning process must take special care to consider how their own deeds or words might have contributed to (or even created) misunderstanding, hurt feelings, or dissension in the planning group. And each participant must be willing to share the fruits of that recognition with the other members of the planning team, through apology to the wronged party (often the group as a whole in addition to some individual member) and through a visible difference in deportment during subsequent occasions throughout the overall religious education planning process.

No person can hope to avoid error. And even the most even-keeled among us occasionally erupts in anger or jealousy. Because there is no possibility of attaining perfection, the only way to avoid becoming the captive of our own faults is to train ourselves to admit our faults and to distance ourselves from them. Perhaps this insight is what led the rabbis of old to state that "there is a remedy for every affliction in the world, and the remedy for the *yetzer ha-ra* (the evil inclination) is repentance."[56] Remorse and restitution constitute a powerful pedagogy through which we educate ourselves in how to behave. Taking responsibility for our own actions is part and parcel of the process of repentance, and the soundest assurance that few breaches will become irreparable.

---

56. Midrash Tanhuma 58:1.

INVITING TRANSFORMATION: VIEWING CONFLICT IN RELIGIOUS EDUCATION PLANNING AS OPPORTUNITY

Conflict throughout the religious education planning process is an inevitable part of human interaction and congregational life. Because of the intimacy and intensity involved in planning religious education, religious education planners enjoy more than their share of conflict—between congregants, between congregants and clergy, and among clergy and other staff. Inability to address conflict in productive ways can defeat the purposes for which the congregation was established. Religious education planners may mourn conflict as evidence and confirmation of human sinfulness. The persistence of conflict offers a continuing opportunity for real spiritual work and growth in religious education. By addressing each new conflict in a religious context—learning to see the person whole, to judge in each person's favor, to take responsibility for our own misdeeds and careless words, and to forgive others as we would hope to be forgiven ourselves, we transform moments of conflict into occasions to build a stronger, more vigorous, more sacred community.

The art of forgiveness is essential to success in planning religious education, as well as to the participants' growth as members of the people of God. Reflecting on the religious nature of the planning process allows for models to emerge that can transform conflict into a constructive force for progress. God's acknowledging sin and forgiving it outrightly can be a model for religious education planning groups. God's bearing iniquity without responding can be a model that helps planning groups continue their work without rancor, while maintaining their dignity and integrity. Allowing for a healing process can empower all participants in conflict. Judging on the merits, not on ascribed or imputed intention, mediates conflict and transforms conflict from being participant centered to being issue centered.

Seeking escape from the inevitable and the unpleasant is a response is both childish and doomed. The inevitable and the unpleasant run faster than religious education planners can ever hope to flee. God summons all of us, including religious education planners, not to be children but rather to rise to a response of adult faithfulness and courage. Engendered by our religious traditions and rooted in biblical constancy, a willingness to *teshuvah* and *seliḥah*, to repentance and forgiveness, is a gift of healing. Each of us, as well as our seeking congregations, can be stronger than we were before the process of planning in religious education revealed the subterranean stresses that are an inevitable part of communal life. The ability to navigate conflict and to forgive wrong can infuse congregational life through the religious education process with a rich spirituality and a deep appreciation for fellow congregants. The ancients reflect this verity of the human heart when they observe, "Who is a hero among heroes? One who controls his evil inclination and transforms an enemy into a friend."[57]

---

57. *The Fathers according to Rabbi Natan*, trans. Judah Goldin, Yale Judaica Series, no. 10 (New Haven: Yale University Press, 1955), chap. 23.

PART 2

DRAWING THE BOUNDARIES

4

KNOWING THE DIFFERENCE BETWEEN STRATEGIC AND OPERATIONAL PLANNING

Paul M. Dietterich

One of the greatest services a religious educator can perform for a church is guiding it through a well-designed process of strategic planning. A process of strategic planning, when it is done well, can be a powerful educational experience for a congregation:

- It can involve and engage people in exploring their faith.
- It can reach people who seldom, if ever, participate in a typical adult religious education program.
- It can unify, direct, and focus all the ministries of a congregation.
- It can enable laypeople and clergy alike to become more articulate about their faith.
- It can help the parish avoid spinning its wheels on efforts that make little or no contribution to its reason for existence.

A congregation should understand plannng itself as an educational experience. The root meaning of the English word "education" is "to lead out." It assumes a past ("already"), a present ("being realized"), and a future ("not yet"). The process of education begins with what is known and can be appropriated from earlier experience. Part of the educator's task is to ensure that what is already known about the heritage of the church is conserved and is made available to people in the present. The process continues by incorporating what is currently being discovered. The religious educator's task is to help a congregation enter into an active encounter with its heritage while learning from its own current lived experience. The process moves toward a new future, the point toward which the "leading out" is done.

"Leading out" involves activities directed toward the future, toward a horizon that lies beyond a person's or a congregation's present limits and has not yet been realized. The religious educator's task is to insist that a congregation not settle for what already is but pursue God's vision, which is revealed to us most clearly in the ministry, death, and resurrection of Jesus Christ—the vision of the kingdom or reign of God. Education has a transformational dimension. It challenges people to participate in shaping something better than what already is.[1] Planning, when designed well, can be a highly significant educational and transformational process for a congregation.

Every religious educator knows that several problems face the churches in North America. In the 1960s James Smart[2] alerted us to a "strange silence of the Bible in our churches," suggesting that our educational approach was failing to equip either members or leaders with knowledge of the Bible. This problem persists. In the 1970s John Westerhoff[3] warned that church educational efforts were not leading children to Christian faith. This problem has magnified. In the 1980s John Hull[4] wondered why Christian adults cannot learn. Many directors of Christian education wonder why Christian adults do not or will not participate in educational experiences designed to help them deepen and broaden their understanding of and commitment to the Christian faith. The Search Institute in Minneapolis revealed in its study of six mainline denominations that as we enter a new millennium contemporary church education is not building up faith communities equipped to demonstrate Christ's ministries of love and justice.[5] Most church educators can

1. See Thomas H. Groome, *Christian Religious Education: Sharing Our Story and Vision* (San Francisco: Harper & Row, 1980), pp. 1–19.
2. James D. Smart, *The Creed in Christian Teaching* (Philadelphia: Westminster, 1962). Also see James D. Smart, *The Teaching Ministry of the Church* (Philadelphia: Westminster, 1974).
3. John H. Westerhoff III, *Will Our Children Have Faith?* (New York: Seabury, 1976).
4. John M. Hull, *What Prevents Christian Adults from Learning?* (Philadelphia: Trinity, 1985).
5. Charles R. Foster, *Educating Congregations: The Future of Christian Education* (Nashville: Abingdon, 1994), pp. 17–36.

give examples from their own experience of adults serving in church leadership positions who are generous with their time and concerned for the church. But they are biblically illiterate and lack the "language of faith," a theological vocabulary that allows them to speak intelligently about their faith. These well-intentioned people often have little or no corporate memory of the biblical story of God's salvific activity. One dismaying effect of this is that all too often the very church leaders who are responsible for making the decisions about the congregation's mission and witness are devoid of a clear understanding of the church's divine calling and mission. It is small wonder that North American churches lack a clear sense of direction and focus, are confused about their identity, and have lost sight of what it means to participate in God's mission.

The challenges loom even greater when we consider the fact that the churches in North America have fallen from their former positions of dominance and prominence and are now relegated to the margins of culture. The culture is so secular that North American churches now find themselves in a missionary environment. Finally, a large percentage of young people baptized and confirmed in the churches during the 1950s, 1960s, and 1970s have rejected the church.

A strategic planning process cannot remedy all of these problems, but it can help. When designed as a process of religious education, a strategic planning process can be an exciting adventure for an entire congregation that stimulates spiritual growth.

- It offers an alternative image to the "school" for organizing religious education.
- It views the educational task as flowing from the congregation's efforts to build up a community of faith that demonstrates through its worship, ministry, and common life what it means to be God's people.
- It is a theological process in that it requires discerning the activity of God and participating in it.
- It is an ecclesiological process because it focuses on the calling, identity, and mission of the church.[6]

---

6. "Ecclesiology is understood to be a theological theory of the church . . . The formal object of ecclesiology, however, is expressed in the description and explanation of the church according to the aspect of its future from the perspective of the gospel. The vision and mission of the church, as well as its tasks and goals, lie within this perspective.

- It is an eschatological process for Christians because it is founded upon Jesus' proclamation of the reign or kingdom of God as the ultimate future which God has in store for the creation.
- It provides a church with a "curriculum," a path to be followed, as an entire series of decisions are made in a particular sequence, each requiring study, prayer, and reflection.

If the role of a director or minister of religious education is properly defined so that he or she is responsible for the faith formation of the entire congregation, including its leaders, then access to these persons is already available. If the church educator's role is narrowly restricted to encompass only "the education program," then at a very minimum the persons responsible for that educational program should engage in a strategic planning process for that aspect of church life.

Most religious educators have learned how to plan on the micro-level, that is, how to develop lesson plans for a class of students. They know how to set learning objectives and how to design activities to help a group achieve those objectives. However, few religious educators have been trained in the planning sciences as they relate to and are used by complex organizations, so they may not know how to utilize a much more complex (and also much more exciting and growthful) strategic planning process as a faith formation process for an entire congregation. The rest of this chapter will be devoted to answering the following three questions and apply them to the church: What is planning? What is strategic planning? What is operational planning?

WHAT IS PLANNING?

Planning is a process of making decisions with futurity. As part of the process of planning, a congregation (or on a smaller level a religious education committee) forms a common perspective that will enable it to proceed into the future in a manner that is faithful to its divine calling and mission. Reaching agreement on this perspective, considering the

---

Ecclesiology is concerned both about the future of the church and about the church of the future." Johannes A. van der Ven, *Ecclesiology in Context* (Grand Rapids: Eerdmans, 1993), p. x.

various members and elements that make up a congregation, is often a major challenge and a worthy educational goal. It involves forming a vision of a desired future set of conditions, or mode of being, that it can expect to reach if it is both faithful and effective. The envisioning process in and of itself is a significant opportunity for significant biblical study and theological reflection. In the process of planning, people not only define the results or end points toward which the efforts of their church and its educational ministries are directed (another significant learning process) but they also devise a path that the church will take in order to "arrive" at those endpoints (still another important learning opportunity).[7]

Planning in the church is the process by which a congregation, parish, or other church body makes decisions about its future direction in this complex and changing environment about and how it will implement those decisions. The planning process enables a church to explore its future direction, to identify alternative futures, to clarify how each alternative would affect the performance of the church, and to make choices about which of those alternatives it wishes to pursue.

There was a time when planning was thought of as a valuable new "tool" for religious education leaders. Planning is no longer thought of in such extraneous terms. Planning in religious education is an inextricable part of the entire fabric of congregational leadership. It cannot be distinguished from the rest of the administrative and theological responsibilities of congregational leaders.

There was also a time when the planning process in religious education was viewed solely as a means to an end— the creation of that all-important *plan*. Many congregational leaders still understand planning in this truncated way. In their eyes, the purpose of strategic planning is to produce a product, *the plan*, which will then be implemented. People with such a "product orientation" usually pressure the planning team to "get on with it" in order to come up with *the plan* as quickly as possible. But taking this approach results in missing a rich opportunity to help the entire congregation participate in a religious education formation process that, (if well designed and managed,) can be exceedingly growthful, unifying, and motivating. The religious educator can help

---

7. Richard L. Daft, *Organization Theory and Design* (St. Paul: West Publishing, 1989), p. 89.

people in the congregation recognize that the process of planning is at least as important as the final plan, if not more so. The process of planning is dynamic; it is filled with opportunities for learning.

Many organizations have learned that planning must be an ongoing and continuing part of their life together. They have discovered that most plans become static shortly after they are created. Worse, plans quickly become obsolete. Most plans have a short life because circumstances change rapidly. Some parts of *the plan* become dated, others require rethinking, others simply do not work, and even cause breakdowns in other parts. Even the process of building *the plan* can become a tedious, paper-pushing project that demotivates people.[8] The planning process, when effectively designed and guided, can help a congregation become a unified faith community, can promote biblical literacy, can help leaders and members alike to become more theologically articulate as they learn to speak the language of faith to one another, and can motivate people to pull together in the same direction.

To help a congregation understand the importance of approaching planning as a process of learning and formation rather than only a product, religious educators can draw upon such biblical images as the wilderness experience of the Hebrew people, showing how it was while the people of Israel were wandering in the wilderness—in between the "already" of slavery in Egypt and the "not yet" of the Promised Future and—that an aggregation of former slaves were formed and bound together into the "people of God." It is in the journey of planning, between the "already" of what the church once was and the "not yet" of what God is calling it to be, that a congregation as a whole can be formed in new and powerful ways as a community of the "people of God."

As part of the journey of planning, the congregation is helped to ask and answer questions, such as What is God calling this church to be and do? What values and principles will guide us on our journey? and How shall we reach our destination? Two different kinds of planning are needed to answer those questions: strategic planning to determine the future direction and destination of the church and operational planning to determine the means of getting there. Each approach to planning

---

8. See Henry Mitzberg, *The Rise and Fall of Strategic Planning* (New York: Free Press, 1994). Mitzberg challenges static and cumbersome approaches to planning and offers constructive ways in which planners can serve as strategic thinkers, analysts, and catalysts to help their organizations move forward in meeting the challenges of the future.

has its own goals, its own methods, and its own technical vocabulary. Each requires its own unique management system. Each has costs and liabilities. Each introduces its own kinds of changes. Each benefits the church in a different way.

WHAT IS STRATEGIC PLANNING?

Strategic planning is the process of making decisions that provide the framework and the substance out of which the church has its being. In the technical vocabulary of the planning sciences, "strategy" (or "organizational strategy") refers to a cluster of five strategic decisions that guide and direct all other decisions and all activities in the church. They are the five most important decisions congregations make:

1. *Vision*: the decision about the vision that will guide the church into the future
2. *Mission*: the decision about the mission of the congregation and its role in the world that describes the identity of the church—what it is and what it does
3. *Key result areas and goals*: the decision about the key areas in which the congregation is to achieve results and what those results are to be, each defined in a broadly worded description of what the congregation will be like when the key results are achieved
4. *Target populations*: the decision about who is to be involved, reached, taught, formed through the ministries of the congregation
5. *Guiding philosophy*: the guiding philosophy that establishes the values, beliefs, strategic practices, and standards that will guide the congregation as a body as it goes about its ministry and mission

These five strategic decisions, when functioning as an "organizational strategy," will have long-term effects. They will send the congregation and all its resources in a particular direction, on a particular course. Having been made, these decisions cannot be reversed without great cost. They form the backbone that will support all other decisions the congregation will make.

Because these five strategic decisions are so important, they should be made in a strategic manner, that is deliberately, with time set aside for study, prayer, and reflection.

> The church . . . periodically needs times of withdrawal from the
> surrounding culture in order to sort out the boundaries by which
> it defines its identity. It especially needs such times when it has
> lost its bearings through an overaccommodation to the surrounding
> world. Such periods of withdrawal are not based on a rejection of
> the world or a lack of commitment to social transformation. Rather,
> as Niebuhr puts it, 'Separating itself from the world it might recover
> its integrity.' The church temporarily stands apart from the world,
> in order to clarify its mission on the world's behalf."[9]

Consider what is involved in these five decisions and the educational
opportunities they provide.

Vision

Vision has to do with promise, future, and hope. A congregation's written
vision is an articulated dream of a compelling future that focuses, directs,
and guides persons and the congregation in all their planning and actions.
The vision that guides a congregation must be a theological statement
that expresses God's vision for humanity. It depicts how a congregation
will participate in the activity of God. To discern God's vision involves
forming a congregation into a discerning community, a people who
are grounded in and informed by Scripture and tradition, a people of
hope who are learning to see with the eyes of faith, a people who are
cultivating faithful imaginations that can discern what is really real. A
discerning community is one in which people together sort, distinguish,
evaluate, and sift among competing stimuli, demands, longings, desires,
and influences in order "to discern what is the will of God—what is good
and acceptable and perfect"[10] For both Christians and Jews, discerning a
vision is a communal endeavor. For Christians, this endeavor is guided
by the Holy Spirit, who works through the interaction of the two or three
gathered together in the name of Jesus Christ as they wait on the Spirit
in humble expectation, silence, and prayer. The process of surfacing,
testing, and transforming vision is much more than a periodic planning
effort, and articulating the vision is much more than a planning tool. The
process of forming a discerning community should be at the heart of the
ongoing life of the congregation.

---

9. Richard Robert Osmer, *A Teachable Spirit: Recovering the Teaching Office in the Church* (Louisville: Westminster/John Knox, 1990), p. 12.
   10. Romans 12:3

Mission

A mission statement serves as a foundation for all major decisions a congregation will ever make. Such a statement should encompass (1) the identity of the congregation (who we are), (2) the nature of our "work" (what we do), (3) our reason for being (why we exist).

A mission statement is designed to provide firm guidance in making important administrative and programmatic decisions. Its purpose is to establish and maintain consistency and clarity of purpose throughout the congregation, to provide a frame of reference for all major planning decisions, to gain commitment from everyone in the congregation through clear communication of the congregation's nature and identity, and to gain understanding and support from people outside the congregation who are important to its continued witness. It guides all congregational decision makers so that any plans developed by any group in the congregation can be tested for compatibility with its mission. The mission statement should be an extension of the vision.

The process of formulating a mission statement is clearly a religious educational process and one in which a religious educator should play a major role. For example, a religious educator can help those responsible for formulating a mission statement reflect on the current context in which North American churches are functioning. The former era, when North America was a "churched culture" has ended and congregations are operating today in an "unchurched culture." Planning team members, and a congregation, can be helped to consider what it means to become a "missionary church" in a secular culture that is indifferent to the church and how this differs from the church's former role as part of the dominant cultural establishment.

Key Result Areas and Goals

One of the most challenging decisions a congregation makes regards the key areas in which it is to achieve results. In the past, congregations tended to adopt the "bigger-better-more" results prized by a consumer economy. They engaged in church growth efforts, incorporated the marketing sciences to become effective vendors of religious goods and services and gain "market share," incorporated commercial fund-raising methods, offered expansive programs, engaged in good works, and identified themselves with the nation state. They were clear about their key result areas. In today's new missionary environment the situation is different. Congregations are unclear about the results they are to achieve. Having been so acculturated for so long, it is a major struggle to break free from cultural bondage and to learn to think in new ways about the church and the results it is to achieve.[11]

The religious educator can help by enabling the planners and the congregation recognize how the North American scenery has changed for the churches, by introducing new ways of thinking about the church's mission, by helping to generate alternative result areas from which choices can be made, and by facilitating the decision-making process.

Key result areas represent those priority areas in which the congregation is to achieve results that will enable the mission to be realized and that will move the congregation in the direction of its vision. Key result areas act as driving forces that affect the direction of the church. They clarify the course or heading the church is taking.[12] They determine the scope of future programming and action. They "drive" the church.

If key result areas are not clarified and articulated and if they are not used to organize the work of the church, then other forces (usually financial) inevitably slip into the driver's seat and take control. Instead of being strategy driven the congregation becomes "survival driven" or "fiscally driven."

Goals are broadly worded descriptions of the end results the congregation is seeking. At least one goal should be developed for each key result area. Goals are not objectives. Objectives are specific and measurable results to be achieved within a given span of time, such as by next year. Goals are broader in scope and describe the future positions the congregation wants to "have" or to "become" at designated future times in order to carry out its vision and mission.

The church educator who is skilled in composing learning goals and objectives can help the planners and the congregation learn the technical differences between goals and objectives and can provide instruction not only in writing the goals but also in the theological reflection required to redefine the goals in this new missionary era.

---

11. See Lesslie Newbigin, *The Gospel in a Pluralist Society* (Grand Rapids: Eerdmans, 1989) and George R. Hunsberger and Craig Van Gelder, eds., *The Church between Gospel and Culture* (Grand Rapids: Eerdmans, 1996).

12. For more information about key result areas in today's North American missionary environment, including several alternative ways of discerning and articulating them, see Paul Dietterich, *Focusing Our Shared Ministry* (Chicago: Center for Parish Development, 1996).

Target Populations

With whom is your congregation to be in ministry and mission? Who are the persons toward whom all your activities are directed? These are strategic questions and answering them require strategic thought. In one congregation a big man with a loud voice and lots of money proclaimed that the congregation's primary target was youth. He insisted that the church add a youth minister to the staff, reasoning that if the church could attract youth, it would also attract the parents of youth, thereby increasing its membership size and financial strength. When confronted with the demographics showing that the community had aged, most of the public school buildings had been closed, and the average age in the community was between sixty and seventy years, he declared the information incorrect and continued to insist on the course of action he was proposing. Fortunately the planners were able to find a way around this person. Otherwise he would have equipped the congregation to minister to a population no longer present in the community.

The decision about target populations is strategic. It influences staffing, budgeting, programming, and the other resources of a church. The religious educator can help the planners and the congregation make this decision based on accurate information and projections for the future, as well as on understandings of what it means to be a witnessing missional congregation.

Guiding Philosophy

Every congregation has its own culture, a kind of congregational personality, that is a reflection of the values, convictions, and behaviors of its leaders and members. It establishes and communicates the expectations people can have of one another and of the congregation itself. These expectations form a guiding philosophy that determines how the congregation will conduct its work, recruit leaders, and establish priorities.

Any number of factors can contribute to the strategic philosophy of a congregation. Christians, for example, can call upon Paul, Peter, John, and other New Testament writers who called for a new kind of radical togetherness to characterize life in the early Christian communities. Communities of Christians were to live together in such a way that they formed a reconciled society of people living under the norms and standards of the reign of God. The following list is far from exhaustive:

Figure 4.1
Practical Behaviors for a Reconciled Community

Showing honor	outdo one another in showing honor (Rom 12:10)
In harmony	live in harmony with one another (Rom 12:16)
Welcoming	welcome one another (Rom 15:7)
Admonishing	admonish one another (Rom 15:4)
Greeting	greet one another with a holy kiss (Rom 16:16)
Waiting for	wait for one another (1 Cor 11:33)
Caring for	have the same care for one another (1 Cor 12:25)
Serving	be servants of one another (Gal 5:13)
Bearing	bear one another's burdens (Gal 6:2)
Comforting	comfort one another (1 Thess 5:11)
Building up	build one another up (1 Thess 5:11)
At peace	be at peace with one another (1 Thess 5:13)
Kind	be kind and compassionate to one another (Eph 4:32)
Subject to	be subject to one another (Eph 5:21)
Confessing	confess your sins to one another (Ja 5:16)
Praying	pray for one another (Ja 5:16)
Loving	love one another from the heart (1 Pt 1:22)
Humility	meet one another with humility (1 Pt 5:5)
Fellowship	have fellowship with one another (1 Jn 1:7)

All of these statements specify practical behaviors that Christians are to practice with one another. They also demonstrate a way of being together that is prized, highly valued, and precious to them. They show that early church leaders were seeking a unique community with a way of being together that contrasts with the world around it, and reveals a different way to be a society.

The planners' responsibility is to identify behaviors, expectations, values, and ways of "being the church" that the gospel calls for and are or should be prized by the congregation. Lacking help, many church planning groups come up with lists of strategic values drawn directly and uncritically from the corporate world: quality, safety, image, responsiveness, financial growth, membership growth, program diversity, and so on. The role of the religious educator is to help the planners reflect on religious practices drawn from Scripture, as illustrated above. The strategic philosophy is usually expressed in the vision and mission statements, but it may help a congregation to be able to read and study such a statement as an additional strategic document shaping the direction of the congregation.

The religious educator can offer the following criteria to the planners to help make these five strategic decisions. In order to achieve the greatest degree of congregational learning, these five strategic decisions should be made

1. with the broadest possible participation by the congregation in order to share the insights and gifts of the whole body;
2. in a spirit of prayer to assure that each decision is guided by the Spirit and to remind the body that this is God's church, not ours;
3. based on careful and rigorous study of Scripture and tradition to insure that they are faithful to and participate in God's mission;
4. with time allowed for reflection so that people have time to ponder, to consider the implications of each strategic decision for themselves and for the congregation;
5. analytically, making use of processes of critical testing and examination in advance of implementation

These strategic decisions should not be based on the whims or the uninformed biases of the decision makers. They require critical analysis. A strategic educational process is needed for a congregation to arrive at informed strategic decisions that unify and give direction and focus to a church or synagogue. It is possible for a *plan* to be created by a planning committee from a congregation but for the process to be so flawed and the theological presuppositions to be so shallow that only the planners own it and are motivated to implement it. The planning system breaks down whenever the planning process is flawed. In such cases, the strategic decisions that emerge will be based on unexamined assumptions about the activity and mission of God, the calling of the church, and the church's God-given mission. Many church bodies build plans but fail to design and enable congregation-wide participation in processes of study and discernment. As a result, they tend to make superficial decisions based on the assumptions of people who have the most power or the loudest voices. Unexamined strategic decisions tend to make the church or synagogue of the future a carbon copy of the church or synagogue of the present.

Few strategic planning resources are available to guide church bodies in processes of Scripture study, theological inquiry, and religious discourse. Most of the literature about church strategic planning assumes what is now an obsolete operating paradigm of the church. The result is that many church bodies think they are engaging in "strategic planning" when in actuality they are not being strategic at all. Unless there is a challenge to the frame of reference for a congregation, there is little chance strategic planning will be done.

The world has changed. The church has been disestablished and needs a new orientation. Unless church leaders and religious educators recognize and understand the depth and scope of the church's changed position in society, they will continue to plan operationally instead of strategically. And as a result, North American churches will continue to be unfaithful and ineffective.

This is where the religious educator comes in.[13] As the professional educator in the congregation and as a person trained to understand and guide processes of learning and study, the religious educator can serve as a guide who

1. stimulates readiness to participate in a strategic planning process,
2. frames the strategic planning process as a Christian or faith formation experience for the entire congregation,
3. teaches church decision makers (and other church members as well) the importance of strategic decisions,
4. uses broadly participatory study and discernment processes that not only "inform" the strategic decisions but also mold the decision makers and the congregation together as a more faithful, unified, biblically and theologically articulate faith community,
5. emphasizes the importance of the process of planning as well as the importance of the plans that emerge from the process,

---

13. Donald G. Emler, *Revisioning the DRE* (Birmingham, Ala.: Religious Education Press, 1989). Emler makes a strong case for the director of religious education as a skilled specialist in the congregation fulfilling the roles of administrator and program developer, educational consultant, learning specialist, researcher-diagnostician-evaluator, and faith interpreter. I am proposing the additional role of planning consultant.

6. establishes the principle that concern for basic strategy is more important than any particular program efficiently managed. Efficiently managed programs can fail if a church or synagogue uses the wrong strategy.[14] The most important task of religious education leadership is to help the congregation think through and define its strategy.[15]

Space limitations rule out a detailed description of both the process of strategic planning and the process of operational planning. Planners can recognize, however, that strategic decisions provide guidance, direction, and boundaries for operational decision making. With the organizational strategy clearly in mind, persons charged with managing various units, committees, task forces, or other groups in the church or synagogue organization have a clear basic structure in which to do their operational work. When the organizational strategy is missing, operational management will inevitably become driven by fiscal concerns: How much does it cost? and Can we afford it? But a well-developed strategic framework and strategic perspective will generate different operational questions: How does our proposed course of action fulfill our vision and mission? To what extent will this proposed course of action achieve our goals? Strategic decisions enable the church to become purpose driven rather than survival driven.

Theological Inquiry and Discourse

Strategic planning needs to be thought of as a theological process. Congregational strategic planning differs from the strategic planning that is done in other organizations because theological inquiry and discourse must be central to the process in religious communities. More specifically, the process should engage congregational leaders and the entire church or synagogue body in biblical and theological study about the activity of God in the world and about the calling of the church or synagogue in today's world. Simple proof texting of biblical phrases or creedal definitions is not helpful. What is needed is to identify and bring to the surface the presuppositions that form decisions and actions.

---

14. Peter Drucker, *Management: Tasks, Responsibilities, Practices* (New York: Harper & Row, 1974), p. 611.

15. Peter F. Drucker, *Managing the Nonprofit Organization: Principles and Practices* (New York: HarperCollins, 1990), p. 3.

As a theological process, strategic planning in the church or synagogue should:

1. call into question all of the fundamental presuppositions on which the church or synagogue and its religious education planners have been functioning;
2. engage the church or synagogue in building new propositional foundations;
3. redefine the identity of the church or synagogue, as well as its religious education mission, on the basis of a different frame of reference;
4. be conceived as a theological process that incorporates theological inquiry, reflection, discourse, and exploration;
5. be understood as a spiritual formation process that leads to major, profound, and long lasting changes in the very identity, mission, and self-understanding of the congregation;
6. be informed by the study of Scripture, reflection on the life of the church or synagogue, sharing of faith, and processes to discern the activity and calling of God;
7. be an experience of church or synagogue; the process needs to be designed in such a way that it actualizes and manifests that which is being aimed for;
8. have internal good in and of itself;
9. be spiritually enriching and uplifting;
10. encourage broad participation, enabling all persons in the church or synagogue body to share their various God given gifts and thereby building up the faith community itself;
11. enable the community to explore, to share, and to grow in its common life and shared ministry as the people of God;
12. enable the entire church or synagogue body to discover the direction of its future life together;
13. make connections with and affect every aspect of church or synagogue life and work: worship, missional concerns, education, leadership activities;
14. draw from and contribute to the ongoing life and practice of the church or synagogue body.

Theological study and religious inquiry invites religious education leaders and members alike to compare a contemporary understanding of the church with understandings of the church portrayed in Scripture.

Jews may reflect on the meaning of being a *faithful community* and Christians may reflect on what it means to be *a body of people sent on a mission*. Such an understanding of the church challenges every local, regional, and national religious education agency, to become a faithful sign, foretaste, and instrument of life in the reign of God. A major part of the religious education mission of the church or synagogue is to become a "demonstration community," a living example of a different way to be a society.[16]

Theological study and religious inquiry should also help religious education in North American achieve freedom from cultural captivity. Christianity in North America has been a part of the political-industrial-social-economic-legal-military establishment. This interrelationship permeates both the church and the larger culture on the subconscious and unconscious levels. It is difficult to know where one leaves off and the other begins. Most church members probably do not know whether they are Americans or Canadians who happen to be Christians or Christians who happen to be Americans or Canadians.

Rigorous theological inquiry as part of a strategic planning process should lead to critical reflection about the relationship of the church to the dominant cultural establishment, about what this relationship currently is, and about what it should be. The Church needs to recognize its own unique identity distinct from culture and thereby escape its current captivity to culture. However, the thought of distancing the church from the pursuits and values of the dominant culture is abhorrent to many church leaders. There will be resistance.

If strategic planning is to be part of the life and work of religious education, it must be grounded in the thought and practice of religious tradition with a strong theological component.

> The first task of the teaching office—the determination of the church's normative beliefs and practices—focuses on the activity of setting forth those teachings by which the church identifies itself as a community. . . This involves the transmission and preservation of the core elements of the heritage of a church community, those items upon which its identity is based. . . The second task of the teaching office [is] the ongoing reinterpretation of the church's normative beliefs and practices in the face of shifting cultural and historical contexts.[17]

---

16. See Hunsberger and Van Gelder, eds., *The Church between Gospel and Culture*.
17. Osmer, *A Teachable Spirit* , pp. 15–17.

Without a strong theological component, only limited reflection will occur about the church's calling. In North American churches congregational planners simply continue to assume the old "establishment church" paradigm and the church simply continues to think of itself as a relatively innocuous vendor of religious goods and services designed only to meet the self-defined wants of individuals and to be the "chaplain" to the nation.

Class of Changes Made
Strategic planning that is done well leads to systemwide changes in the church. Such changes *reorient* the church's understanding of its identify and its calling and mission in a secular culture, producing a new frame of reference or worldview. The vision, the mission, and the goals require extensive changes in how the church defines and lives out its understanding of its calling and mission.

Work Pressures
Strategic planning cannot be done effectively by operational managers. While the operational managers keep the ship afloat and care for its day-to-day management , strategic planners must have no responsibility whatsoever for operational decisions. They must not become caught up in the immediacy of work pressures.

Decision-Making Method
In strategic religious education planning, a database is created to undergird each strategic decision. The data is carefully analyzed, leading to careful, thoughtful, prayerful decisionmaking. In strategic planning, religious education strategic managers make decisions deliberately, thoughtfully, prayerfully, based on the best and most complete information available.

Authority of Planners
Strategic planners must be placed high in the church's organizational structure. In congregational and parish planning, this usually means that the planning team reports directly to the council. In a regional church body (synod, conference, diocese, etc.) the strategic planners should report directly to the annual meeting and should be under the direct

supervision of the bishop or regional executive. When the religious education department of a congregation or regional body engages in strategic planning, those planners should report directly to the committee responsible for religious education. The point is that strategic decisions are so far-reaching and so profound that the final decision-making body must make them. Therefore the religious education planners should report directly to that central body. In contrast, operational managers usually have the authority to make decisions and implement them. In most church bodies, religious education strategic planners have no such authority. They recommend decisions to a higher, more central body. Once the higher body makes the decision, the strategic planners can then recommend implementation procedures.

Information

Strategic planning requires a substantial information base to inform strategic religious education decisions. In order to determine the current and future situation facing the church body and to identify major problems and issues that the strategic plan must address, a profile needs to be constructed. This profile serves as a major learning resource. It is carefully examined, analyzed, reviewed, and discussed broadly throughout the religious education system in order to identify the strategic decisions that the strategic plan must address. The profile must contain valid and reliable information in at least four areas: (1) the theological heritage of the church organization and how that heritage is expressed in church life and work, (2) the external environment, including trends projections that reveal changes that will be occurring, (3) the constituency of the church body in order to clarify who is involved and who will be participating in the church in the future, and (4) a description of how the church organization currently functions and how it will need to function in the future.

In addition, it is essential for religious education strategic planners to have strong communications capability in order to keep the entire system aware of all strategic documents as they emerge and in order to prepare people for knowledgeable participation in strategic decision making.

Feedback

Due to the nature of strategic decisions, the impact of these decisions may not be felt for months or years after they are made. The strategic planners must therefore develop a process for monitoring the effects of all strategic decisions over an extended period of time. This process will provide the planners with information necessary for adjusting decisions or making additional decisions.

Timing

Time must be allotted to gathering the information needed to inform and support strategic decisions. When risks are identified, each risk option must be examined critically and carefully and must be played out in scenario form as part of making the strategic decision.

Strategic planning's priorities differ from those of operational planning. The futurity of decisions is important. The long view is more important than the short view. Where operational decisions are made hastily and on the run, strategic decisions must be made reflectively, with sufficient time for pondering and analyzing each decision. The group responsible for guiding the strategic planning process must be free from day-to-day operational concerns. It must be given the time required to think and ponder, pray and reflect.

Strategy Making

An integrated organizational strategy is created at a point in time. In operational planning strategy evolves as a series of decisions become precedents. But in strategic planning the organizational strategy is carefully crafted and is presented as a complete document for action by the decision-making person or body.

Implementation

A major investment of time and energy must go into planning the implementation (or transition management) process. Research and experience indicate that truly strategic plans requiring the reorientation of the church organization require a process plan for strategic management. This includes fostering a strategy supportive climate and culture, building a transition plan, managing the transition into the new strategic framework, and instituting strategic controls. All strategic changes must be integrated into and assimilated by the church system.

WHAT IS OPERATIONAL PLANNING?

Planning also involves the creation of specific steps to achieve the desired future. It is not enough to clarify and choose a future direction for the church, thus answering the question, Where are we going? Another question, How shall we get there? must be answered. A management system must also be planned and developed to assure that the church body will move in the direction of its goals and will do so on a specific schedule, with a specific timeline, with clear responsibilities carried out by specific leaders and leadership groups, and within a certain budget.

So there is planning—and then there is planning.

Not all planning processes are the same. Different approaches to planning lead to making different kinds of decisions. Each approach produces different results. Each approach requires different kinds of management systems. Some approaches to planning are more effective than others, depending on the circumstances. If used inappropriately, some can actually damage the church and its religious education efforts.

Most church bodies are managed operationally. The major question operational leaders ask is, How are we to make efficient use of our scarce resources in order to achieve our goals? Operational management involves a major investment of time and energy devoted to problem-solving activity: how to enlist and train leaders, how to develop and produce a variety of programs and services, how to deal with conflict, how to assimilate new members, how to generate the money required. In terms of operational thinking, if solutions can be found for these problems and if the problems are addressed efficiently, the organization's resources will be well used.

What exactly is operational planning and how does it work?

Definition
Operational planning is the process of making decisions with short term effects. Operational decisions are made on a short-range planning horizon; operational leaders deal with the immediate, day-to day managing of the church organization or one of its religious education programs. These decisions involve little risk, although they may carry some costs. Once made, it is possible for the church body to reverse operational decisions without damaging itself very seriously.

A Sequence of Operational Decisions
Operational planners such as pastors, directors of religious education, or directors of central office religious education are fundamentally problem solvers. Since their primary concern is efficient use of the church's scarce resources, operational planners spend much of their time identifying and

solving problems related to resource use. In operational planning, the planning group usually makes the following decisions in the following sequence:

1. *Problem Definition*: The planning group clearly defines the specific problem that congregation is facing. Unless it defines the problem accurately, the planning group has little hope of identifying a solution.

2. *Problem Analysis*: The planning group identifies the factors contributing to the problem. It is these factors that will need to be addressed in any solution.

3. *Setting Objectives*: Objectives are precise, measurable, and timebound descriptions of desired end results. The exact outcomes that are desired are defined.

4. *Establishing Essential Conditions*: Every solution must meet certain criteria, usually associated with cost, quality, and time, if it is to be supported enthusiastically. These are the essential conditions. Other criteria, which it would be helpful if the solution could meet, are desirable conditions. Prior to devising a solution, the planning group needs to clarify the essential conditions, which the solution must meet, and differentiate them from the desirable conditions. The best solution is one that meets all of the essential conditions and most of the desirable conditions.

5. *Generating Alternative Solutions*: With the problem clearly identified, the major contributing factors or forces identified, clear and precise objectives established, and the essential conditions clarified, the planners then generate a number of alternative solutions. Brainstorming processes are often helpful in generating these alternatives. The goal is to facilitate distinguishing one option from among a number of viable options. But the alternative solutions must be viable. They must address the problem as defined, diminish the power of the major factors contributing to the problem, achieve the objective, and be capable of implementation within the essential conditions.

6. *Choosing One Option*: Having assembled a number of viable alternative solutions from which to choose, the planners must now decide on one option to implement. This usually involves weighing the costs and the benefits of each of the alternative solutions and selecting the one with the least cost and the most benefit.

7. *Creating the Implementation Plan*: Implementing the option is the next step. This usually includes constructing program plans, budgets, and timelines. Depending on the complexity of the solution, the planners

may develop a variety of timelines, PERT charts (program evaluation review technique), or Gannt charts, which show all the steps that will need to be taken and the sequence in which they will be taken.

8. *Assigning Responsibility*: Having drawn up all the detailed implementation plans, the planners must then identify the persons or groups to implement the plans. These persons will need to be enlisted, trained for their work, and provided with the resources they need to do it. They need to be supervised, supported, and rewarded in some ways.

9. *Implementing the Plans*: Operational management is the process a planning team uses to assure that the various plans are actually implemented in the ways they were planned.

10. *Monitoring and Adjusting*: As any plan is implemented, especially for the first time, each step of the plan requires a continuous monitoring and adjusting to assure a good "fit" between the problem and the solution. Monitoring involves regular checking on the implementation process to see what is actually occurring. Adjusting means making the little (and sometimes big) changes needed in the plan or in the implementation process so that the solution will work well, the objectives will be achieved and all essential conditions will be met.

Operational Managing

Operational managing is the process of implementing operational decisions. Most religious educators and other church leaders are operational managers. They operate in an atmosphere of immediacy. They handle their work effectively on a day to-day basis within a framework of operating plans and general economic principles (such as those governing costs, cash flow, and budgets).

Most operational managers gather information on the fly, integrate it hurriedly, juggle many issues simultaneously, make decisions hastily, and try to balance naturally opposed forces. Unless provided for by clear organizational design, neither strategic planning nor strategic transformation can help operational managers as they fashion hasty, improvised solutions.

The priorities involved in operational management are usually wrong for strategic planning and are always wrong for strategic transformation. Operational responsibilities focus on the specific and the present, whereas strategic planners focus attention on the general and the future. Various constituents place demands on the operational manager for immediate action.

Operational managers live under constant pressure to be productive. They tend to develop an "activities" orientation rather than a "results" orientation. (Their reports to their constituents usually highlight their activities rather than the redemptive results of those activities. The church rewards them for being so busy, not for the results they have achieved.) Most church bodies are not clear about the results they expect from operational managers, beyond satisfying various political needs. Because of the pressure to be productive, most church leaders are operational in their thinking, planning, and managing.

Theological Inquiry and Discourse

Operational management assumes and occurs within the existing frame of reference of the church: the cognitive, affective, and behavioral lens through which things are interpreted and lived out. A church's frame of reference includes existing assumptions, expectations, beliefs, values, patterns of behavior, purpose, goals, ways of doing things, structures, processes, norms, and standards. The frame of reference of a church is its "worldview" or operating "paradigm," its way of seeing and interpreting reality.

This frame of reference may be clearly articulated in writing and made broadly available to the operational managers. More commonly, however, the frame of reference of most North American church bodies is not clearly articulated. It is not in writing. It is implicit, assumed, and unexamined, often invisible to the operational planners themselves. Yet decisions are made from this frame of reference, regardless of how implicit and invisible it may be.

Working in a context that pressures planners to produce lots of programs and quick results, most operational managers make decisions based on a multitude of implicit presuppositions about what the church and religious education is called to be and do. When asked to make these presuppositions explicit, operational managers often resist, objecting that doing so would slow them down and interfere with "getting on with it."

Most operational managers in both church and religious education, however, have either never examined critically the presuppositional world in which they operate. Some have tried but found the task overwhelming. Other planners recoil at the thought of such a process not only because it is hard work but because it may force them to adopt ways of working and behavior that planners know church organizations neither value nor reward. Work pressures for planners do not allow them to consider such examinations. Furthermore, there are few resources available to help planners engage creatively in such a difficult task.

As a result, most church leaders and religious educators assume

- some undefined and unexamined understanding of the church's calling and mission,
- some undefined and ambiguous guiding vision,
- some key areas in which the church must achieve results in its ministry and mission if it is to be both faithful and effective,
- some goals to give the church a sense of direction for the future,
- some larger populations that their solution must satisfy,
- some set of values and norms that serve as a strategic orientation for the church.

Few operational church leaders raise or even consider theological questions like, What is God calling the church to be and do in today's postmodern world? Some are actually hostile to theological reflection. As one operational and very pragmatic manager put it, "Theology just gets in the way."

Class of Changes Made
Most operational plans introduce low-level incremental changes into the church. Such changes are usually made operationally and on the run. They are introduced in piecemeal fashion in one part of the church system either to anticipate some emerging challenge or to correct some problem that has already occurred.

Incremental changes assume the existing frame of reference of the church and do not challenge it. They affect only part of the church system and may not be noticed in other parts. They have short-term effects.

Work Pressures
Operational managers generally do not plan well because of diverting motivations, inexperience, lack of training, or lack of feedback. Because of the many pressures placed on them and the lack of organizational

attention to unrealistic workloads, they just do not have the time to engage in strategic planning, even given the inclination and the skill.

The operational manager's most valuable resource is time. But to a great extent, time is not his or her own. Operational managers simply cannot function in unhurried, reflective modes if the demands of their jobs do not provide for time allotted to strategic planning. Without an adjustment in workloads, strategic planning will simply be added on to already pressured workloads. To treat the planning process as an "add on" is to build failure into the church organization. Outmoded arrangements of assigning work must be jettisoned if strategic planning and strategic transformation are to be able to flow unimpeded to their respective destinations. Nothing is more dangerous to a church organization than unrealistic work expectations that clog planning channels.

Decision-Making Method

Some operational managers pride themselves on working through the sequence of steps in operational problem solving in a matter of seconds. They make hasty decisions. Many seek a quick fix and an easy answer. Many operational managers resist spending much time on problem identification and problem analysis for fear that the problem will become more complicated if it is analyzed too much and will ultimately require a more complex solution. Some operational managers actually belittle problem analysis because they think that it slows them down. They sometimes may speak disparagingly of "the paralysis of analysis."

Authority of Planners

Operational managers, whether an individual DRE or a church council, tend to have the authority and the power to choose among competing values. They are able to make decisions, allocate funds, deploy personnel. They can decide how time will be invested, what the priorities will be, and what tasks must be done before others. Although they usually must report to one or another church legislative body, when it comes to the day-to-day management of the church, these religious educators do have the authority to make decisions independent of their respective authorizing bodies. However, making and implementing a wide range of operational decisions without seeking permission from others would be considered overstepping their responsibilities and privileges.

Information

Operational managers recognize the importance of information and try to gain immediate access to channels of information related to a particular problem they are trying to solve. They gather as much information as can be garnered quickly. They make most of their decisions on the run, based on partial information.

Feedback

The feedback system of most operational managers is short run and almost immediate. They make a change and usually get immediate feedback from those affected by the change. Many operational managers deliberately seek feedback. (How do you like the new microwave oven in the kitchen . . . the new hymns we sang last Sunday . . . the way we now conduct business in staff meetings?") They adapt to feedback and respond to it by making quick adjustments.

Timing

Operational managers react quickly to unanticipated problems. When a problem arises, operational managers swing into action very swiftly. They are often evaluated in terms of their ability to function quickly and effectively in response to crises. In the same way, operational managers tend to take advantage of change opportunities. One operational manager, for example, when confronted by unanticipated problems, always initiates the problem solving and operational planning process by asking, "What opportunity does this give us?"

Strategy Making

The decision about the church's organizational strategy is not made at one point in time, deliberately, by the church body. When the church is run by operational managers making piecemeal decisions on the run, the church's organizational strategy evolves over time by the sheer accumulation of operational decisions that tend to form patterns that have the effect of being strategic.

Implementation

Depending on the skill of the operational managers and the pressures under which they are working, implementation of the operational plans may vary. In many cases, operational plans are carefully introduced and integrated into church life and work. In other cases, even the operational plans themselves are introduced hastily, and on the run. Insufficient attention has been devoted to preparing persons for the changes, to quality control, to training those who will implement the plans, or to monitoring and adjusting the plans. Since most operational plans call only for tuning and adapting adjustments to the existing work and structure of the church, they can be introduced quickly and with a minimum of effort.

CONCLUSION

Both operational planning and strategic planning are appropriate administrative processes under the right conditions. Operational planning in religious education is essential to getting things done in a timely manner and with attention to quality, budgets, and human resource utilization. Once the strategic framework has been crafted and the religious education enterprise has decided on strategic management, operational planning within that framework is essential.

Strategic planning, with a transformational perspective in today's post establishment church world, is essential because it enables the church to redefine itself and religious education in a new frame of reference. It helps the congregation discern and discover how to participate in God's vision and mission. It enables the congregation to become focused and purposeful. When well managed, strategic planning leads to a reorientation that assures the introduction, integration, and assimilation of major and profound changes in ways of perceiving, thinking, and behaving as the church.

Too often strategic decisions are made by default, instead of a well-designed strategic planning process. As operational managers make operational decisions on the run, the church body's strategy becomes determined over time by the sheer accumulation of operational decisions that tend to form patterns that have the effect of being strategic.

When a religious education enterprise commits itself to strategic planning, it must do so with the full realization that it must either segregate strategic planning from the operational manager's work responsibilities (with different persons performing the different functions) or make provision for its operational managers to shift gears as they move back and forth from strategic to operational decision making. Unless provision is made for this shifting of gears, usually by the adjustment of workloads, operational managers will become confused and even more pressured, resulting in diminished effectiveness and increased stress.

The different and conflicting decision-making styles, values, and skills needed for operational versus strategic planning are shown in figure 4.2 below. In most complex organizations, the strategic planning process is turned over to a planning group that has no other responsibilities. Operational planning is assigned to program managers. These organizations have determined that the two sets of competencies are sufficiently different that the same person cannot do them both or at best will not have peace of mind while attempting to perform them both.

Other organizations have learned that with proper training, adjustments in workloads, and clear expectations among all concerned persons and groups, the same persons can perform both functions—if the persons themselves and the organization recognize that the two planning functions call for opposite working behaviors. Without this recognition, people will feel pushed and pulled in both directions simultaneously. They will violate the primary concern of strategic planning: that strategic decisions must be made strategically. In making the transition into strategic planning, careful attention must be given to the conflicting dynamics of operational and strategic decision making in religious education.

Figure 4.2
Requirements of Operational and Strategic Planning

Factor	Operational Planning	Strategic Planning (as a Transformational Process)
Theological inquiry and discourse	Receives little or no attention; existing theological frame of reference is assumed	Undertakes theological exploration of the church's calling and mission; redefines the church's identity and work
Class of changes made	Makes turning and adapting changes within the existing frame of reference	Reorients the church to a new frame of reference, intentionally bending, sometimes breaking the frame of reference of the entire church system
Work pressures	Values program productivity; is pressured to produce quick results	Has time to identify and reflect critically on presuppositions; organizes and ponders decisions
Decision-making method	Makes intuitive, implicit decisions on the run	Makes analytical decisions, with broad participation
Authority of planners	Has both formal and informal authority to make and implement decisions	Has formal authority only; enables broad involvement to identify optional courses of action and facilitate choices among them

continued

Figure 4.2, *continued*

Factor	Operational Planning	Strategic Planning (as a Transformational Process)
Information	Possesses immediate access to channels of information; makes decisions based on partial information	Involves broad participation in gathering and analyzing information, including the results of theological inquire; decisions grow out of communal reflection and sharing
Feedback	Adapts quickly to feedback on decisions	Encourages entire church body to become a learning system: examining, interpreting, and utilizing feedback gathered over time
Timing	Reacts quickly to unanticipated problems; takes advantage of chance opportunities	Has freedom from day-to-day operational concerns; uses the process as an opportunity to transform the life and practice of the church body: carefully times every step to maximize participation and learning
Strategy making	Strategy evolves as series of decisions become precedents, made over time in stepwise fashion	Integrates organizational strategy to create intentionally at one point in time
Implementation	Does quick tuning and makes adapting adjustments	Deliberately embeds new ways of perceiving, thinking, and behaving: fosters a strategy-supportive climate, manages transition; change may be fast or slow

5

ASSESSING THE NEEDS
OF A CONGREGATION

Gilbert R. Rendle

A needs assessment is critical in planning religious education appropriate to the specific people each congregation seeks to serve. People who do spiritual seeking within religious organizations today come to the local congregation with a plethora of divergent questions, expectations, interests, and personal histories. Planners in religious education find themselves asking, What form of ministry should be used? At the heart of the question is the desire to discern the specific call that God has given to the particular congregation.

In earlier generations cultural standards were closely followed by most congregations, and differences among groups of people in the population were minimal. In such an environment, religious education programs in congregations were designed as "one-size-fits-all." These programs were the expected norm. Religious education programs did not change. People conformed to the religious education offered by the congregation. However, today cultural expectations are increasingly diverse and differences among subgroups of people are highly recognized and supported. The expectation is that religious education will shape itself to meet these differences. Planners in religious education need to know as much about the people it seeks to serve as it does about the faith the congregation seeks to share.

A needs assessment is a process of collecting and interpreting data to describe what people report as important to them. The goal of collecting

131

data is the accurate description of people and perceived needs. The data collected forms a database that guides decisions made by leaders.

Congregations are ministering to increasingly different people with church resources often strained and limited. Effective congregations led by competent planners of religious education need to make decisions about where to (and where not to) use their resources of dollars, staff, time, and facilities. Without a database built on current and future needs of the people who are the target of the congregation's ministry, these decisions will not come easily and will be accurate. However, with a database that develops from an ongoing process of listening to and learning about people, the congregation will have an opportunity to monitor the effectiveness and the appropriateness of its planning in religious education. An accurate database establishes a foundation for and a realistic pathway to planning subsequent assessment initiatives.

This chapter addresses the purpose and design of a religious education needs assessment for planning in religious education. It also offers basic techniques of data gathering and analysis. Two approaches to religious education needs assessment will be reviewed: (1) through problems and (2) through opportunities for ministry. There are times when an assessment is initiated as a part of an overall problem-solving process. On other occasions an assessment may be a response to an opportunity for ministry, in which case a competency model approach is appropriate.

There are benefits in a well-designed religious education assessment of congregational needs. Techniques of data gathering, ways in which questions shape responses, and a conceptual framework will be offered to better understand and to better identify the appropriate audience to be assessed. Assessing the religious education needs of a congregation includes gathering and analyzing data about people who are and people who will be participants in religious education. The fundamental reason for gathering and analyzing data is to enable congregational leaders to do critical decision making.

Religious education is not data driven and does not easily conform to a quantitative bottom line. A necessary discernment process is at the heart of making decisions to be faithful to the call of God. This work of discernment can be informed and supported by what is learned from an assessment process. But the discernment must also be sensitive to (1) the purpose and identity of the congregation and (2) the resources available to the congregation. A shared variance model of decision making will be discussed as a means of balancing the discernment process and helping to keep needs assessment learnings in perspective for decision making. Finally, it is important to recognize that each congregation, by its size and its style, will have different modes in which to approach a religious education needs assessment.

WHAT IS A NEEDS ASSESSMENT?

In order to move beyond the familiar territory in which the congregation most comfortably works, it is necessary to assess the religious education needs of the people. The term "need" simply means the difference between the present situation and a more desirable one.[1] A "needs assessment," then, is a process that identifies and analyzes the reported needs of an individual, a group, or the whole congregation. It is an intentional process of collecting and interpreting data to describe what people report as important to them in their desire to move from the present state of affairs to a more desirable one. A needs assessment is most often initiated, designed, and implemented by a planning team such as a committee or a work team on religious education. The planning team identifies a problem or an opportunity in religious education to which it feels called to respond but for which more information is needed.

Whose needs (the congregation's or the individual's) are being addressed? Religious education planners must raise this fundamental question from the inception of a needs assessment. The world of marketing distinguishes between the needs of the "seller" and the needs of the "buyer." The needs of the buyer are the domain of marketing. And while the language and the disciplines of marketing are often uncomfortable for the congregation, which understands itself not to be a business, the implications and the learnings of marketing are becoming more germane to the work of ministry.[2] In particular, a congregation needs to understand the difference between "selling," which focuses on the needs of the seller/provider/institution (the congregation) and "marketing," which focuses on the needs of the buyer/customer/member (the person

---

1. Gary D. Gilmore, M. Donald Campbell, and Barbara Becker, *Needs Assessment Strategies for Health Education and Health Promotion* (Dubuque: Brown & Benchmark, 1989), p. 4.

2. For an in-depth introduction to the importance and the discipline of marketing for the local congregation see Norman Shawchuck, Philip Kotler, Bruce Wrenn, and Gustave Rath, *Marketing for Congregations* (Nashville: Abingdon, 1992).

or group the congregation seeks to serve). The aim of marketing is to be "consumer oriented." This means to be aware of and responsive to the needs of the buyer/customer/member and to understand the buyer so well that the service or product fits the person and sells itself.[3]

The "selling congregation," then, is more aware of and sensitive to its own need to increase the number of people who support its programs and ministry. For example, the parish may develop a religious education youth program that plans meetings around social events and then work to convince young people to schedule these events into an already overcrowded school and social calendar. The "marketing congregation" instead works to become much more aware of and sensitive to the needs of the persons it seeks to serve. Religious education opportunities are designed to meet those needs. It is person oriented rather than program driven. The marketing congregation might work with its young people to discover the needs of this audience. It then might develop a program of hands-on weekend mission work in neighboring volunteer agencies. Reflection times can be designed into the ministry to determine how the young people fit into their larger community through these experiences.

In other words, a needs assessment is intended to be a "marketing tool." It seeks to more fully understand the needs, hopes, goals, or style of the persons to be served in order to find appropriate ways to serve them. Needs assessment is not a means to serve the needs of the religious institution. Rather, it seeks ways to serve people.

Perhaps one other caution needs to be stated before moving on to address the concepts and techniques of developing a religious education needs assessment in the congregation. The needs assessment is one tool that fits into and supports the greater task of discernment of ministry that leads to faithful decision making. The purpose and the reward of an effective assessment is to take information about persons or situations and represent this audience in some quantifiable form as "facts." "In ordinary circumstances, people analyze facts in order to come to a conclusion. While this is a useful exercise, it is not the same thing as discerning God's call."[4]

---

3. James M. Hardy, *Managing for Impact in Nonprofit Organizations* (Erwin, Tenn.: Essex, 1983) p. 46.

4. Suzanne G. Farnham, Joseph P. Gill, R. Taylor McLean, and Susan M. Ward, *Listening Hearts: Discerning Call in Community* (Harrisburg, Pa.: Morehouse, 1991), p. 12.

Decisions of planning in religious education necessarily depend on a mix of facts and data along with an understanding of the purpose, the identity, and the theology of the congregation. Decisions come from an intentional effort to listen to the call of God in the midst of the specific and immediate situation of ministry described by the assessment. There will be ongoing references in this chapter on how planning an assessment in religious education fits into the fuller discerning and decision making of congregational leaders.

WHY DO A NEEDS ASSESSMENT?

The argument so far is that planning an appropriate needs assessment in religious education is at the heart of an effective congregational life. Religious educators work to understand the needs of the people and, based on those needs, to develop ministry opportunities and religious education programs and events designed to address those identified needs. Including appropriate assessment produces a number of advantages to religious education planning and decision making.

A well-designed needs assessment provides information that assists planners of religious education to understand the people to be served and provides (1) a logical starting point based on data for individual action or program development, (2) a sense of ownership in programs by the people who shared their information in the assessment, (3) a database that provides direction and guides efforts toward identified goals, (4) direction and validation for the use of resources (staff, money, space, etc.) based on the goals identified through the needs assessment, (5) authorization to continue (or discontinue) already established programs or events when they can be demonstrated to be (or not be) linked to the identified needs, (6) a means to monitor program effectiveness (by doing a follow-up needs assessment after a program or event), and (7) a method to move from a general awareness of needs to the specific needs felt by the particular people in the congregation or surrounding community.

There is excellent descriptive material available to congregations today that identifies the needs of segmented groups of people in communities.[5] The religious education planning group must take responsibility to move away from general descriptions of national or regional

---

5. For example, Tex Sample, *U.S. Lifestyles and Mainline Churches* (Louisville: Westminster/John Knox, 1990), offers an application of a VALS (values and lifestyles)

publications and ask specifically how those issues are understood and experienced by the people in the immediate ministry area. For all of its importance, an assessment of a group or of a whole congregation does not have to be difficult and elaborate. What it must do is accurately describe the people under consideration.

WAYS TO APPROACH A NEEDS ASSESSMENT

A needs assessment supports the goals of religious education. While a needs assessment does not have to be complicated, there are helpful ways to think about developing an assessment process to support the goals of the religious education planning team. There are two basic models for needs assessment: (1) a problem model and (2) an opportunity model.[6] Each of these two models requires its own strategy.

A Problem Model

A problem is not necessarily a crisis. It can be a deviation from a desired standard that is important enough to motivate people to find a solution to it. For example, in a needs assessment that has been replicated in

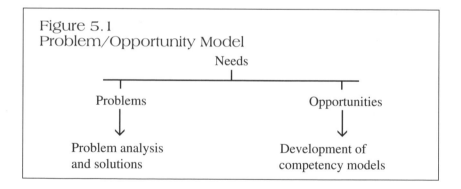

Figure 5.1
Problem/Opportunity Model

Needs

Problems — Opportunities

Problem analysis and solutions — Development of competency models

---

marketing analysis to issues of local church ministry; George Barna, *The Frog in the Kettle: What Christians Needs to Know about Life in the Year 2000* (Ventura, Calif.: Regal, 1990), provides a summary of social changes and demographic/psychographic shifts applied to the church. Along with an ever expanding list of books and resources from the church press is an equally expanding and accessible amount of secular materials found in publications such as "Marketing Tools Alert," a news supplement to *American Demographics,* or in the business and management sections of most bookstores.

6. Larry Nolan Davis, *Planning, Conducting, and Evaluating Workshops* (Austin, Tex.: Learning Concepts, 1974), pp. 35–37.

churches and in denominations, it was discovered that baby boomers (people born between 1946 and 1964) grew up without a substantial biblical background. These adults report not being familiar enough with biblical writings to be able to understand references to the Bible in the preaching and the teaching of the church. The studies suggest that these adults do not relate the biblical message to their daily experiences. The need of this audience is identified as "biblical illiteracy." Churches are responding with renewed religious education programs of Bible study and "teaching" sermons. A number of denominations are addressing this problem through national programs of group Bible study. While not a crisis, biblical illiteracy is a significant deviation from a previous norm and is therefore a problem "need" to be addressed.

When dealing with a needs assessment in response to an identified problem, it is important for the religious education planning team to "play detective." Once the data is collected to define the "problem," it is important for the planning group to follow problem analysis and problem solution steps carefully to track down the direct connection, if any, between a proposed religious education program or event and the desired change identified by the needs assessment.[7] When data that identifies a need has been collected, the onus is on the religious education planning group to follow effective problem-solving methods to respond appropriately.

In the case of one urban church that was working cooperatively with other center city churches, the problem was "understanding why members would not take interest in or respond to a pressing need that had become a goal of the church." A needs assessment done among church members indicated valuable information. For example, one driving reason that many members chose to travel into the city from surrounding suburban areas was the opportunity for hands-on involvement in working with people facing problems in a community characterized by cultural, racial, and economic diversity. The needs assessment in the community and around the congregation indicated that the one singular area of unmet need was an emergency shelter for homeless men in the city. The community had shelters for women and children, but there were no adequate options for adult men. After several attempts from the planning group it was apparent that the members of

---

7. Gene E. Custer, *Planning, Packaging, and Presenting Training: A Guide for Subject Matter Experts* (San Diego: University Associates, 1984), p. 25.

the participating churches were not interested or motivated to work to change the status quo for homeless men, despite educational efforts to describe and to explain the desperate situation surrounding the churches.

The problem of city housing for homeless men had to be restated to identify the critical need to be addressed. The religious education planning team had to do the necessary homework to define the right problem to be solved. In this case, the planning team set aside two hours in an afternoon to do a force field analysis of their situation. A force field analysis states the goal to be addressed and then identifies driving forces and restraining forces that hold the situation in a status quo, and therefore unsolvable, position.[8]

A force field analysis assumes that for every problem there are driving forces trying to move the situation to resolution and there are opposing restraining forces that balance out the driving forces and maintain the status quo. Kurt Lewin, the developer of the force field analysis, believed

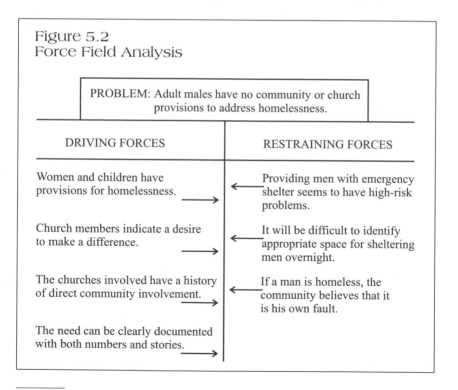

Figure 5.2
Force Field Analysis

PROBLEM: Adult males have no community or church provisions to address homelessness.

DRIVING FORCES	RESTRAINING FORCES
Women and children have provisions for homelessness.	Providing men with emergency shelter seems to have high-risk problems.
Church members indicate a desire to make a difference.	It will be difficult to identify appropriate space for sheltering men overnight.
The churches involved have a history of direct community involvement.	If a man is homeless, the community believes that it is his own fault.
The need can be clearly documented with both numbers and stories.	

_____

8. Marvin R. Weisbord, *Productive Workplaces* (San Francisco: Jossey-Bass, 1988), pp. 77–79.

that a problem is moved by increasing drivers or reducing restraints. Reducing restraints is more effective, since increasing the driving forces attracts increased restraints. For example, physically pushing against an opposing player in sports invites that player to push back harder in order to maintain balance. Reducing restraining forces is a more effective strategy because it helps to empower the natural driving forces that move toward change. With this awareness the religious education planning team carefully listed as many drivers and restrainers as possible, a few of which are identified above. (Note that driving and restraining forces do not need to be corresponding opposites.)

As the religious education planners worked, they discovered a powerful restraining force was the community assumption that if a man was homeless it was his own fault. This assumption did not apply to women and children. The community work ethic asserted that if a man was responsible and did what he needed to do, he would not be homeless. The religious education planners began to understand that this community assumption was the critical problem. The planning team developed steps to educate people around this issue. Stories from interviews with a number of homeless men, conducted at a soup kitchen in one of the churches, were used to educate the church members. A number of the homeless men had recently been deinstitutionalized from a mental hospital by state law but were not able to care for themselves. One man's salary was adequate to rent an apartment, but when he and his wife separated, he had to move out. But he could not afford to rent a second apartment for himself. These stories and a number of others were taken by the religious education committee to Sunday school classes, board meetings, and social gatherings in each of the churches. Finally interest grew in doing something about housing for homeless men.

Problem solving is a favored activity of many planning groups. Given a problem, many people want to move quickly and directly from the initial statement of the problem to the implementation of a solution. One trap is moving too quickly and solving the wrong problem. The use of effective problem-solving methods guards against this trap. In regard to the city housing for homeless men, the congregation needed a restatement of the problem. Assumptions that people hold significantly affect how a problem is perceived.

An Opportunity Model

If the strategy for a problem needs assessment focuses on analysis and problem solving, then the strategy for an opportunity-model needs assessment focuses on the utilization of a "competency model" that defines goals. Competency model refers to a list or a description of the behaviors that the religious education planning team identifies as necessary or desirable to fulfill the opportunity.

Congregations searching for a new pastoral leader are familiar with competency models since as the search committee defines the behaviors a new pastor would be expected to exercise with the congregation in order to meet the perceived needs. A similar definition can be brought to church members or to persons the church is seeking to serve. This method of needs assessment is not primarily concerned with what is wrong but with what is possible. It lends itself to the pursuit of new opportunities.[9]

Figure 5.3
Steps involved in Using a Competency Model

1. *List what is expected:* Begin developing a competency model by listing expected and critical behaviors.
2. *Assess the current proficiency:* Describe some measure or judgment of the current level of proficiency for critical behaviors among the target group.
3. *Identify the gap between proficiency and current:* Identify needs that, if addressed, will bring the current level of performance up to the level of the competency model.
4. *Specify each need:* Specify those needs that are educable/trainable.
5. *Design training:* Design programs/experiences/events to educate or train the persons involved.
6. *Measure performance after intervention:* Measure or judge the level of performance/knowledge after the intervention.

A number of congregations use the competency model approach in receiving new members. For example, the leadership of the congregation may determine that being prepared for membership should include competency behaviors such as the following:

---

9. Davis, *Planning, Conducting, and Evaluating Workshops*, p. 52.

Figure 5.4
Competency Behavior for Preparing New Members

1. *Beliefs and facts:* Identify major beliefs and basic historical facts of the faith.
2. *Congregational history and ministry goals:* Be familiar with basic historical facts and current ministry goals of the local congregation.
3. *Congregational structure:* Have a working knowledge of the structure, committees, programs, and leaders of the congregation.
4. *Recent members:* Be familiar with others recently joining the church.
5. *Participate:* Know about and participate in ongoing groups, activities, or programs of the church.

Once the model is developed, new members can be "tested" for their competence in each of these areas prior to any membership process. The resulting information will offer clear guidance to the leaders of membership orientation or training classes. Once these needs of new members are determined, appropriate religious education programs, experiences, or events can be planned. After the new members complete their membership preparation, the religious education planning group can then ask questions to determine the effectiveness of the religious education opportunities and programs.

In one congregation the competency model is being used by the religious education planning group to address leadership development issues among elected church leaders. A major goal of the religious education ministry is to provide leadership training and development supportive of church leaders in their families, in work places as well as in the congregation.

The competency model can be applied to the whole ministry of the church. The teachings of W. Edward Deming and the Total Quality Movement have given rise to a number of significant attempts to understand and influence the leadership of the congregation by identifying competencies and assessing needs to meet them.[10] This requires a clear understanding of the core purpose of the local congregation and the

---

10. James D. Anderson and Ezra Earl Jones, *The Management of Ministry* (San Francisco: Harper & Row, 1978); Ezra Earl Jones, "The Primary Task of Ministry," *Quest for Quality in the Church* (Nashville: Discipleship Resources, 1993), pp. 27–34.

Figure 5.5
Competency Model for Church Leaders

1. Be aware of their personal leadership style
2. Be aware of the effect their leadership style has on others working
   with them
3. Build an agenda
4. Lead a meeting
5. Manage normal conflict so that it is does not disruptive meetings

development of clear competency models for each part of the church "system" that will support that core purpose of ministry.

DEFINING THE "AUDIENCE" AND FOCUS OF THE ASSESSMENT

Current members of a congregation tend to reinforce the present religious education ministry. In addition to assessing the needs of people already active in the congregation, it may be important for the religious education planning team to gather data from people who are not active or who are not yet related to the congregation. To work with only the people who are active in the life of the congregation may be comfortable and relatively easy. However, data gathered from these people alone is very limited and may not be accurate.

When the religious education planning team uses a process of needs assessment, the team must be clear about what "audience"—what group or subgroup of people—will be the appropriate focus of the planning. A tool that helps identify the appropriate audience for such an assessment is a congregational adaptation of the "current clients-current services" matrix often used in business.[11]

In quadrant 1 the religious education planning team seeks to understand the response of persons who are already involved in the ministry of the congregation to the programs or processes already in place. Typically, a planning team tests satisfaction in this quadrant by quantifying the

---

11. J. William Pfeiffer, Leonard Goodstein, and Timothy M. Nolan, *Applied Strategic Planning: A How to Do It Guide* (San Diego: University Associates, 1986), pp. 127–28.

Figure 5.6
Matrix Model

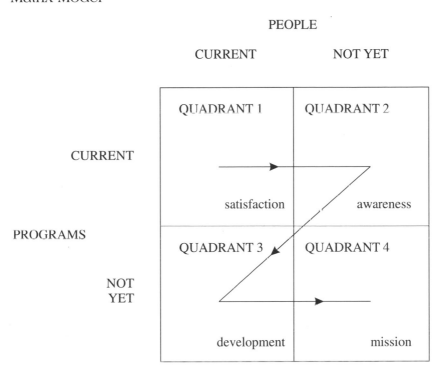

PEOPLE

CURRENT   NOT YET

Quadrant 1   Identifies persons who are already involved in the religious
             education of a congregation
             Tests current *satisfaction*
Quadrant 2   Identifies persons who are "not yet" involved in the reli-
             gious education ministry
             Examines the issue of *awareness*
Quadrant 3   Identifies needs of people who are currently involved in
             religious education or stay on the periphery
             Examines what hidden needs *can be developed*
Quadrant 4   Identifies the needs of people who are "not yet" partici-
             pating in the religious education ministry
             Examines the necessary *mission* to serve the "not yet"
             audience

number of persons attending and/or by asking satisfaction questions about the time, place, leadership, or content of the programs offered. Religious education planning teams are comfortable assessing this area and have an easy time gathering data.

In quadrant 2 the religious education planning team seeks to understand the response of persons who are not yet involved in the congregation to the ministry currently offered. Often assessment in this quadrant examines the issue of awareness. In one situation, a church consultant who was working with an awareness assessment for a large urban church took an active role in gathering data from "not yet" people. This Presbyterian church was situated on a busy intersection in the city and its large, imposing building overshadowed a bus stop on the corner. The consultant stood at the bus stop for several hours and simply asked people waiting for the bus if they could direct him to the nearest Presbyterian church. Amazingly, the overwhelming number of people did not know or they offered directions leading in every possible path away from the Presbyterian church in whose shadow they stood. A major task in quadrant 2 needs assessment is to adequately define or describe the specific group of "not yet" people that the planning team hope to understand. The next step is to develop direct steps to gather information from this group of people.

Quadrant 3 is the quadrant of development. This quadrant works with people who are already involved or affiliated with the congregation in an attempt to identify needs that may have been hidden or are as yet unheard by church leaders. In quadrant 3 religious educators often find that specific steps need to be taken to hear from the people who are on the periphery of active church life.

In quadrant 4, that of mission, the religious education planning team is again working with people who are not yet a part of the ministry of the congregation. In quadrant 2 the planning team assessed these "not yet" people in an effort to understand how to make this audience aware of and feel included in the present ministry of the congregation. In quadrant 4 the religious education planning team seeks information that will help the team to understand these "not yet" people in order to develop new religious education opportunities and programs of ministry designed to address unmet needs. This is perhaps the least comfortable and most difficult quadrant for most religious education planning teams, since it requires working past natural barriers to make contact and learn about persons who are not in relationship with the congregation. Needs assessment in this quadrant typically leads congregations to deal with significant change.

The "Z model" within the four quadrant matrix shows that as the religious education planning team proceeds from quadrant 1 through quadrant 4, both the risk and the difficulty of ministry increases. The four quadrants help the religious education planning team focus the purpose for a needs assessment and the appropriate target audience.

MODELS AND METHODS: COLLECTING DATA

The goal of a needs assessment in religious education is to design a process for gathering the appropriate information from a clearly identified group or from representatives of a group. Collecting information (descriptive data) from and about the people the religious education planning team seeks to serve is at the heart of assessing the needs of a congregation. There are numerous instruments and methodologies for collecting data in congregational life. Much of what is available is informal and task specific. Models and methods of assessing needs are designed to collect data around an identified question or problem. The intent of a needs assessment is to offer insight that will help answer the specific religious education planning questions being asked.

A helpful resource that includes many examples of needs assessment instruments and methodologies is the *Handbook for Congregational Studies*.[12] This publication, as well as resources often available through judicatory offices and organizations such as The Alban Institute,[13] may offer instruments that can be appropriately used in the congregation. Already existing instruments may be adapted to fit the local situation or they may offer guidance in creating an instrument appropriate to the religious education planning questions in the congregation.

---

12. Jackson W. Carroll, Carl S. Dudley, and William McKinney, eds., *Handbook for Congregational Studies* (Nashville: Abingdon, 1986).

13. The Alban Institute is an organization committed to understanding the local church congregation. It provides training, consulting, and a full list of publications designed as resources for congregations. It may be contacted at 7315 Wisconsin Avenue, Suite 1250W, Bethesda, MD 20814 (1-800-486-1318) for a publications catalog and information about their services.

Figure 5.7
Four Areas of a Congregational Needs Assessment

Program: Organizational structures,
the *what* of a congregation's life,
plans, and activities through which a congregation expresses
its mission and ministry both to its own members
and those outside the membership;
Process: Reflects the *how* of members' relationships
with one another.
Processes have to do with the underlying flow
and dynamics of a congregation
that knit it together in its common life
and affect its morale and climate;
Social context: The setting, local and global,
in which a congregation finds itself
and to which it responds,
points to the *where* religious education is offered;
Identity: Persistent set of beliefs,
values, patterns,
symbols, stories, and style
that make a congregation distinctively itself,
identity points to *who* the people are.

Four areas are most consistently explored in assessing needs in the congregation: program, process, social context, and identity.[14]

Despite the differences in the four areas identified, it is possible with considerable reflective accuracy to gather information from people to describe each.

A number of basic techniques are used in gathering data in a needs assessment. The technique chosen or the particular data gathering instrument used must be selected only after the religious education planning team has clarified the reasons for collecting information, has identified the group or subgroup of persons involved, and has determined what questions need to be answered. Then the planning team will want to consider the instrument or technique, as identified below, that will most effectively gather the needed data.

---

14. Carroll, Dudley, and McKinney, *Handbook for Congregational Studies*, p. 11.

Congregational Records

Many congregations are coming to realize the importance of keeping religious education programmatic records which in some cases, record not only how many persons attended but also name them. The audience then can be described as a group in order to understand who is being served by a specific religious education program. However rudimentary the records are, records are a natural place for the planning team to start as it attempts to understand people's level of satisfaction with current programming.

This approach is also useful in examining newly initiated programming. It is important, however, to move beyond such records. Measuring only attendance and satisfaction invites the planners to fall into the trap of thinking that the religious education programs in themselves are the purpose of the congregation. The question that needs to be asked is, In what specific ways does the religious education program contribute to the congregation's purpose or call to ministry?[15]

Surveys

Surveys are written instruments that invite people to respond with information about themselves, their feelings, or their perceptions. Surveys usually contain two types of questions: (1) questions eliciting background information, such as: age, sex, tenure of membership, marital status, and (2) questions eliciting need oriented information such as: asking information about the felt needs, interests, individual concerns. Once different needs or interests are identified, this information can be analyzed by age, sex, tenure, etc., as a means of understanding the different needs or interests held by the subgroups of people served by the congregation. Surveys need to be (1) brief so that people can complete them in a reasonable amount of time and (2) clear and concise so that people can easily understand the questions.

There are several different forms of surveys, conducted such as single step and multiple step. Single step surveys, as the name indicates, are conducted once and the information collected is interpreted by the religious education planning team. These are the surveys most commonly used by congregations. They are completed by persons attending the main worship service(s) or religious education classes or events.

15. Anderson and Jones, *Management of Ministry*, pp. 138–39.

This is the most effective way of getting a high number of completed returns from the most active group of persons in the congregation. To survey people other than active attendees, other methods of contact and information collection, such as mailing, hand delivery, or visits to natural gatherings, need to be considered.

Multiple step surveys are designed to gather information and also solicit the help of respondents in interpretation and further clarification. Multiple step surveys are adaptations of the Delphi technique, which was originally designed for future forecasting but has been developed to identify needs and problems and to assess potential solutions.[16] A survey consisting of a limited number of broad questions is sent to a representative group of responders—often a predesigned mix of decision makers, participants, and "experts" or professional workers in the field. The respondents are usually contacted before the survey is sent to ask for their participation in completing all rounds of the survey, since each individual's participation is critical in survey development and interpretation. Responses are analyzed and then a second, more focused survey is developed. Respondents are then sent the results of the first survey and are asked to answer more specific questions in a second survey. These responses are analyzed and another survey is developed from the second survey responses in an effort to further sharpen and clarify the issue at hand. The usual number of rounds is three to five.

Interviews
"Often people are able to get in touch with their deepest needs and yearnings as they are given the opportunity to verbalize them." [17] Anderson and Jones question whether persons participating in programs of ministry are approached so frequently that the real information about their own lives and their desires is left unspoken. Interviews, or "intentional conversations" with persons, can follow a number of different strategies.

Random Interviews: One congregation utilizes an annual random telephone interview process in which one-tenth (every tenth person on the membership list, beginning with a different name each year) of the congregation is telephoned and asked to respond to a brief list of previously identified questions. Telephone interviewers are trained to

---

16. Joel Kurtzman, *Futurecasting* (Palm Springs, Calif.: ETC Publications, 1984), pp. 62–73.

17. Anderson and Jones, *Management of Ministry*, p. 140.

cover the agreed on questions and record the responses. Other concerns or issues that the persons wish to talk about are gathered also.

Interviewing A Specific Audience: Often it is important to identify the specific persons (or the subgroup of persons) from whom information is needed. One congregation recognized the development of a large group of persons who had once participated in the congregation's religious education program, but were becoming inactive. The planning team was not aware of any complaints about the religious education ministry and realized that it needed to hear from people who had decided not to participate. Since these persons might not want to "raise complaints" about the religious education planning team, additional steps were taken to gather the information. A neutral person who was not a member of the congregation was contracted to make fifteen telephone contacts with persons whose names would be provided. Specific questions were supplied to this interviewer with instructions to also gather responses or issues that the interviewed persons wanted to share. A letter was then sent to the fifteen identified persons stating that they would be phoned by the interviewer sometime during a specified five-day period. All persons would be asked a number of questions about their experience with the religious education programs being reviewed by the planning team. The name of the interviewer and the interviewer's relationship to the planning team were given in the letter. The letter indicated that responses were very important to the development of the religious education ministry of the congregation. Respondents were encouraged to offer the planning team very honest responses. To encourage candidness, the letter explained that the person calling was not a member of the congregation. The caller would report findings to the religious education planning team only. The caller had been asked not to report any names or attach any names to particular responses, but to offer a descriptive summary report of all responses. Not surprisingly, the well-prepared and well-focused strategy resulted in 100 percent cooperation. The religious education planning committee obtained responses that their inactive congregational members would probably not have shared directly.

An Ongoing Interview Database: A third strategy, beyond random interviews and interviewing an identified subgroup, is the development of an ongoing interview database. This is done best by staff persons or key congregational leaders who maintain contacts with members. It may be the pastor, rabbi, or religious educator who contacts members in the course of home visitations, committee meeting conversations, hallway conversations, and so on. The religious education planning team identifies one to three significant, open-ended questions (questions that require more than a yes or no response). Whenever the opportunity presents itself, the leaders ask the agreed upon questions. Following the conversation, when the respondent is no longer present, the leader notes on a three-by-five-inch file card the essential points of the person's response. The file cards are stored in a file or a drawer until a sufficient number of responses have been collected. The responses are reviewed and are grouped by similarities in search of patterns in the responses. Subgroup notations can be made on the card (member/nonmember; active/inactive; new member; participant of which group) to help identify and cluster responses when reviewed.

For one pastor this process culminated in a descriptive report of hopes and concerns of congregational members that gave motivation and direction to the religious education planning team as it announced the beginning of two new programs of child care and church school. Using information from the ongoing "interviews" with members, the religious education planning team was able to ascertain that the congregation, which was composed primarily of older persons, was anxious to bring children and younger families into the religious education ministry. However, the responses also indicated that these "emptynesters," retired adult members, felt that they had straightened up and fixed up the church, just as they had done in their homes as their own children grew up and moved away. These older members were bothered by the noise and the chaos that children bring to a parish facility.

The religious education planning team was effective in initiating the new programs because the team members were able to hear and to take into consideration both the members' hopes of including children and the concerns about the ensuing "mess" as new religious education ministries were developed to include children.

The beginning of a leader's tenure in the congregation is a natural time to begin these ongoing interviews. Individual or small group meetings can also be initiated to help the new leader get to know members of the congregation. The "getting-to-know-you" process is a time when members expect and appreciate the leader's inquiry about personal hopes and concerns with issues facing the congregation. The continuing development of an ongoing interview database through a leader's election, call, or appointment is a valuable tool that allows the congregational leader to track patterns of responses. By prior agreement with the religious education planning team concerning which issue or opportunity to explore, the leader can intentionally use regular meetings with members to systematically ask, What do you think about . . . ? or What concerns do you have about . . . ? Noting responses on file cards allows for the identification of patterns that emerge in the accumulation of a number of responses. It is an ongoing means of "taking the pulse" of the congregation.

Nominal Group Techniques and Focus Groups

At times it is more efficient and productive to talk with people in groups, inviting their direct participation in gathering information. The nominal group technique gathers people in groups of five to seven for a structured and intentional process. Participants are invited to prepare written responses to a focused question. Each person is asked to share responses in a round-robin fashion with the full group. The group clarifies the responses through discussion, and participants then rank order the responses and discuss the rank ordering. The group then discusses a final rank order.[18]

Focus groups are somewhat less formal. Fairly homogeneous groups of five to ten people are gathered by a leader prepared to stimulate and track the pattern of the discussion.[19] Focus groups are usually exploratory groups used to generate ideas and opinions, uncover attitudes, or test new ideas. One congregation realized it had a large number of business leaders who were active in worship but did not participate in religious education or spiritual development events. The religious education planning team set a breakfast meeting in a local restaurant that could provide space for private conversation. The hand-written invitations were delivered to eight business leaders from the congregation. The discussion topic was "what my church needs to understand about business and my role as a business leader in the community."

Another religious education planning team developed a number of "coffee and conversation" events as it tried to understand a group of people who were "not yet" active church participants. The planning team

---

18. A. L. Delberg, A. H. Van de Ven, and D. H. Gustafson, *Group Techniques for Program Planning* (Glenview, Ill.: Scott, Foresman), 1975.

19. Philip Kotler and Alan Andreasen, *Strategic Marketing for NonProfit Organizations,* 4th ed. (Englewood Cliffs, N. J.: Prentice-Hall, 1991), pp. 248–53.

finished a demographic and psychographic analysis of the community[20] and identified several significant concentrations of persons in the neighborhood with lifestyles that were not heavily represented in the congregation. Members of the religious education planning team went to the few people in the congregation who did reflect these lifestyles in the community and asked each of these people to invite two to four of their friends to accompany them to a "coffee and conversation" sponsored by the planning team. The conversations were held in homes and the topic was "helping our church understand our community." The interests and concerns of the target persons were explored. For example, people were invited to talk about leisure time (when they had it, how they used it, how much they had) and their personal, professional, or family goals. It is also helpful to ask such groups what magazines they read and what radio stations they listen to, since these two media are among the most highly segmented and are targeted for specific audiences. The planning team can review these magazines and radio stations with particular attention to advertisements that offer insight into the hopes, goals, and concerns of a particular group of people. Based on learnings from these conversations, the religious education planning team was able to consider what role of ministry their church could offer to engage these people as new members.

Inferential Learning

There is a rapidly growing wealth of resources available to and written for religious organizations which describe the needs and hopes for a large number of subgroups of people in our communities.[21] The segmenting and targeting techniques of the marketing industry offer in-depth insight and understanding of numerous groups of people identified by age, gender, race or ethnic origin, personality type, socioeconomic class, and

---

20. There are now a number of services available to churches and religious organizations that provide at reasonable cost demographic and psychographic studies that are geographically specific to the location of the church and the immediately surrounding community. These studies are highly accurate and sophisticated marketing analyses designed for use by religious organizations. Along with describing the vital statistics of an area, they offer insight into the behavioral lifestyles of people in the community (using a segmenting system that describes 50 different identifiable lifestyles). Examples of such providers include Percept, 151 Kalmus Drive, Suite A104, Costa Mesa, California 926277 (1-800-442-6277); Visions-Decisions, P. O. Box 94144, Atlanta, Georgia 30377 (1-800-524-1445); and many national judicatory offices.

21. See footnotes 13, 20.

lifestyle. Notable examples include the growing amount of materials being written about groups such as the baby busters (the children of baby boomers) and empty nesters (those whose children have grown up and left home). Once an identifiable subgroup of persons has become the focus for a needs assessment, it is possible to locate both secular and ecclesiastical descriptive resources. The religious education planning team may want to jointly read or study such materials and develop its own ideas, assumptions, or hypotheses determining how these learnings apply to the persons the parish has identified.

A next step involves gathering available representatives of each group to meet with representatives of the religious education planning team as a focus group to sharpen the learnings, offer ideas, or develop appropriate survey or interview strategies to identify specific needs.

Theology, Identity, and Spirit

Parts of our congregational or community life are not easily reduced to questionnaire or surveys. Such parts are nonetheless formative influences and need to be understood. Walter Wink assures us that every congregation has an "angel" that speaks for it, just as every corporation has a corporate "culture" that determines how it relates to its customers and its environment.[22] Congregations that I work with easily understand the idea of an angel of the congregation and can often accurately talk about the message(s) of the angel. One Roman Catholic congregation was particularly uncomfortable with this notion until we began to talk about the voice of its saint (the church was named for St. Vincent). Participants could then talk about the voice that guided them. The angel of the church, according to Wink, has two voices: the voice of personality that speaks of its past and tells where it has come from, and the voice of vocation that speaks of where God calls the congregation to move in the future.

The responsibility of religious educators is to encourage both voices to be recognized and honored in the present moment. This often means trying to "hear" unquantifiable but powerful information that speaks of needs and hopes that the religious education planning team must consider. There are tools available to help. James Hopewell's analysis of congregational worldviews can help identify how the "critical mass" of

---

22. Walter Wink, *Unmasking the Powers* (Philadelphia: Fortress, 1989), pp. 69–86.

Figure 5.8
Voice or "Angel" of Your Congregation

1. Who is the voice of your congregation's "angel"?

2. How has the voice or "angel," guided the congregation?

3. Is there a message for the future from this voice or "angel"?

congregational members understand themselves theologically.[23] Sometimes specific tools are not available, but processes are. Several colleagues and I have worked to find ways to "interview" congregations and
help individuals tell their stories. We have found that people intuitively
know and can put into words their experience with their faith or with
their congregation. For example, one exercise invites people to select
a Scripture story that describes the story of the congregation in the
present moment. One congregation struggling with evangelism in the
neighborhood easily identified the biblical story of the man at the side
of the pool called Bethesda who had not been healed after thirty-eight
years. The man at the side of the pool had no one to help him in the water
for healing.[24] When asked why they chose this story, they answered that
their church had been sitting at the edge of the "water" at the corner of
4th and Oak Streets for many years and had never been able to "make it
in" when the community was troubled. It was time, participants said, to
take the plunge and get into the community. In their agreement around
that biblical story, need was identified and hope was spoken.

Similarly, individuals can be asked to pick the hymn or gospel song
that sings the song of the congregation in the present moment. Congregations often enjoy developing historical time lines on large sheets
of newsprint. People remember and chronologically list by decades on
newsprint important people, events, and learnings from past and present
moments of their ministry. Then participants talk about their dreams for
the future. By beginning in the present moment and working back into
the past, then returning to the present and working into the future, both
the voice of personality and the voice of vocation of the congregation

---

23. Barbara G. Wheeler, James F. Hopewell, eds., *Congregation: Stories and Structures* (Philadelphia: Fortress, 1987).

24. John 5

Figure 5.9
Our Congregation's Story

1. What scripture, hymn or song describes your congregation in the present moment?
2. Why did you select this particular story?

can be heard. Needs and hopes can be identified and placed in sequence on the newsprint to offer a description of where people understand both the history and the future of the parish. Needs do not always have to be quantifiable in order to be identifiable.

MODELS AND METHODS: ANALYZING DATA

The purpose of gathering data for a religious education needs assessment is to assemble the most accurate description possible. One of the most powerful tools in determining appropriate next steps in religious educa tion planning is to accurately describe what is in the current moment. There are several helpful guidelines for describing what is.

First, description and evaluation are two different approaches. One speaks of what is and the other gives voice to what a religious education planning committee thinks should be. In the process of a needs assessment the religious education planning committee must simply describe the situation as accurately as possible. Planning team members must withhold evaluation of what should be until the description is complete and accurate. If the needs assessment is problem oriented, the religious education planning team's judgment of what "should be" will be given voice as problem solutions are considered. If the needs assessment is opportunity oriented, the team's "should be's" will be given voice as the planning team identify criteria of competencies that it plans to meet. But the primary and most difficult task in the needs assessment is first to describe, without evaluating, until the need or the hope of the identified person or group is accurately understood.

It is critically important for religious educators to remember that a needs assessment is a descriptive process. While a needs assessment normally involves data gathering (some of which is usually quantifiable in number form), it is not "research" undertaken to "prove" some principle or truth about the people involved. There is always the question of whether what is being identified is an actual need or a perceived need. Actual needs, if they can be identified, are less the domain of a needs assessment than are perceived needs. It is perceived needs that religious education planners are obviously more aware of and therefore the ones that are reported in any needs assessment process.

There are two kinds of realities. One is the actual reality of the situation. The other is the perceived reality. Of the two, it is the perceived reality that is most important to the people who perceive it, and this is the one that people are most highly motivated to address. If this perceived reality is not included in addressing the situation, people will have little interest in working with what someone else has decided is the true need. In that sense, an assessment in the religious education ministry is not seeking to determine needs that are true beyond any shadow of a doubt. The more functional purpose is "to describe workable processes which assess issues of individual and group importance"[25] (the perceived need) in order to identify the appropriate place or style to begin.

Relieving ourselves of the task of researching "actual" needs is important to being able to truly listen to and describe the perceived needs of the people. It is important to find an appropriate starting place that people will accept—one that individuals feel is important— if religious educators hope to involve these people in programs of religious education or personal change.

Second, data collected must be described as simply as possible to aid analysis. When gathering data from church records, it is more helpful to graph or "picture" the information than it is to put it in numeric form. For many people, graphs or representations lead more quickly to ideas and understanding while numbers lead to calculations. Similarly, when gathering data from surveys and interviews, responses are best grouped in simple frequency distributions converted to percentages.[26]

Third, it is critical that religious education planning not be data driven (fig. 5.10). The value of data is in accurately describing what is, not necessarily in telling planners what they should do next. It is

---

25. Gilmore, Campbell, and Becker, *Needs Assessment Strategies for Health Education and Health Promotion,* p. 5.
26. For example, see Carroll, Dudley, and McKinney, *Handbook for Congregational Studies,* p. 161.

possible for data to suggest its own "solutions," which may or may not be appropriate for the specific congregation or planning group. For example, a large church located downtown in an economically depressed small city established a religious education futuring committee to assess the needs of the church and its ministry over the next five years. As they gathered descriptive data, it became clear, by all objective measures of church growth, that the congregation was located in the wrong spot. The majority of their members lived outside the city limits in a developing suburban area. While the population in the city was continuing to decrease, the population in the suburban ring around the city was growing by leaps and bounds. Normal traffic patterns did not bring people into the city past this church any more, but rather took people around the city on a bypass. Parking was limited and increased crime around the church made it less and less attractive for current members to come to evening programs. In fact, the data was overwhelming in suggesting that the church was in the wrong location. Leaders were feeling "driven" by this information to consider relocation. It was not until they rehearsed their history and recalled the commitments of the church that leaders began to describe the purpose of the church's religious education ministry. The leaders realized the strength of the commitment that had been made to the very city that they were feeling the congregation must leave. This congregation realized that the call to ministry was a call to stay and minister in that city. Rather than allow the data to tell them to relocate, the religious education planning committee began to review the data to test if the programs were appropriate for staying in the present location. The planning committee resisted being data driven by clarifying their purpose in collecting the data.

MODELS AND METHODS: DECISION MAKING

A Shared Variance Model

As stated earlier, a needs assessment is a valuable tool for congregational leaders as the religious education planners move toward decision making and development of future ministries. Effective use of a needs assessment instrument enables the religious education planning team to be clear about which persons the planners are seeking to serve and to be clear about the specific needs, hopes, or concerns of those people. By itself, however, a needs assessment may not be sufficient to lead to

Figure 5.10
Steps to Take to Avoid Being Data Driven

1. Clarify the purpose of the needs assessment.
2. Plan your questions prior to collecting data. Identify, what planning questions your religious education planning group is seeking to answer.
3. Be open to unanticipated data's reframing questions. If unanticipated data is collected, allow it to reframe your question or to form other planning questions for a second round of data collection before assuming that it is an answer. Guard against implementing a ministry or a program of religious education that may not reflect the mission of your congregation.
4. Decide who will use the information. Make this decision prior to data collection.
5. Establish and agree on the criteria to analyze data prior to data collection.

appropriate decision making. It is possible for people to share needs, hopes, or concerns with a congregation that is unable or is not called to address those identified needs, hopes, or concerns.

In other words, to have identified a need for religious education is not the same as being committed to respond to it. Decision making for congregational leaders must be a discerning process in which information and learnings from an assessment play a helpful and critical part. They must also be weighed with other "listenings" and criteria. One approach to decision making is a "shared variance model" (fig. 5.11) that the religious education planning team or decision makers use to look for places where three critical variables come together: the missional objectives, the resources of the congregation, and the learnings from a needs assessment.

"Shared variance" refers to the overlap of the three critical variables. To identify the overlap is to identify the part of the potential ministry of the congregation that truly "belongs" because it is consistent with all of the critical components necessary to address it. The "perceived and identified needs" in this model refers to the information and learnings that come to the religious education planning team through the needs

Figure 5.11
Variables of Shared Variance

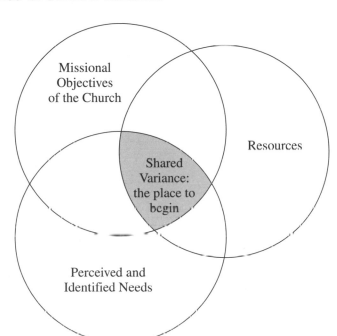

assessment. But as indicated above, to have identified the need is not necessarily to be called or committed to meeting it.

The second variable is the "missional objectives" of the congregation. These missional objectives grow out of the history, the identity, and the theological understanding of the congregation. Finally, the third variable of "resources" (members, staff, time, finances, facilities, energy) must be considered to raise the more practical issue of whether the congregation has what is required to respond with religious education ministry. It is in the shared variance—the overlap of such critical factors—that the congregation must do its discerning and decision making to ask if the religious education planners have found their next "place to begin" in ministry.

Consider the congregation located in an urban crisis environment. Through the years many persons were drawn to that church because of its high profile and effective community ministries. Suburban members regularly drove past many other congregations in order to attend the congregation located in the city. Members made it clear that there was a felt need for offering more programs of religious education and spiritual development, especially for their children and youth. "After all," members pointed out, "many of the churches we drive by have the kinds of programs that we need." However, the full decision-making process in this congregation had to account for not only the needs that members felt for their children but also for the call that the church felt for community ministry. Then there was the reality of limited resources of time, staff, members, and finances. Despite the need clearly expressed by members, religious education leaders were forced to make critical decisions about how and with whom the planning team would respond with ministry. In this case, the planners could not provide all of the programs for children and youth that were desired.

Consider the rabbi who spoke of the dilemma that arose when he encouraged younger adult members of the congregation to participate. These young adults came out of the consumer orientation of the last several decades and were very clear with him about the services and the programs they wanted. However, the rabbi felt at times that what people wanted in religious education was not always consistent with the traditions and the values of the congregation and the faith.

IMPACT OF CONGREGATIONAL SIZE

The style in which a congregation addresses a religious education needs assessment must fit the character of the congregation. The size of the congregation is one strong determinant of a congregation's style. Organizational development and systems theory have helped us to understand that the size of a congregation is, perhaps, the most critical single variable in understanding the role that leaders will assume, the expectations that members will bring, and the style in which the congregation will function.[27] The larger a congregation is, the more formal the planning and therefore the needs assessment tend to be. Similarly, the larger the

27. For a concise and very helpful demonstration of these differences by size, particularly as it relates to ministry to new members, see Arlin J. Rothauge, *Sizing Up a Congregation for New Member Ministry.* It is available from The Episcopal Church Center, 815 Second Avenue, New York, N.Y. 10017.

congregation the longer the planning cycle (that is, problem or opportunity identification, data collection, data analysis, project or program development, implementation, evaluation, problem or opportunity identification). Conversely, the smaller the congregation the more informal and the shorter the religious education planning cycle will be. This also holds true for small cells or ministry areas within a large church.

In other words, the needs assessment is a process of collecting and interpreting data to describe what people report as important to them in the desire or need to move from the present state of affairs to a more desirable one. But the needs assessment must be done appropriately according to the size and the style of the congregation and its religious education planning group.

For example, one large and very formal congregation that developed a very professional style among its staff and professional expectations among its members regularly evaluates every religious education offering by asking participants to fill out evaluation sheets at the conclusion of programs and events. These sheets are then summarized, reviewed by staff, and shared with the appropriate religious education planning committee as an ongoing formal process of assessing the needs of members and the effectiveness of programs and events. This style fits well the size and the expectations of this particular congregation. The planners are currently in the third year of a full church missional strategic planning process. They have very effectively gathered large amounts of written data to describe their present situation of ministry and to build a strong consensus for developing future goals of ministry.

Such a style would not fit congregations that have less formal expectations and shorter planning cycles. One such smaller congregation that has developed a notable track record for effective and well-timed adult religious education programs and events is based on the work of a small planning team that meets monthly. Any formal data gathering is done by administrative committees or staff people collecting it for their own purposes. Then the planning team appropriates it for conversations as needed. The meetings begin with a thorough, lengthy, and highly anecdotal assessment of the needs of the church, church members, or the surrounding community based on their rather extensive network of relationships and associations. Personal thoroughness and sensitivity to the network undergirds the ireffectiveness as planners anecdotally describe (i.e., do their needs assessment of) their congregation. Then, usually over coffee and often within a brief half hour, the planners make decisions about the next steps for the adult religious education program of the church. The decisions made by these planners are often remarkably accurate for the needs identified. The formal style of the larger church would frustrate this planning team in the smaller church. The informality and conversational nature of the smaller church would exasperate the professionalism and the efficiency of the larger church. Yet each church clearly found the style and the timing to match its size and expectations and developed an appropriate process. In between these two polar examples is a full continuum of alternatives and choices of how formal, how extensive, and how lengthy the process of needs assessment must be.

CONCLUSION

Without having a clear sense of people's needs religious educators risk falling into a trap that is best expressed in an aphorism from the quality improvement movement: "When we don't know what to do, we do what we already know how to do." In other words, religious education planners repeat old programs, continue established groups, and choose familiar curriculum because planners know how to do these things, whether or not the irefforts are of importance or of help to the people each seek to serve.

Curiously, a modern adaptation of an ancient Sufi legend appears with some regularity in a number of books about leadership and management. It tells of a passerby who encounters a man on his hands and knees under a street lamp. When he offers to help, he finds that the man is looking for his lost house keys. After looking for several minutes, the passerby asks, "Where did you drop them?" The man answers that he dropped them outside his front door. "Then why look for them here?" asks the passerby. "Because," comes the reply, "there is no light by my doorway."

This story suggests that planners of religious education find it difficult to move beyond the known and comfortable corporate and missional circles of light that each has become used to.[28] This occurs despite the

---

28. Peter M. Senge, *The Fifth Discipline* (New York: Doubleday, 1990), p. 60; Roger Harrison, "Strategies for a New Day" in *The Planning of Change,* by Warren G. Bennis, Kenneth D. Benne and Robert Chin (New York: Holt, Rinehart &Winston, 1985), p. 129; Ezra Earl Jones, *Quest for Quality in the Church* (Nashville: Discipleship Resources, 1993), p. 37.

fact that planners are increasingly aware that the needs of the religious education and the spiritual development of the people of congregations require a newness that better reflects the times and the tastes of a new day. In the words of one of the hymns of the Christian church "New occasions teach new duties . . ."[29]

Planners of religious education are becoming more and more aware that the "paradigm is shifting" and leaders are finding that the learned and comfortable circles of light that have been used in the past are not necessarily shining in the most helpful places. To be effective in this new day the efforts in religious education, discipleship training, and spiritual development need to be more focused and directly related to the needs, goals, and styles of the people in the congregations and communities that surround the church. With a clear sense of the needs of the people through an effective assessment, religious education planners can move out of old circles of light to serve more effectively people who are searching.

29. "Once to Every Man and Nation." #242 in *The Methodist Hymnal* (Nashville: Board of Publication of the United Methodist Church, 1964–66).

6

ENGAGING EFFECTIVE
PLANNING TEAMS

Estelle Rountree McCarthy

The scene is a religious education committee meeting at Any Congregation. The conversation sounds like this: "We've lost our senior high advisers. Can we find anybody to take over for the rest of the year?"

"Last summer's intergenerational Sunday school was well attended and people were really turned on by it. Shall we plan one again this year? I know, I know, it's just around the corner but with so many other things to take care of, it just slipped through the cracks."

"All the experts say it's a good idea to have a planning retreat with the new members of the committee. An overnight. Is there a time that would not conflict with busy schedules? What about May 17? That's the men's golf tournament? Oh, the men's golf tournament. What about the week before? Oh, no, Mother's Day!"

"And there's teacher training . . . They won't come? Well, they certainly need to!"

Finally at 10 P.M. Doris explodes. "I am so tired of these endless details and of problems that need solutions. Lurching from crisis to crisis. Planning one event after the other. Tonight it has finally hit me, something I've been vaguely uneasy about for months. Is it worth it? What are we trying to do anyway? Sometimes I think we're in the business of oiling machinery, never mind whether or not it's a necessary, useful machine, as long as it's working well . . . or even working at all! What's it all for? What is it all for?"

After a shocked silence, Jeannine, who has no tolerance for a silence lasting longer than sixty seconds, bursts out, "Doris, I'm surprised at you, good member that you are, even thinking those kinds of questions. Of course it's worthwhile! We all know that." Several people nod agreement.

"Well," retorts Doris, somewhat belligerently (she finds herself " 'ticked off' " by Jeannine's sanctimonious tone), "if you're so sure, Jeannine, just tell me, what is it all for? What is our purpose?"

"I'm sure we all agree, Doris," Jeannine replies rather coldly, "that our purpose is to teach Scripture. I personally am appalled, as practically everyone I know is, at the biblical ignorance of this parish. It's our heritage and our children don't know it. Of course I try my best to teach at home, but I get very little help from the congregation. I certainly want Roberta and Steve to be able to name the books of the Bible and recite the Ten Commandments and . . . well, I'm not so sure we shouldn't start teaching the catechism again, you know those cute little books."

"That's learning the Bible?" Joel comments.

"It comes to about the same thing, Joel," Jeannine retorts, feeling slightly on the defensive, her voice becoming more and more strident. "Well, surely we all agree about teaching the Bible," Jeannine asserts, addressing the group.

"Ah," says Bill, who loves a good argument and rises hungrily to the bait, "I'm not so sure it's that simple, Jeannine." Everyone settles down for a sermonette. "It seems to me that there's more to learning the Bible than just being able to recite facts. What seems to be of particular importance, to me at least, is applying the lessons of the Bible to life. In the men's class, which as you all know I've been teaching every other month for . . . let me see . . . is it ten or twelve years? Let me think, it was the year after George became pastor. Oh, that would make it eleven years ago this March."

"And your point, Bill?" Joel nudges.

"Well, yes, the point is . . . After we teach the facts, or as I would put it, the text, we need to struggle to find out what the Bible means for us today—to apply the text. And sometimes that is uncomfortable, yes, it is. But it's got to be done."

Lynn, the single young adult on the committee, breaks in. "Bill, I do believe this is just about the first time you and I have ever agreed about anything on this committee. Of course we need to see what the Bible is saying to life. What it is saying about war and peace, about abortion rights and gay rights. And it is uncomfortable at times, but so necessary."

"That's not exactly what I had in mind, Lynn" Bill is beginning to feel mighty uncomfortable.

Gladys, recently divorced at age forty-five, speaks up. "It's all well and good to talk about the importance of the Bible . . . and having it at the top of our religious education program. . .and, mind you, I'm all for the Bible," she hastens to add. "But what has made the difference in my life is the support we give one another. What I've been through these past few months was bearable only because of the support and friendship of our sharing group. I'm beginning to find out who I really am. For all these years I was just a doormat. But now I'm becoming me, a beautiful person."

Bill interjects, "That is wonderful, Gladys, but I don't see much connection between the Bible and theology and . . ."

"There certainly is, Bill Grainger!" Gladys is angry. "And it wouldn't hurt you one bit, and might even help you if . . ."

Miss Mary Graham, a retired school principal and resident saint of the congregation, breaks in quietly, "I think all of these goals seem good. But the fundamental matter we just must be concerned about is passing on our precious heritage to the next generation. I was reading a book by Walter Brueggemann last month.

"Walter who?" asks Bill.

"Walter Brueggemann. And he said something that really impressed me. In fact I even wrote it down. He said the church was always but one generation from extinction. Isn't that true! It's bringing up the next generation 'in the nurture and admonition of the Lord' ("Whatever that is", Joel says softly to Doris) "that is of critical importance," says Miss Mary Graham, gently but ever so firmly.

Since nobody in their right mind would be up to disagreeing with Miss Mary Graham, the conversation peters out, and the meeting breaks up shortly thereafter. The postmeeting conversation takes place in twos and threes. "Gladys seems so overly emotional" and "wish Bill wouldn't go on and on" and "can you believe reviving the catechism?" and "what are we trying to do?"

This "slice of life" from a parish religious education planning committee is not a verbatim account. Most religious education planners, however, can identify with most parts of it, and perhaps laugh at themselves.[1]

---

1. This opening scenario is available on the videotape "What's It All For?" available from Video Education Office, Presbyterian School of Christian Education, 1205 Palmyra Ave., Richmond, VA 23227. It can be helpful to religious education planning teams as they examine their effectiveness.

It does not take much experience or sophistication to conclude that this planning committee is not doing effective, quality work. Why not? For one thing, it is apparent that what is often called the "climate" of the group, or the group culture, is not conducive to doing quality work. There are undercurrents of unexamined disagreement, conflict, and denial. Communication is poor. There is a hurried atmosphere that implicitly says that there is no time for anything but quick decision making. Although the committee has a stated purpose,—to be responsible for the religious education ministry of the parish—when that purpose is discussed, even briefly, there seem to be many interpretations of what the purpose actually is. So in effect, there is no overarching purpose with which all can agree.

More subtle perhaps is a lack of vision held in common by the committee—a long-range hope, a desired future—that makes purpose worthwhile and quality important. Thus there is little motivation or corporate energy for doing more than crisis management. This religious education planning committee found itself reacting to short-term problems instead of planning for the future and dreaming of possibilities.

The simulated committee conversation at the beginning of this chapter serves as a jumping-off point for exploring the topic of this chapter: an inquiry into the nature of religious education planning teams and what makes them effective. Much has been written about what makes effective teams. Theories about effective teams, as well as resources

---

Figure 6.1
Simulated Committee Response

If this conversation were happening in your religious education planning team, how would you participate? Consider each of the following items and discuss how to increase the effectiveness of this planning team:

1. Ways to respond to the undercurrents of unexamined disagreement, conflict, and denial
2. Ways to improve the poor communication
3. Ways to change the hurried atmosphere
4. Ways to clarify the team purpose and vision

and opportunities for becoming more effective team members, abound. What can be added that will help religious education planning teams who are involved in the educational work of the congregation?

Perhaps one contribution that this chapter can make is to explore the development of theories and practices in contemporary North American culture and their adoption and adaptations by religious groups in their efforts to increase the effectiveness of their teams or work groups. This chapter will survey some of the theories and practices regarding groups and teams that have been developed outside religious institutions since the mid-1940s. This chapter will suggest implications for religious education, will provide examples from religious education practice, and will discuss guiding principles for religious education. Finally, it will reflect theologically on these theories and practices from the perspectives of the Jewish and Christian traditions.

DEFINITIONS

Teams are not new. They have existed for hundreds of years in all aspects of life: family, workplace, sports. Since the term "team" has specific meanings within the larger category of group, looking at some contemporary definitions of team(s) can be a helpful beginning point.

Teams are task-oriented groups that have "a goal or combination of goals—to solve a specific problem, to plan a specific action, to produce a specific report, to make specific recommendations, and so forth."[2] Work teams are "small groups of interdependent individuals who share responsibility for outcomes of their organization."[3] A team consists of "two or more people: it has a specific performance objective or recognizable goal to be attained; and coordination of activity among the members of the team is required for the attainment of the team goal or objective."[4] It is "a small number of people with complementary

2. Gordon L. Lippitt, *Team Building for Matrix Organizations,* Reprint Series (Washington, D.C.: Project Associates, 1969), p. 4. This resource is available from Project Associates, Inc., 506 Lamar Rd., Washington, D.C. 20016.

3. Susan A. Wheelan, *Group Processes, A Developmental Perspective* (Boston: Allyn & Bacon, 1994), p. 218.

4. Carl E. Larson and Frank M. J. LaFasto, *Team Work: What Must Go Right/What Can Go Wrong* (Newbury Park, Calif.: Sage, 1989), p. 19.

skills who are committed to a common purpose, performance goals and approach for which they hold themselves mutually accountable."[5]

Teams shift their exclusive reliance on "one-alone and one-to-one direction to one-to-all." This notion of team does not replace the need for the individual's actions; however, the team goal is to find the fullest advantages of the whole.[6]

Thus planning and management experts are in remarkable agreement. All stipulate that a team is a particular kind of group distinguished by its focused sense of purpose. Teams are goal oriented. Teams are performance based. Teams are production oriented, and committed to specific outcomes. Definitions of teams include the concepts of cooperation, coordination, and interdependence.

Think of the varied religious education teams in particular congregations: committees for overall planning such as the religious education committee; subcommittees for various agelevels or for family life, vacation church schools, or children and worship; short-term task groups for purposes like building a new educational facility, planning youth Sunday, or working toward a mission trip; teams for teaching in many places and settings.

ASSUMPTIONS ABOUT TEAMS

Teams are not the only way to involve persons in effective planning. Experience shows that one person working alone may do successful planning. As long as the individual is working within the framework of communal goals, such solo efforts can be quite fruitful. A sense of rugged individualism can be used to further the collective strength of a team. The intent is to harness the energy for the full team. Research indicates, however, that team planning is generally a key to effectiveness.[7]

The professional literature that is particularly relevant for the contemporary parish dates primarily from the 1950s to the present. The

---

5. Jon R. Katzenbach and Douglas K. Smith, *The Wisdom of Teams: Creating the High-Performance Organization* (Boston: Harvard Business School, Harvard University, 1993), p. 44.

6. Robert R. Blake and Jane Srygley Mouton, *The Managerial Grid* (Houston: Gulf Publishing, 1964), p. 303. See pages 1–4 for the self-assessment of managerial styles.

7. Katzenbach and Smith, *Wisdom of Teams,* pp. 18–19. John M. Bryson, *Strategic Planning for Public and Nonprofit Organizations,* (San Francisco: Jossey-Bass, 1995), pp. 219–20.

pioneering work done in human relations training, management, organization development, and systems theory during this period have had marked influence on team effectiveness.[8] The literature developed outside religious structures about theory and practice has provided most of the theory and practice that are advocated today in church and synagogue. Religious institutions have welcomed and embraced many of these findings from the so-called secular sphere.[9] While welcoming insights, aims, and practices from nonreligious institutions, church and synagogue will need to evaluate usefulness and consequences from the point of view of their own mission, purpose, and theological positions.[10]

CHARACTERISTICS OF EFFECTIVE TEAMS

A survey of the literature about teams in secular institutions—industry, business, and service organizations—since the end of World War II uncovers a general consensus about characteristics of effective teams. Specific emphases in particular periods will be treated later in the chapter. At this point a summary of characteristics of effective teams as described by relatively recent writers and practitioners will be presented. Note that these characteristics clarify what is meant by "effective."

Fran Rees offers "ten essentials of teamwork" that seem to capture the consensus of critical characteristics needed for effective teamwork. These characteristics are displayed as circular, not linear or hierarchical.[11]

---

8. Gregory E. Huszczo, *Tools for Team Excellence* (Palo Alto, Calif.: Davies-Black, 1996), pp. 101–3. For further examination of the impact that social scientists have make on religious education see: pages 173–83 in "Group Dynamics and Religious Education," C. Ellis Nelson, in *Religious Education: A Comprehensive Survey*, ed. Marvin J. Taylor (Nashville: Abingdon, 1960).

9. Alvin J. Lindgren and Norman Shawchuck, *Management for Your Church: How to Realize Your Church's Potential through a Systems Approach* (Nashville: Abingdon, 1977), pp. 20–28.

10. Ibid., pp. 50–56. Lindgren and Shawchuck suggest that the theological dimensions of a church are the primary issue involved in the creation of a mission statement. The six dimensions of creating a mission statement include Bible study, theological and doctrinal concepts of church, tradition, the needs of the world and contemporary society, the local scene and the presence of the Holy Spirit.

11. Fran Rees, *How to Lead Work Teams: Facilitation Skills* (London: Pfeiffer, 1991), p. 39.

Leading teams have certain characteristics in common. They exist for a specified purpose, and hold goals in common. Their concept of leadership sometimes includes a formal leader; at other times a leadership arises from the group. They pay attention to individual needs as well as to group goals. They view conflict as constructive because communication is open and the members trust one another. All team members are actively involved. The team has power to make decisions.

Jon Katzenbach and Douglas Smith set forth the following basic characteristics. The emphasis here is on performance that leads directly to results.

1. Teams are accountable.
2. Teams need education in necessary skills.
3. Members are committed to a common goal that is meaningful.
4. Members emphasize performance and team basics instead of "trying to become a team."
5. They do not understand teamwork as being the same as team. Performance is the primary objective.
6. A team remains the means, not the end.[12]

Looking back at the religious education committee scenario in terms of the effective team characteristics stated above gives some insight into why the committee's life and work was ineffective. Although the committee had an overall purpose approved by the congregation, specific understandings of the purpose and goals varied widely. The group was fragmented and there was no sense of leadership. Group members seemed incapable of listening to one another, partly because they were so engrossed in their own personal agendas. Conflict wasted energy and was hurtful to persons. Disagreements and hostility seemed to spring from unresolved conflicts originating in other times and places. Though the religious education team had the power and responsibility for making decisions, it seemed severely hampered by internal troubles that consumed the team's energy.

This religious education committee needed agreement about and commitment to a common goal that could lead it forward. It needed to

---

12. See Katzenbach and Smith, *Wisdom of Teams,* p. 8, for a graphic of the team basics and pages 49–129 for team performance.

learn listening skills and conflict-resolution skills and how to participate responsibly in its own life.

Certain theories and practices propounded in the years since World War II have molded the contemporary understanding of team effectiveness.

Two streams of theory and practice have given rise to present-day understandings about team effectiveness. The first system is the human relations movement. The second system is the organizational development movement, with particular emphasis on systemic thinking. Both streams are grounded in the behavioral sciences.[13] Both are process oriented. Both have important consequences for planning in religious education.

HUMAN RELATIONS LABORATORY TRAINING

A breakthrough event in the 1920s and 1930s was the now classic Hawthorne study, of the Hawthorne Illinois plant of the Western Electric Company, authored by a group of Harvard professors.[14] The initial hypothesis was that a group's output is connected with the lighting of the work area. The research group set up elaborate conditions to study effects on production. After five years, the study of a group of women workers revealed that the experimental group's production output increases when they worked under reduced lighting. Other conditions were altered— rest periods, methods of pay, refreshments, and a short work week. Researchers found the output curve rising regardless of other changes that were made. When all changes were eliminated and the women went back to working under the original conditions, their output rose even more.[15]

After extensive analysis the researchers agreed that the most significant factor in production output was a sense of group identity, social

13. Gregory E. Huszczo, *Tools for Team Excellence,* pp. 102–3. Concern for both production capability and people emerged as an attempt to bring the previously separated foci into one unifying direction of leadership and team development.

14. G. Homans, "Group Factors in Worker Productivity," in, *Basic Studies in Social Psychology,* ed. H. Proshansky and B. Seidenberg (New York: Rinehart & Winston, 1965), pp. 592–604. The Hawthorne study is described in *The Human Problems of an Industrial Civilization,* by Elton Mayo (Boston: Division of Research, Graduate School of Business Administration, Harvard University, 1933).

15. Fred N. Kerlinger, *Foundations of Behavioral Research,* 2d ed. (New York: Holt, Rinehart & Wilson, 1964), p. 155.

support, and cohesion that came with increased worker interaction. The key, they determined, was a sympathetic supervisor who encouraged worker participation in decisions. The Hawthorne study did not prove its initial hypothesis. Rather, it showed that it was possible to take a random collection of employees and build them into a highly productive work team, even if physical conditions were not ideal.[16] The research demonstrated that extra attention paid to people causes them to change. This is known as the Hawthorne effect.[17]

The Hawthorne study and the Hawthorne effect have encouraged religious educators. Congregational teams are usually composed of persons with differing backgrounds, abilities, and levels of commitment. The Hawthorne study suggests that sensitive and caring leadership generates active participation from all and that respectful interactions among all increase team productivity. A word of caution: although change is aided by the Hawthorne effect, it is not wise to institutionalize the process to achieve results.[18]

About a decade after the conclusion of the Hawthorne study, the laboratory human relations movement was born (also known as sensitivity training, T-group [training group], or encounter group). Laboratory training, as it was also known, was intended to offer new and improved methods for group facilitation. It sought more effective human *"responses to* and . . . *control of* change."[19] Matthew Miles describes this movement as "intensive group self-study procedures, usually taking place in a residential setting and designed to bring about increased sensitivity and skill in relation to social-psychological phenomena occurring in interpersonal group and organizational situations."[20]

The purposes of the human relations laboratory, according to William Dyer, were to focus on group processes, problem solving, and sharing information in an open way. Participants were helped in establishing and sharing information as well as in forming a highly cohesive group climate. Other group processes included building norms of shared and

---

16. William G. Dyer, *Team Building: Issues and Alternatives* (Reading, Mass.: Addison-Wesley, 1977), pp. 7–9.
17. Fred N. Kerlinger, *Foundations of Behavioral Research*, p. 345.
18. Gregoary E. Huszczo, *Tools for Team Excellence*, p. 197.
19. Bruce Joyce and Marsha Weil, *Models of Teaching* (Englewood Cliffs, N.J.: Prentice-Hall, 1972), pp.75–92.
20. Irving R. Wesheler and Edgar M. Schein, eds., *Five Issues in Training* (Washington, D.C.: NTL-NEA, 1962), p. 4.

collaborative action.[21] Notice the emphasis on group rather than team. Also note the assumption that the learners could acquire skills through the process of participation.[22] Early leaders of this movement included Leland Bradford, Kenneth Benne, Ronald Lippitt, and Kurt Lewin. The pioneering group, the National Training Laboratory (NTL), was begun by them and others in 1946 in Bethel, Maine. During the 1960s and 1970s to "have a T-group experience—preferably at Bethel—was *de rigeur* for middle-managers of corporations and also for national staffs in religious institutions.[23]

Emphasis at Bethel and at laboratories that appeared in other locations throughout North America was specifically focused on group process. The content was the group dynamic itself. The themes of human-relations training include (1) building bridges between the world of the human sciences—sociology and psychology, (2) understanding learning as an inductive and experience-centered matter, and (3) increasing the capacity for inventing and developing of experimental teaching methods. The central experience was the training group (T-group). The T-group was not a therapy group, though its emphasis was definitely on feelings. It focused on both individual behavior in the group setting and small group phenomena.

Since the ultimate purpose of the NTL at that time was to promote the spread of more effective leadership in occupational and organizational pursuits, many institutions sent their top leadership to these training sessions in the 1950s and 1960s.[24] The basic notion was that individuals or groups from an institutional setting would "come apart" to become more sensitized to social interaction and then return to their places of work with fundamentally new insight born of small-group experience. They would understand from experience how their actions in group settings affected other members. They would know some small-group theory. They would have experienced and dealt with confrontation, conflict, and new ways of problem solving. It was widely believed at

---

21. Dyer, *Team Building,* p. 22.

22. Joyce and Weil, *Models of Teaching,* p. 76.

23. For new staff members at national and middle-levels, attendance at one or more human relations laboratories constituted a rite of passage into "full-staff-hood," or as a more current phrase might put it, "political correctness."

24. Wesheler and Schein, eds., *Five Issues in Training,* pp. 3–6. By 1962 there were 4,000 NTL alumni, including persons from educational groups, health organizations, volunteer agencies, industry, and business.

the time that such experiences would result in increased effectiveness in deliberation and action back home. As the movement spread, increasing emphasis was placed on individual self-awareness and the importance of releasing individual potential.[25]

Leadership

Two aspects of leadership were important in the T-group movement. The first was of the "trainer," who was the group facilitator. The trainer acted as coach and referee. As coach, the trainer kept the group moving; as referee, the trainer helped enforce already agreed-on guidelines and at times kept the group from going beyond what it could handle safely. Trainers offered substantive content sparingly, since the group itself provided its own content. They proposed procedures and at appropriate times clarified and summarized.

The second aspect of leadership was that leadership from the group itself was encouraged. For "leadership to arise from the group" was a mark of success in T-groups. If the designated leader spoke little and the group managed its life together, so much the better. Collegial relationships were encouraged. One person might serve as gatekeeper, another might serve as summarizer, someone else as tension reliever. The group was encouraged to take responsibility for its own life.

Four objectives of learning in the T-group include (1) to develop the mental ability to observe oneself and others, including a sensitivity to self and others; (2) to learn about control, specifically how a group can learn to be self-managed; (3) to develop the awareness that communication is on-going at various levels within any one group; and (4) driving to gain competency in group problem solving.[26]

Contributions of Human Relations Training

It would be difficult to overstate the contribution that the human re-lations movement has made to the development of effective teams. Using emerging research in psychology and sociology, it brought to consciousness the importance of personal self-esteem and interpersonal relationships to team functioning. It put into words and gave theoretical

25. For an examination of exercises, see the multivolume *Handbook in Human Relations Training,* by Pfeiffer and Jones. Both content and methodology are discussed.

26. J. R. Kidd, *How Adults Learn* (New York: Association Press, 1977), p. 261.

underpinnings to what many organizations through experience "knew" already: no matter how noble the purpose and how important the work, unless a team paid careful attention to its internal life, its productivity was impaired or blocked, and team ownership of the final "product" was often low. It showed that attention must be paid to the affective domain, specifically, awareness of feelings and emotions. Intentionality was vital in working through them successfully. Attending solely to the cognitive domain denies human nature.

A second major contribution of the human relations movement was to offer experiential processes and training to groups for overcoming barriers to healthy interpersonal relationships. A theorist and writer popular in the 1960s and 1970s was William Schutz, whose book *JOY* helped to put the human potential movement in the hands of the public.[27] Schutz's work popularized the human relations movement and suggested procedures that summarized much of what the human relations movement was about. Schutz wrote about the need to get in touch with and be aware of feelings. He emphasized the individual's basic need for inclusion, control, and affection. Schultz's methods are designed to help individuals recognize their feelings and modes of behavior and to help persons in groups increase awareness, experience telling the truth, and understanding of responsibility and choice.[28] Schultz suggests a number of exercises, many of them games, that call forth feelings of inclusion, control, and affection.[29]

All of these movements, and others, have helped church and synagogue as well as "secular" institutions. Many religious institutions and denominations adapted these learnings from the movement to their own settings and purposes. In the 1960s, the former Presbyterian Church (U.S.) devised a five-day workshop and a twelve-hour workshop that drew directly on the NTL experiences in Bethel, Maine. The five-day

---

27. William Schutz, *Joy: Expanding Human Awareness* (New York: Grove, 1967).

28. Jack K. Fordyce and Raymond Weil, *Managing with People*, 3d. ed. (Reading, Mass.: Addison-Wesley, 1971), pp. 186–87.

29. There are other helpful resources. H. Lewis and H. Streitfield in *Growth Games* (New York: Harcourt Brace and Jovanovich, 1970), list games that build warmth and trust and help break through blockages. The Pfeiffer and Jones handbooks (see footnote 25) give many exercises that can be used to increase awareness and open up new dimensions of effectiveness for teams. One of the most helpful books, still used as a textbook, which offers both theory and training, is David W. Johnson and Douglas K. Johnson, *Joining Together: Group Theory and Group Skills*, 3d. ed. (Englewood Cliffs, N.J.: Prentice-Hall, 1987).

workshop was an "away from home" experience; the twelve-hour work-shop was recommended as both an "away from" and an "at home" experience. These workshops were immensely popular and gave thousands of church leaders across the denomination an opportunity within the framework of their own tradition to experience the centrality of inter-personal relations in both learning and planning. A look at experience-based training reveals these areas of emphasis: perception of persons, responsible membership in groups, and communication. Relevant doctrinal and biblical study, interspersed with training exercises, was added to give a theologically based framework.[30]

In the 1960s the National Council of Churches held an annual ten-day sensitivity training experience for church leaders at the American Baptist assembly grounds at Green Lake, Wisconsin. It was the place to be if you could not go to Bethel.

In 1970 Nancy Geyer and Shirley Noll wrote a book entitled *Team Building in Church Groups*. The influence of the human relations move-ment is evident in its goals for team building: (1) to express feelings, ideas and questions related to the tasks, (2) to listen and respond directly to the feelings and ideas of other members of the team, (3) to act and feel as individuals sharing equal responsibility with every other individual on the team, and (4) to enable the team to fulfill its task more effectively.[31]

Suggestions for Effective Planning Teams in Religious Education

In his chapter in the book *The Pastor as Religious Educator*, G. Temp Sparkman includes the following aspects of "groupness," which seem to derive from the human relations movement: (1) successful teams receive the unique gifts that each member brings and builds its life in accordance with such gifts; (2) participants affirm each other in their giftedness; (3) participants bring individual ambitions for personal development and willingly invest them in the group; (4) participants share the group's common understanding of the overarching purpose of the group, though they do not necessarily devote themselves with equal intensity to all of the group's goals; (5) participants are drawn with earnestness, in some

---

30. Unpublished handbooks. The former Presbyterian Church (U.S.), which helped form the Presbyterian Church (U.S.A.) in 1983.

31. Nancy Geyer and Shirley Noll, *Team Building in Church Groups* (Valley Forge, Pa.: Judson, 1970), p. 7.

cases, passion, into some challenge facing the group; (6) participants unapologetically disagree with each other and in good spirit confront each other's weaknesses; (7) participants contribute to and share fully in the group's successes and failures; and (8) participants recognize and accept that the group and its work impinge on other groups within and beyond the larger organization.[32]

Those responsible for planning religious education in the church and synagogue need to be attentive to persons and their interrelationships. Almost all religious institutions affirm this practice and build it into their literature. Yet congregations vary tremendously in their practices. Religious education groups can improve their overall effectiveness through following four suggestions for leaders and other members of teams.[33]

First, as a religious education planning team begins its work together, it needs experiences that help each person get to know members on a more than superficial level. Do not assume that because members grew up together or have been together in the same congregation for years, that they will know one another as persons or feel comfortable with one another. Sometimes the reverse is true. Knowing someone's name, social security number, and occupation does not necessarily mean being in touch with that person. As a new religious education planning team is constituted, or as new members join, plan experiences that offer persons nonthreatening, enjoyable ways to reveal aspects of their lives and personalities.

Do not shortchange this process of getting to know one another. Never omit this important activity in the interest of saving time. To do so will almost always hinder teamwork. Providing opportunities not only in the beginning but during the course of the team's work together is very important. A team in one parish regularly begins its monthly meeting "getting on board with one another," describing what has happened to each since the team last met, sharing concerns and celebrations—the ups and downs of life, the tragedy and the wonder. This procedure was suggested by a member of the team, not staff. As planning team members share something of their own lives, they find themselves appreciating each person as a human being and working together more effectively. A

---

32. G. Temp Sparkman's chapter "The Pastor as Leader of an Educational Team" in *The Pastor as Religious Educator*, ed. Robert Browning (Birmingham, Ala.: Religious Education Press, 1989), pp. 132–35.

33. See Martha Leypoldt, *Learning Is Change* (Valley Forge, Pa.: Judson, 1971).

word of caution is due here. One church leader years ago was heard to remark that the team he was a part of learned to know and care for each other very well, but "didn't accomplish one damn thing!"[34]

Second, educate and train religious education planning groups in essential skills that enhance interpersonal effectiveness. Skills can be learned in listening, in communicating, in roles that are necessary parts of group life. Such education can occur at the beginning of a planning team's life together or it can be a part of each meeting or as need arises. Consider budgeting the time that is necessary for new religious education planning committees or new teaching teams to become more proficient in these areas.

Third, when the planning team evaluates its effectiveness in religious education, not only at the end of a particular phase in the team's life but throughout its life together, include questions that evaluate feelings, attitudes, and group interactions. Use some of the evaluative tools in Martha Leypoldt's book *Learning Is Change*.

Fourth, remember that religious education planning team members themselves have skills in this area from their own work or volunteer experiences. Many staff members and lay leaders can discover a myriad of skills possessed by team members as they take time to talk with them and be present to them.

The T-group laboratory "away from home" methodology was transferred into the organizational setting in the 1950s and 1960s as the best method known at the time. There were problems with it, however. First, the T-groups with participants who were "away from home," began their group experience with individuals who were strangers to one another. Members had never met each other before and were unlikely to work together in the future. On the other hand, work groups that were formed "back home" had a long history with each other. Second, T-groups disbanded and never met again. On the other hand, work groups "back home" continued intact after the sessions were over, and members had to be responsible for issues that had been raised. These differences revealed the importance of the environment. The T-group approach tended to ignore structural, economic, environmental, and political factors. It did not

---

34. Robert C. Worley, "Church Education as an Organization Phenomenon," in *Foundations for Christian Education in an Era of Change*, ed. Marvin J. Taylor, (Nashville: Abingdon, 1976), pp. 123–24.

take into account the complex nature of organizations and relationships to their surroundings.[35]

Gradually the T-group methodology shifted from unstructured groups to a more focused, defined process of training a group of interdependent people in collaborative work and problem-solving procedures.[36]

ORGANIZATIONAL DEVELOPMENT

The interest in more focused group training brought forth organization development (O.D.), with its emphasis on work teams. Note that the operative word in human relations training is "groups." Laboratory training emphasizes self-understanding and improved interpersonal relationships. The operative term in organization development is "teams." It emphasizes performance and purposes to be accomplished—work to be done.

Since 1955 theory about organizations has developed at an accelerating pace. The development of technology, increasing pluralism, and the development of new theoretical concepts have resulted in new organizational practices.[37] It is impossible in this brief essay to trace these theories in detail, certain facets that bear on effective teams will be examined as organizational development is considered from a systems approach.

"Organizational development" is a term used to describe sustained systematic effort to improve an organization's culture or climate.[38] "It

---

35. Ibid., pp. 121–22.

36. Dyer, *Team Building,* p. 23. For a review of the literature on the impact of the group dynamics movement first known as the National Training Laboratory (NTL) in Group Development see Cyril O. Houle, *The Literature of Adult Education* (San Francisco: Jossey-Bass, 1992), pp. 228–32.

37. Worley, "Church Education," pp. 124–26, suggests that "tilting or focusing of congregational resources to the church school has allowed educators and other church professionals to ignore the educational needs of the total congregation." He suggests that this myopic vision has caused religious educators to become distanced from the educational tasks that they must accomplish. For a chart that shows five organizational theories and their influence on congregations, see Lindgren and Shawchuck, *Management for Your Church,* pp. 26–27. Note that the theory of human relations influenced congregations as the term "the fellowship of faith" emerged and as planners leading groups encouraged respect for relationships within the environment that included feelings, mutual acceptance, and goals (pp. 22–23). Also see Paul B. Maves's chapter in *Religious Education: A Comprehensive Survey,* ed. Marvin J. Taylor (Nashville: Abingdon, 1960), pp. 132–42.

38. Fordyce and Weil, *Managing with People,* p. ix.

is a response to change, a complex educational strategy intended to change the beliefs, attitudes, values and structures of organizations so they can better adapt to new technologies, markets, challenges, and the dizzying rate of change itself."[39] It is a way of managing change and a way of focusing human energy on specified outcomes.[40] Gordon Lippitt describes it as the process to initiate, create, and confront the necessary changes that organizations must make to become or to remain viable. These changes often include adapting to new conditions, solving problems, and learning from experience.[41] Most religious institutions are by nature "conserving." They have a difficult time confronting changes and adapting to new conditions. This can be true in religious education, as any planner or teacher who has recommended changing the hour of service or Sunday school knows.

The function of organizational development is to develop the total organization. Special emphasis is placed on the management of organizations. Formal work teams are the key item.[42] Management is collaborative and shared. Focus is not on the manager but on the work group.

Organizational development views the organization as an interdependent, interactive system. An action in one part of the system inevitably affects other parts. A systems approach to organization emphasizes interrelatedness, connectedness, interdependence, and interaction.[43] Particular units often relate to units in other systems. The term "matrix" is used to denote working across divisional and organizational lines, using resources within any part of the system or other systems. The old way of looking at levels in an organization as existing autonomously is passé.

For instance, a religious education planning committee that wishes to propose plans for including children in corporate worship will need to interface with the worship committee or liturgy team, the pastor

---

39. Warren G. Bennis, *Organization Development: Its Nature, Origins, and Prospects* (Reading, Mass.: Addison-Wesley, 1969), p. 2.
40. Fordyce and Weil, *Managing with People*, p. 15.
41. Lippitt, *Team Building for Matrix Organizations*, p. 1.
42. Wendell L. French and Cecil H. Bell Jr., *Organizational Development* (Englewood Cliffs, N.J.: Prentice-Hall, 1973), p. 15.
43. Timothy Arthur Lines, *Systemic Religious Education* (Birmingham, Ala.: Religious Education Press, 1987), pp. 42–46. This text offers a review of literature and an integration of a systems approach to religious education. For further study see "Prisoners of the System, or Prisoners of Our Own Thinking," chapter 3 in Peter M. Senge's *The Fifth Discipline* (New York: Doubleday, 1990), pp. 27–54.

or rabbi, the director of religious education, and the governing board. A wise planning committee may initially propose a team composed of representatives from each of the responsible groups. Similarly, a youth group that is serious about going on a mission trip to Mexico will need to contact other interested parties: the youth committee, the mission committee, the budget committee, parents, church staff. The basic principle is that there is no "outside" to the interrelationship, the problems, the new efforts, the plan.[44] The congregation is one and therefore each and every choice impacts others parts and pieces of the religious education effort. There is one religious education system in place in any one congregation.

In a provocative essay, Robert Worley lifts up another important characteristic of systems: their vulnerability to other systems, whether a competing system or the very system of which the work team is a subsystem.[45] Other systems are increasingly encroaching on what has traditionally been thought of as "sacred time." Witness mandatory Sunday morning practice sessions scheduled on Sunday mornings. The Jewish community, of course, has had to face this situation for centuries.

Wendell H. French and Cecil H. Bell Jr. delineate seven characteristics of organization development: (1) an emphasis on group and organizational processes in contrast to substantive content, (2) an emphasis on work teams as the key unit of learning, (3) an emphasis on collaborative management of the work team, (4) an emphasis on the culture of the total system and its influence on the work team, (5) an emphasis on action research, (6) a view of change as an ongoing process, and (7) a primary emphasis on human and social relationships.[46]

Leadership in Work Teams

Leaders in work teams in a systemic approach have learned much from the human relations movement. However, leaders in organizational development assume a more active role insisting that the hierarchical or benevolent patriarchal (matriarchal) style change in favor of a participative team-task-orientated style. As one writer notes, former managers will need to adapt to new situations and to acquire new skills. They

44. Peter M. Senge, *The Fifth Discipline*, p. 67.

45. Robert C. Worley, "Church Education as an Organizational Phenomenon," pp. 119–20.

46. French and Bell, *Organizational Development*, pp. 19–20.

need to think and act like team members relying on former authority. These new leadership roles necessitate a shift from old mental models of leading groups. Leaders need to move from thinking of themselves as supervisors to thinking of themselves as teams and to begin to view a facilitative team leader's style instead of a directive team leader's style. They need to balance managing with facilitating. In a departure from early styles in organizational development, they need to be more self-reliant when leading groups and teams, not relying heavily on consultants.[47]

Two major roles of leadership in work teams is to facilitate and to motivate toward accomplishing the agreed-upon goals. Different situations demand different leadership, responses, but in general, work teams involved in effective planning require leaders to perform six basic functions in helping groups to (1) decide with clarity their purposes and objectives, (2) become conscious of their own procedures in order to improve their problem-solving capability, (3) become aware of talents, skills, and other resources existing within their own membership, (4) develop group methods of evaluation so that the group will have ways of improving its process and become aware of how others think and feel, (5) accept new ideas and new members without conflict, and accept discipline in working toward long-range objectives and profiting from failure, (6) create new task forces or subgroups as needed and terminate them when it is wise to do so.[48]

Leaders who are working with religious education planning teams becoming with being educated as leaders of work teams. Educating lay leadership in the basics of team development is essential. Staff persons who support planning teams must be aware of the need to understand both old models of leadership in work teams and newer principles of effective work teams. Working with planning teams in religious education takes both deliberate time and careful education of the chairpersons who will lead work teams. Leadership of religious education planning teams will not include manipulating staff or coaching every play from the sidelines. The unique role of leading a work team requires a set of skills that can be developed. Planning in religious education will benefit from leaders who develop this skill set. In fact,

---

47. Rees, *How to Lead Work Teams,* pp. 11–15. For a discussion of "natural leaders in a learning organization," see Senge, *Fifth Discipline*, pp. 357–60.
48. Lippett, *Team Building for Matrix Organizations,* p. 114.

effective leadership in congregational life is possible only when leaders become effective in developing viable teams.[49]

Contributions of Organizational Development

The broader notion of organizational development, systemic thinking, has much to offer in guiding the development of effective work teams including four basic characteristics. First, work team goals flow from the purposes of the organization itself. These goals must be clarified as common to the work of the team. Second, the organization must emphasize change. The work team must be proactive in its efforts to realize goals, not reactive.[50] Third, team members are not simply linked to one another. As a team, they are linked to other parts of the organization, both locally and in broader arenas. What happens in a work team affects other parts of the system in some way, large or small. Fourth, teams formed across work areas can often be more effective than teams drawn from only one area. This is because teams that spend their planning hours focused on one specific part of an organization's life often begin to think alike and frequently begin to miss imaginative ways to recast problems, issues, and opportunities.

The insights and practices gleaned from both the human relations stream and the organizational development stream have had a tremendous impact on the literature and practice of team building. The most effective management style is one that develops teams that pay attention both to persons and to purposes. Task and membership are both important. When task is stressed to the exclusion of team members, the relational dynamic is lost and individuals are viewed as machines completing a task. Consistent in both streams has been the overarching goal of more effective performance by teams related to the purposes of the organization or institution. Consistent in both streams has been the underlying assumption that effective teams are key to fulfillment of purpose.

Recent Developments

In the 1980s and 1990s the work of two persons, among others, has transformed the way of developing and leading teams and understanding

---

49. Varney, *Building Productive Teams,* pp. 132–33.
50. Huszczo, *Tools for Team Excellence,* pp. 21–35.

processes. The first is W. Edward Deming, a statistician, who worked as a consultant in Japan following World War II. His method provided the key to Japan's rise to industrial excellence. His work did not gain widespread acclaim in the United States until the mid-1980s.

The so-called Deming method is built on the idea of quality performance and continual improvement and is characterized by cooperation and win-win approaches. It takes systemic theory seriously and asserts that team performance is judged by its contribution to the aim of the entire system, not for its individual product or profit. The Deming method emphasizes (1) constancy of purpose, (2) leadership of management toward continual improvement rather than performance evaluation and merit rating, (3) a vigorous program of education and retraining, (4) driving out fear among employees, and (5) breaking down barriers between departments and units. The Deming management method focuses on process rather than specific tasks. The Deming cycle is "Plan—Do—Check—Act."[51] This method implies that processes can be improved. The intent is to initiate constant improvement into each cycle of change.

Among other things, Deming's thought reminds religious educators that their work is to contribute to the larger purposes of church or synagogue, not to build their own "empires" or to defend their own turf. Planning in religious education constantly examines processes for transformation. Therefore, the entire religious education leadership of the congregation must plan together. Caring for the needs of the community and congregation is the responsibility of those who design the congregation's religious education plan. When new community needs are identified, the entire staff examines the present ministry offerings to determine how to respond. Perhaps the critical learning from the Deming cycle is that planning in religious education begins with a plan and proceeds to an implementation of that plan.

A second influential person of the 1990s is Peter M. Senge, author of *The Fifth Discipline: The Art and Practice of the Learning Organization*. The organizations that will truly excel in the future, says Senge, will be learning organizations which have the ability to learn faster than their

---

51. Mary Walton, *Deming Management at Work* (New York: Putnam, 1990), pp. 21–22. This cycle was originally named after Walter Shewhart, who pioneered statistical quality control. The Japanese named this the "Deming cycle." The four stages in the PDCA cycle include plans for a change, the change itself, check on the results of the change, and, depending on the result, the necessary improvements beginning a new cycle with new information. For further reading on the PDCA cycle, see Mary Walton, *The Deming Management Method* (New York: Putnam, 1986), pp. 86–88.

competitors. Leaders of learning organizations know "how to tap people's commitment and capacity to learn at *all* levels in an organization."[52]

Senge too focuses on the importance of systemic thinking as a discipline for seeing wholes, interrelationships, and patterns of change. He rejects the idea that the world is composed of separate, unrelated forces. He advocates building a shared vision, a picture of the future, a specific destination that includes translating individual vision into shared vision. Organizations can continually expand their capacity to create their future. Learning means "recreating ourselves." Learning means "metanoia"—a fundamental shift or movement of mind.[53]

Teams, not individuals, are the major learning unit in modern organization. If teams do not learn, the organization does not learn.[54] The "fifth discipline" is systems thinking, which holds together the other four disciplines: (1) personal mastery (not over people but a special level of proficiency)—the discipline of continually clarifying and deepening our personal visions; (2) mental models—turning the mirror inward and scrutinizing our internal pictures of the world; (3) building a shared vision—a shared picture of the future we intend to create; (4) team learning—beginning with dialogue and discerning patterns that underlie learning. Teams have patterns that undermine their own learning. These patterns can be defensiveness, shifting blame, preempting learner needs, or being blind to the needs of a community. Whatever the underlying patterns are, they need to be identified. When the patterns are identified, they can be changed. Team learning is vital to the health of a learning congregation.[55]

Senge reminds religious educators that a shared vision for the future and a belief that such a future is possible moves a learning congregation toward that future. Churches and synagogues call this belief hope.

Since 1980, research and writing about congregations has proliferated.[56] Much of this material takes seriously the systemic nature of congregational life and helps place work teams in the context of the life

---

52. Senge, *Fifth Discipline*, p. 4.
53. Ibid., pp. 13–14.
54. Ibid., p. 10.
55. Ibid., pp. 4–10.
56. For a review of the literature in adult religious education see Houle, *The Literature of Adult Education* pp. 255–59. Timothy Arthur Lines, *Systemic Religious Education* (Birmingham, Ala.: Religious Education Press, 1987), pp. 211–21. Planning for strategic and spiritual change in congregational life is addressed by Roy M. Oswald and Robert E. Friedrich Jr., *Discerning Your Congregation's Future* (New York: The Alban Institute, 1996).

and work of a particular congregation. Planning in religious education is informed with a knowledge of congregational dynamics.

Suggestions for Effective Planning Teams in Religious Education

Work teams who wish to improve their planning effectiveness in religious education may benefit from the following five suggestions, which grow out of the organizational development movement. First, the purpose of any work team is derived from the purpose of the larger institution. Many work teams in the parish take their purpose not only from the congregation but also from a denominational stance and/or a particular theological tradition. Sometimes these purposes may be in conflict. For example a congregation may choose curriculum resources that are consistent with its own particular identity, but are not recommended by the denomination.

Second, understandings of purpose that are held by members of the religious education planning team need to be surfaced in a welcoming, nonjudgmental manner. Often team members have never brought to consciousness or have never articulated their own understanding of why they have been asked to serve, and to what end. Look again at the scenario that begins this chapter to see the negative results of being judgmental and inhospitable.

Third, purposes of work teams are derived from a shared vision of possibilities toward the future. A work team involved in religious education planning should not necessarily derive its purpose from what it already knows and is doing. Outside resources may be needed to enlarge perspectives and encourage new approaches. If a religious education committee is considering changing its time of study to avoid conflict with the major weekly worship service, the committee may use peer teaching. Representatives from a congregation that has effectively resolved this issue may be willing to come to the committee planning session and offer the experience of their congregation to the planning team.

Fourth, if a congregation (or a denomination) is unhealthy, religious education planning work teams will feel it. If professional staff members are waging "turf wars" with each other, there will be little interdependency and trust among teams.

Fifth, if the head of a parish and its governing body become disengaged from the ongoing life of the congregation, the religious education planning team's work will be hindered. The pastor or rabbi rarely attends religious education planning committee meetings and does not do direct teaching, giving as a reason that "if it ain't broke, don't fix it." Yet if someone claims, the clergy is unable to interpret the planning committee's thought.

Reflections

The theory and practice of effective religious education planning teams has been examined through significant insights gained from general research and writing. Religious communities need to scrutinize the assumptions undergirding these practices for compatibility or congruence with the Jewish and Christian traditions. For congregations who wish to be faithful as well as effective, the major standards of reference will be religious, biblical, and theological. What theories and practices are "at home" in a theocentric setting? What, for example, would religious institutions choose not to use because of their convictions about what it means to follow the God of the Scriptures?

As the two streams, human relations and organizational development, are revisited to evaluate their significance for religious institutions, it seems clear that the human relations movement is broadly humanistic in nature. It values human life and believes in human beings as creative persons who can change and grow. There is a pervasive optimism and a belief that problems are solvable, if persons come to understand one another and are willing to be vulnerable risk takers. There is a distinct moral code of honesty, openness, and respect. Although this humanistic outlook derives primarily from Greek understandings of purpose and meaning, Jews and Christians who are informed about their faith can see much within this humanistic tradition that is congruent with their own beliefs and traditions.[57]

At first glance the systems approach to organizational development seems to be primarily humanistic also. On closer examination the underlying beliefs of enlightened self-interest appear to be stronger, that is, performance is related to production and attention to the market. Concerns for individuals and groups seem to be means rather than ends. Theory and practice emphasize an end-product of quality that will appeal

---

57. For a review of the literature see Houle, *The Literature of Adult Education*, pp. 255–59. Also see Lindgren and Shawchuck, *Management for Your Church*, pp. 22–28.

to consumers. Jews and Christians may feel awkward or uneasy with some of this philosophy.

To point out areas of compatibility only is to miss important, differences that exist between these two streams and Jewish/Christian traditions. Central to Christians and Jews is the conviction that religious institutions derive their identity and purpose from the nature and purpose of the God of the Scriptures. God is for them the first and final authority. Therefore to be in relationship with God and with God's will and purpose is fundamental. Perhaps the difference can be couched in the concept of faithfulness. This concept is an essential modifier to effective teams for the Jewish and Christian traditions. To be effective is to beg the questions: For what? For whom? How? Why? Faithfulness in the Jewish/Christian context denotes unique answers to these questions. Faithfulness is a covenantal relationship. If it is ignored, the very nature of the congregation's life and the purpose of its existence and, of course, team effectiveness will be undercut. Discernment is critical; a key question for religious educators is, What is God doing in this world and how can we participate in God's work?

Peter Rudge, in his book about ecclesiastical administration, has helpfully provided categories for examining similarities and differences between institutions that are basically humanistic and those that are religious.[58] Roughly analogous to the conception of an organization, says Rudge, is the doctrine of religious community. Organizations and religious communities both emphasize personal relationships, the communal life, and groups of people who have common interests and are dependent on one another. A religious institution, parish, or congregation, including its religious education planning teams have a sense of mystery, of "the Other in the midst." And this gives rise to an atmosphere of modesty and humility on the planning team. Through an open process of discernment, religious education planning teams explore God's guidance. It is the corporate discernment which is explored in the planning process.[59] How does this sense of divine initiation inform the planning team throughout the entire planning process? For instance, is prayer simply a device for beginning a planning session or is it a time of invocation and discernment? Do members of a religious education planning team regularly pray for one another and for their work together?

---

58. Peter F. Rudge, *Ministry and Management: The Study of Ecclesiastical Administrators* (London: Tavistock, 1968), pp. 37, 38.

59. Roy M. Oswald and Friedrich, *Discerning Your Congregation's Future*, pp. ix–xv.

How are the prophetic voices of team members who cannot join the consensus included in the planning process?

Analogous to the relationship of an organization to its environment, according to Rudge, is the doctrine of the relationship of religious institutions to society. Organizations in industry and even some charitable institutions accept the world as it is, and the organization's task is to deal with the consequences. There is an accommodation to environment as long as the organization's purpose can be fulfilled. Jewish and Christian institutions, by their very nature, seek to discern what God is doing in the world and to participate with God. At times religious communities care for the world; at other times they seek to transform the culture, either through changing persons or changing structures or both.[60] At the same time institutions are aware of human finiteness.

What are the implications here for faithful, effective planning teams in religious education? A major implication is that religious education planning teams always have an eye out for the impact of the work on the prevailing culture. Religious education planning teams are preparing members for work in the world. "Congregations exist for mission as fire exists for burning," the theologian Emil Brunner has said.[61]

Rudge says that organizational goals are analogous to purposes in religious institutions. Religious institutions are goal-oriented. Peter Senge points out that there is something more important than goal—a vision that has drawing power and provides motivation.[62] Faithful work teams are goal-oriented, pointing beyond themselves to God's great purposes, or God's vision for God's whole creation. At the same time, for faithful work teams the process (or journey) is the goal also. Growth in individuals and growth in the planning team go hand in hand with accomplishment of purpose. In religious institutions both persons and goals, as they relate to God's purposes, are seen as essential.

Rudge says that the nature of leadership is analogous to the doctrine of ministry. Religious institutions have learned much about shared leadership from other institutions. Broadly speaking, leadership belongs

---

60. See the occasional publication *Laynet*, edited by Edward White, for helpful insights and practices. Available from Denyse Stoneman, Marketplace Ministries, Box 7895, Madison, WI 52707.

61. Quoted in Donald G. Miller, *The Nature and Mission of the Church* (Richmond, Va,: Knox, 1957), p. 69.

62. Senge, *The Fifth Discipline*, pp. 207–32. Senge's notion of "shared vision" incorporates being immersed in an overarching goal. A team that experiences a shared vision is unaware of the extent of the courage needed to fulfill the vision (pp. 208–9.)

fundamentally to the community of faith, not to individuals (or to staff members). A servant leadership found in Jewish and Christian traditions is emphasized because it is derived from the nature of God, not simply because it "works."[63] Effective planning teams in religious education carry hope for the future.

63. In *Five Challenges for the Once and Future Church* (New York: The Alban Institute, 1996), pp. 73–80. Loren B. Mead suggests four classic patterns for involvements in God's mission: receiving, offering, identifying, and serving.

7

EVALUATING THE
PLANNING PROCESS

Trenton R. Ferro

The term "evaluation" often elicits negative reactions[1] that stem from unpleasant personal experiences. Many evaluations are poorly planned and constructed, lacking in clear, positive purposes and criteria, fail to involve those to be evaluated, and are administered unfairly.[2] According to Malcolm Knowles, evaluation "is the area of greatest controversy and weakest technology in all of education, especially in adult education and training."[3]

Directors of religious education and other prospective evaluators of the planning process often refer to this activity as entering an esoteric field of knowledge and practice. Evaluation as an arcane science is only reinforced by many books devoted to the topic of planning and developing religious education programs that offer little or no discussion

---

1. This phenomenon has been noted by a number of authors, including Dennis H. Dirks, "Evaluation," in *Harper's Encyclopedia of Religious Education* ed. Iris V. Cully and Kendig Brubaker Cully, (San Francisco,: Harper & Row, 1990), p. 233, and Michael Scriven, *Evaluation Thesaurus,* 4th ed. (Newbury Park, Calif. : Sage, 1991), p. 145.

2. Trenton R. Ferro, "Evaluating Young Adult Religious Education," in *Handbook of Young Adult Religious Education*, ed. Harley Atkinson (Birmingham, Ala., : Religious Education Press, 1995), p. 367; "Evaluating the Family Religious Education Program," in *Handbook of Family Religious Education* , ed. Blake Neff and Donald Ratcliff (Birmingham, Ala. : Religious Education Press, 1995), p. 227.

3. Malcolm Knowles, *The Adult Learner: A Neglected Species,* 3 rd ed. (Houston: Gulf, 1984), p. 134.

either of the value of evaluation or of evaluation purposes and processes themselves.[4]

GETTING STARTED WITH EVALUATION

What Is Evaluation?
Attempting to define "evaluation" provides some insight into the complexities and confusion surrounding the term. Many useful books on the subject fail to define it.[5] Some authors do offer definitions, and surveying them will help the reader understand the concept of evaluation. Stephen Brookfield asserts that , "evaluation . . . is inescapably a value—judgmental concept. The word value is at the heart of the term, with all the normative associations this applies."[6] Scriven offers a similar statement: "The key sense of the term 'evaluation' refers to the process of determining the *merit, worth,* or *value* [emphasis in the original] of something, or the product of that process."[7] According to Dirks, "evaluation is determining what we are doing in comparison with what we ought to do" and involves three distinct activities: gathering information, forming judgments on the basis of factual data, and making decisions to correct or improve the program planning process.[8]

Michael Quinn Patton, a theorist and practitioner in the field, offers this comprehensive definition:

> The practice of evaluation involves the systematic collection of information about the activities, characteristics, and outcomes of

---

4. See publications cited by Ferro in "Evaluating Young Adult Religious Education," pp. 367–68, and "Evaluating the Family Religious Education Program," p. 228. There are more complete treatments in the religious education literature, some of which are cited later in this chapter.

5. A definition is lacking, for example, in the following: Scarvia B. Anderson and Samuel Ball, *The Profession and Practice of Program Evaluation* (San Francisco: Jossey-Bass, 1978); Richard A. Berk and Peter H. Rossi, *Thinking about Program Evaluation* (Newbury Park, Calif. : Sage, 1990); Arden D. Grotelueschen et al., *An Evaluation Planner* (Urbana : University of Illinois, Office for the Study of Continuing Professions, 1974); Joan L. Herman, ed., *Program Evaluation Kit* (Newbury Park: Sage, 1987); Jacqueline Kosecoff and Arlene Fink, *Evaluation Basics: A Practitioner's Manual* (Newbury Park: Sage, 1982); and David Royse, *Program Evaluation: An Introduction* (Chicago: Nelson-Hall, 1992).

6. Stephen D. Brookfield, *Understanding and Facilitating Adult Learning* (San Francisco : Jossey-Bass, 1986), p. 264.

7. Scriven, *Evaluation Thesaurus,* p. 139.

8. Dirks, "Evaluation," , p. 233.

programs, personnel, and products for use by specific people to reduce uncertainties, improve effectiveness, and make decisions with regard to what those programs, personnel, or products are doing and affecting. This definition of evaluation emphasizes (1) the systematic collection of information about (2) a broad range of topics (3) for use by specific people (4) for a variety of purposes.[9]

Leonard Rutman and George Mowbray define program evaluation as the "use of scientific methods to measure the implementation and outcomes of programs, [sic] for decision-making purposes."[10] Finally, Blaine Worthen, James Sanders, and Jody Fitzpatrick: "Put most simply, we believe that evaluation is determining the worth or merit of an evaluation object (whatever is evaluated)." They go on to point out that evaluation is a process of identifying, clarifying, and applying defensible criteria to determine the value, quality, utility, effectiveness, or significance of the object being evaluated, in terms of this discussion, the religious education planning process.[11]

These definitions suggest that on the one hand, evaluation is a process that is similar to needs assessment and research, both of which require planned and organized collection of data and careful analysis and interpretation of those data. On the other hand, the purposes of program planning evaluation differ from other data collection modalities in that evaluation is conducted in order to place a value upon or to make a judgment about program planning and the various program components. Combining these two elements provides a working definition for this chapter: evaluation is the process of collecting and analyzing data in order to make an informed and valid decision about the religious education planning process.

Why Should Evaluation Be Done?

There are several major reasons for evaluating planning: (1) to make sure that what is being planned in religious education is consonant

---

9. Michael Quinn Patton, *Practical Evaluation* (Beverly Hills, Calif. : Sage, 1982), p. 15.

10. Leonard Rutman and George Mowbray, *Understanding Program Evaluation* (Newbury Park, Calif. : Sage, 1983), p. 12.

11. Blaine R. Worthen, James R. Sanders, and Jody L. Fitzpatrick, *Educational Evaluation: Alternative Approaches and Practical Guidelines*, (New York : Longman, 1997), p. 5.

with congregational purpose and direction; (2) to make sure that the
planning itself is on course; (3) to be able to change the direction of,
expand, or contract what is being planned as new information and data
are discovered; (4) to cope effectively with change; and (5) to bring
about change. Existing congregations—congregations with a history—
have experienced change and continue to do so. The locales in which
these congregations are situated may have changed (urban to inner city
to renovated inner city , suburban to urban, rural to suburban, and so
forth), or the primary population from which the congregation drew
its membership may have moved or diminished. Such congregations
need to decide whether they will continue serving the needs of those
persons still attending (often an aging cohort) or refocus their attention
on the existing broader neighborhood. They must decide whether their
emphasis should be internal (on the current membership) or external
(exposing themselves to a change in function, services, and membership). Congregations experiencing such change need to make decisions
about their emphasis and direction, in short, about their mission. No
organization can be all things to all people, including congregations.
Therefore, they must evaluate their planning: what are they doing and
why are they doing what they are doing?

New congregations, although unencumbered by a history, need to
make similar decisions. What is to be their focus, their purpose, their
direction? Why are they starting a new endeavor? Why are they starting
it in the particular place where they plan to develop? How will they be
known, be identified, be recognized? Evaluating their planning can help
both existing and new congregations make purposeful and meaningful
choices about the nature and content of their programming—and help
them be sure that they are remaining true to the course they have outlined
in their mission statement.

*   *   *

One major reason why evaluation is so often problematic, misun-
derstood, and misused is that planners and facilitators who conduct
evaluations have not determined clearly what they want to evaluate—or
and why. The literature on evaluation provides some insight into the
diverse reasons for conducting program evaluations. Anderson and Ball
list six major purposes for evaluation: (1) to contribute to decisions
about program installation; (2) to contribute to decisions about program
continuation, expansion (or contraction), or "certification" (licensing,

accreditation, and so forth); (3) to contribute to decisions about program modification;(4) to obtain evidence to rally support for a program;(5) to obtain evidence to rally opposition to a program; and (6) to contribute to the understanding of basic psychological, social, and other processes.[12]

Robert Fellenz, Gary Conti, and Don Seaman give the following reasons for conducting evaluations: (1) to determine how well the program objectives are being achieved, (2) to make decisions related to program improvement and future operation, (3) to meet the requirements of the program sponsor, (4) to provide a feeling of worth or accomplishment to the program staff, (5) to describe what happened so that other educators can determine if they wish to duplicate the program, (6) to become or remain accountable, and (7) to provide learning experiences for anyone interested in the program.[13] Evaluation is conducted to improve processes and assess outcomes, to determine what happened with the participants, and to decide the merits of the program itself.

Two discussions from the religious education literature also address the purposes of evaluation. John Elias states:

> The major purpose of evaluation is to improve the program by providing information to planners about all aspects of the program. Good evaluation leads to better decisions about continuing or discontinuing programs or teachers, improving practices and procedures, and adding specific strategies and techniques. A second legitimate function for evaluation is that it provides a measure of accountability to the parent organization, leaders, and participants.[14]

Dirks is more specific and direct in his observation: "One of the primary purposes of evaluation is to assure that what we do helps achieve our objectives. This requires clearly established goals and criteria of effectiveness if evaluation is to be meaningful."[15]

The purposes for evaluating the planning process, then, can be multiple. Evaluations are conducted in order to see what in the planning

---

12. Anderson and Ball, *Profession and Practice of Program Evaluation,* pp. 3–4, 15–35.

13. Robert A. Fellenz, Gary J. Conti, and Don F. Seaman, "Evaluate: Student, Staff, Program," in *Materials and Methods in Adult and Continuing Education* , ed. Chester Klevins (Los Angeles : Klevens, 1982), pp. 342–43.

14. John L. Elias, *The Foundations and Practice of Adult Religious Education* (Malabar, Fla.: Krieger, 1982), p. 273.

15. Dirks, "Evaluation", p. 233.

process is working or effective, to see what in the planning process is not working or not effective, to determine what in the planning process needs to be changed—and how. Evaluations are conducted in order to determine how the planning process is going. Are the elements planned consistent with our original goals and objectives? Have all the key persons been included in the planning process? Is the planning keeping pace with the previously established time line? Is appropriate attention being given to both program content and logistical matters? What are the necessary next steps to be taken in the planning process? Evaluations in a planning process are conducted in order to assess what has been done and to determine what can or might or ought to be done.

Purposes typically determine what is to be evaluated, the types of assessment to conduct, and methods of data collection to be employed in the evaluation process. Time spent on making evaluation decisions early in the planning process will spare planners and facilitators the great disappointment that comes when they discover, too late, that the best opportunities for collecting useful and valuable data slipped by because evaluation of the planning was an afterthought rather than an intentional undertaking.

What Should Be Evaluated?

Evaluating the planning process seeks answers to the questions raised in the previous section. The content of evaluation is the flip side of the purposes of evaluation: Does the program that is being planned meet the mission of the religious organization? Are both the program content and the logistical support needed to deliver the program receiving sufficient attention in the planning process? How will the planner decide if the program being planned, once it is actually delivered, is effective? Asking the question, What should be evaluated? drives the selection of which planning processes or what specific aspects of the planning process are to be examined in order to collect the data necessary for making an informed decision, on the one hand, of the programs or portions of programs to be evaluated. These aspects may include, but are not limited to, inputs, program design, actual delivery processes, materials and methods under consideration, prospective situations and locations, and other elements of the planning process.

Not every person, thing, process, or outcome needs to be evaluated in every religious education event or program. As Knowles points out, evaluation has become a sacred cow.[16] In order to say that they have conducted an evaluation, many planners are seduced into using generic or standardized evaluation forms or procedures. However, facilitators and planners of religious education who are truly committed to helping both the organization and its individual members grow and develop will definitely be interested in the specific results of their planning efforts.[17] They will want to improve, change, and adapt the planning process, or aspects of it, so that the programs they are planning will be of greatest benefit for the intended participants. Consequently, it is better by far to concentrate on a few aspects and elements of the planning process than to conduct a massive, often time-consuming, and expensive evaluation effort that will result in the production of a report that gathers dust on a shelf. The question, then, of what to evaluate becomes vitally important. In order for evaluation to be successful in the local congregation, synagogue, or other religious organization, the planner of religious education needs to consider carefully what other persons in that organization need to be involved in the evaluation process.

Who Should Do the Evaluation?

Successful evaluation in the local congregation, synagogue, or other religious organization includes knowing who in the planning process should do the evaluation. Following the advice of Dirks[18] and the process outlined in this chapter, those who must live with and use the answers, decisions, solutions, and results of an evaluation (the persons who are called "stakeholders" in the evaluation literature) must be the ones who ask the questions and seek out the data that will be used to craft the answers. The concerns of these stakeholders will vary. Some will be concerned about the potential effectiveness of the program currently being planned; others will be concerned about what may happen to current programs; still others may be more concerned about scheduled dates, times, and locations. Often stakeholders will have multiple concerns. In addition to the items just listed, stakeholders may

---

16. Malcolm S. Knowles, *The Modern Practice of Adult Education: From Pedagogy to Andragogy*, rev. and updated ed. (New York: Cambridge, 1980), p. 198.

17. For a more complete discussion of the program planning process, see Trenton R. Ferro, "Setting Up a Young Adult Religious Education Program," in *Handbook of Young Adult Religious Education,* ed. Harley Atkinson (Birmingham, Ala.: Religious Education Press, 1995) pp. 345–66.

18. Dirks, *"Evaluation," pp.* 233–34.

also be interested in how well the program of religious education is being planned and conducted, which methods and activities are being planned, and what the cost the planned program may be.

Involving the stakeholders in the total evaluation process decreases exponentially the inherent tensions that arise within religious organizations when decisions are made about program planning. Stakeholders should take part in spelling out the purposes of the planning process, in designing the evaluation process, in collecting the data, and in making value judgments based on the gathered data. Instead of the religious educator making decisions unilaterally, the DRE now shares the decision making with all who have a vested interest. If persons in the organization feel that programs that have meaning for them are being altered or eliminated without their involvement and input, they will resist the planning process. It does not matter how well the religious educator may have planned the evaluation or how solid and accurate the data or how correct the eventual decision; those left out of the planning and evaluation process will object to any decisions that jeopardize programs near and dear to their hearts, lives, and experience. On the other hand, if the planner allows these same persons to take responsible roles in the evaluation process, these potential objectors may become allies. They will be able to see the evidence for themselves and will share responsibility in making decisions during the planning process. They will see that the planning process produces programs that fit their religious organization's mission, that these programs can be healthy and viable, and that these programs can accomplish their purposes.

When Should Evaluation Be Done?

The answer to this question depends on the answer to the Why? and the What? questions discussed above. Data need to be collected when they are available, especially when the religious education planning process is being evaluated. Herein lies one of the primary reasons for making evaluation planning an integral part of the program planning process. If decisions about evaluation are made only after programs are over, significant opportunities for data collection are lost and certain important questions about programs can never be answered. If no thought is given to evaluating a program until it has been completed, the only data available are those related to results of the program. DREs are able, then, to answer only such questions as the following: How many persons actually attended the program? How much money was made or lost on the program? How did the participants react to the program? Under these circumstances, DREs are able to evaluate only the results of their planning efforts; they are unable to evaluate the process itself. For example, if they have exceeded expected costs or have taken too long to complete the planning, they will probably be unable to conduct useful assessments that would help them understand why they have exceeded their budgets or their time limits. The opportunity to collect the necessary data to answer such evaluative questions will have passed.

This failure to make evaluation planning a part of the overall religious education planning process is possibly the primary reason why evaluations frequently prove to be inadequate and uncomfortable or why they provide less than satisfactory feedback—and the reason why many persons react negatively to the very idea of evaluation. Since "the evaluation" is usually thought to be the final activity in any program, it is usually the last programmatic element to receive attention during the religious education planning process (if it receives any attention at all). Consequently, evaluations often are conducted with little or no planning or forethought. If evaluations are to be anything more than pro forma endeavors ("Oh, we pass out an evaluation form after all our programs!"), the planning of evaluation requires attention, along with the other elements of the program planning process,[19] from the very beginning.[20]

Summative Evaluation. The recognition that evaluation can be conducted from the very beginning of the program planning process, not only at the end of the program, is discussed extensively in the evaluation literature as *formative* and *summative* evaluation.[21]

---

19. See Ferro, "Setting Up a Young Adult Religious Education Program," pp. 345–66.

20. This point is emphasized by Herman, *Program Evaluation Kit*; Alan B. Knox, *Helping Adults Learn* (San Francisco: Jossey-Bass, 1986), pp. 164–69; and Worthen, Sanders, and Fitzpatrick, *Educational Evaluation,* pp. 192–203.

21. For more complete discussions comparing and contrasting formative and summative evaluation, see Anderson and Ball, *Profession and Practice,* pp. 3–35; Harold Beder, "Program Evaluation and Follow Up," in *Managing Adult and Continuing Education Programs and Staff* , ed. Philip D. Langerman and Douglas H. Smith (Washington, D.C.: National Association for Public Continuing and Adult Education, 1979), p. 265; Robert O. Brinkerhoff et al., *Program Evaluation: A Practitioner's Guide for Trainers and Educators* (Boston: Kluwer-Nijhoff, 1983), pp. 38–39; Byron R. Burnham, *Evaluating Human Resources, Programs, and Organizations* (Malabar, Fla. : Krieger, 1995), p. 5; David Deshler, ed., *Evaluation for Program Improvement* (San Francisco: Jossey-Bass,

Usually carried out at the conclusion of a program, *summative evaluation* focuses on results. It seeks to answer questions like the following: How effective was the program? Did the program accomplish what we had hoped it would accomplish? Did the participants benefit from it? Did the participants like it? Summative evaluation considers whether objectives have been met, activities completed, and participant competence improved.

Although summative evaluation is usually conducted near or at the end of a program, the results of this type of evaluation have tremendous impact on the program planning process. If planned and conducted carefully, summative evaluations provide valuable data for the planning of subsequent activities and programs. Through summative evaluation, program planners in the religious organization will have gained insight that will help them decide whether to continue or to discontinue a program. Often the planners will also gain information that can help them plan new and different programs. Furthermore, the planners, will be able to make appropriate alterations, deletions, additions and changes to those programs which they do decide to continue so that those programs will be even better the next time they are planned, developed, and offered.

Formative Evaluation. Formative evaluation is designed to answer questions such as: How are we currently doing in the planning process? Are we on course? Are we remaining true to our mission, purposes, and goals? What can be done to improve what we are presently doing? Conducted both before and periodically throughout the program planning and implementation stages, formative evaluation seeks to improve both the program planning process itself and the actual program while it is in progress. "Formative evaluation focuses on the interactive elements of the program, stressing process and indicators of progress."[22] Because

---

1984), Herman, *Program Evaluation Kit,* Theodore J. Kowalski, *The Organization and Planning of Adult Education* (Albany, N. Y. : State University of New York Press, 1988), pp. 151–52, 168; John A. Niemi and John M. Nagle, "Learners, Agencies, and Program Development in Adult and Continuing Education," in *Managing Adult and Continuing Education Programs and Staff,* ed. Philip D. Langerman and Douglas H. Smith (Washington, D.C.: National Association for Public and Continuing Education, 1979), pp. 167–68; Royse, *Program Evaluation,* pp. 38–43, 65–70; Scriven, *Evaluation Thesaurus,* pp. 168–69, 340; Edwin L. Simpson, "An Interactive Model of Program Development," in, *Materials and Methods in Adult and Continuing Education: International Illiteracy,* ed. Chester Klevins, (Los Angeles: Klevens, 1987), p. 159; Worthen, Sanders, and Fitzpatrick, *Educational Evaluation,* pp. 14–18, 108–10, 200–202, 484–87, 498–500.
   22. Simpson, "An Interactive Model of Program Development," p. 159.

they "are employed to adjust and enhance interventions," formative evaluations "are not as threatening and are often better received by agency staff than other forms of evaluation."[23]

The Timing of Evaluation

The timing of evaluation, then, depends on what the facilitators, the planners, and the sponsoring religious organization wish to accomplish through the evaluation process. If the emphasis is on the continuous improvement of the religious education planning process, the evaluation needs to be ongoing (formative evaluation). A continuous improvement emphasis using formative evaluation of the planning process includes evaluating the programs and their settings; making appropriate accommodation for shifting participant interests; changing activities to increase participation; and similar considerations. If the concern is with outcomes, meeting objectives, assessing changed attitudes and behaviors, and making decisions about future programs, then evaluation needs to be conducted at one or more points following the completion of the program (summative evaluation). Very often those with a vested interest in the success of the programs offered by the religious organization (the stakeholders) will actually want to gather data for the purposes of both formative and summative evaluation. In order to accomplish either, however, the planning of the evaluation must be part of the program planning process. When to evaluate, then, is connected with the questions, Why evaluate? and What should be evaluated?

Summary

Why is planning important in the whole process of evaluation? If evaluation is not planned, the religious educator and other parish leadership are limited in terms of (1) what can be evaluated, (2) when it can be evaluated, and (3) how it can be evaluated. Failure to plan the evaluation process in religious education can also be symptomatic of other serious, endemic problems: lack of direction, lack of purpose, lack of focus, and lack of good practice in current programming activities. The purpose of evaluation is to make a decision about something. If no decision is required, evaluation is not necessary. Evaluating planning in religious

---

23. Royse, *Program Evaluation,* p. 38.

education is driven by the desire to answer questions about what is, about what might be, and about what ought to be.

WAYS TO EVALUATE THE PLANNING PROCESS

Planners of educational programs in religious settings often will want to assess their programs at two levels. The more familiar or "micro" level (discussed under the headings of "Informal Evaluation" and "Formal Evaluation" later in this chapter) is the level at which planners, facilitators, and other stakeholders evaluate the effectiveness of specific planning processes related to classes, courses, workshops, and other programmatic religious education activities. Before proceeding to that more extensive discussion, however, another level of evaluation should be mentioned: evaluation at the "macro" level, that is, the examination of the total set of spiritual, learning, growth, developmental, social, and other activities offered by the congregation, church, agency, or other religious organization.

Macro Evaluation
Every institution should have a statement of mission and purposes that undergirds its structure, culture, and programs.[24] Every religious organization, as well, needs to identify its mission and basic purposes.[25] Although religious groups on the surface may appear to do about the same thing, each religious group actually possesses its own unique values, vision, and set of purposes. Organizational uniqueness motivates what that group does and contributess to an organizational culture that controls how the members of that group go about carrying out those purposes. Avery Dulles, for example, through the application of the discipline of comparative ecclesiology, demonstrates that congregations, synagogues, and other religious agencies are organized and function

---

24. See the discussions in Knowles, *Modern Practice*, pp. 68–72, and Michael J. Offerman, "Matching Programmatic Emphases to the Parent Organization's Values," in *Strategic Planning and Leadership in Continuing Education* ed. Robert G. Simerly (San Francisco: Jossey-Bass, 1987), pp. 71–86.

25. Ferro, "Setting Up a Young Adult Religious Education Program," p. 350, and Sharan B. Merriam and Trenton R. Ferro, "Working with Young Adults," in *Handbook of Adult Religious Education* ed. Nancy T. Foltz, (Birmingham, Ala. : Religious Education Press, 1986), p. 71.

according to certain models: as institution, as mystical communion, as sacrament, as herald, and as servant.[26]

This mission statement, often included in the organization's articles of incorporation and/or its constitution, becomes an important guide or "rule" against which to measure current programs and activities. Do these various endeavors represent the purposes for which this church, parish, synagogue, or agency was organized? Do the various programs and activities that the organization plans, sponsors, and supports help advance its mission, or do they detract from and becloud its raison d'être? Application of this one "screen" alone, as Knowles describes the process,[27] may provide sufficient cause for removing or altering a particular programmatic undertaking, offering, or activity. Thus the mission statement must be given great weight in evaluating the religious education planning process.

The purposes identified by the religious organization for achieving its mission can usually be spelled out in terms of the major functions undertaken by the group. These functions can be made part of a model, a program evaluation and planning matrix,[28] that can be used as a screen at the macroevaluation level. As an example, a local congregation, synagogue, or assembly might identify as its major functions teaching, preaching, individual pastoral care, organizing, and celebrating.[29] Another schema, based on New Testament Greek, might be *kerygma* (preaching), *didache* (teaching), *koinonia* (fellowship), *diakonia* (ministry or service), and *martyria* (witness).[30] If the current or proposed program or activity fits within the functions identified by the religious organization as appropriate and necessary for advancing its mission, then planning can proceed. If it does not fit, then the planners need to reconsider. On occasion, planners may feel strongly that a proposed program should be part of that organization's activities. In that instance, the planners need to make the case to their broader membership and work toward changing their mission and functions. Such examination

---

26. Avery Dulles, *Models of the Church*, (2nd) ed. (Garden City, N. Y. : Image, 1991).

27. Knowles, *Modern Practice*, pp. 123–25.

28. This model and its application and use are developed more fully in Ferro, "Evaluating the Family Religious Education Program," pp. 236–39, and Merriam and Ferro, "Working with Young Adults," pp. 74–80.

29. As developed by Henri Nouwen, *Creative Ministry* (Garden City, N. Y.: Image Books, 1971).

30. Discussed in Ferro, "Evaluating the Family Religious Education Program," pp. 236–39, and Merriam and Ferro, "Working with Young Adults," pp. 74–80.

and discussion is necessary from time to time in any vibrant and dynamic organization.

Informal Evaluation

While some evaluators consider informal evaluation—one approach to "micro" evaluation—to be repugnant,[31] such a process has an important and useful place, especially for formative (or process) evaluation. As Knowles observes,

> Informal evaluation is actually going on all the time. Some kinds of judgments are being made continuously about the worth of a program. Participants are constantly making complaints or paying compliments. Teachers and leaders are never without feelings about how well or how poorly things are going. The directors of programs are sensitive both to these judgments and to their own feelings. . . . But it does not serve the same purpose as periodic, systematically planned evaluation.[32]

However, it must be understood that informal evaluation need not be unplanned, unmanaged, or unaware of values and assumptions. These major concerns probably cause the reactions of the detractors noted above by Knowles.

Religious educators can and should be consistently conscious about what they are doing. They need to be aware of their own feelings and reactions, as well as the feelings and reactions of those with whom they are involved in the planning process. They can be asking themselves and their colleagues questions like these: How is it going? Will it work? Are all the pieces in place? Has anything been left out? Is the process worth the time, the effort, and the current and prospective financial outlay? What would happen if . . . ¿'

Religious educators also carry out informal evaluation of programs already in progress. They do so for a number of reasons: (1) to increase participants' awareness of their own developing and changing

---

31. See, for example, Anderson and Ball, *Profession and Practice,* pp. 62–63, and Robert E. Stake, "The Countenance of Educational Evaluation," in *Educational Evaluation: Theory and Practice* by Blaine R. Worthen and James R. Sanders, (Belmont, Calif.: Wadsworth, 1973), pp. 107, 125.

32. Knowles, *Modern Practice,* p. 203; see also Elias, *Foundations and Practice of Adult Religious Education,* p. 275.

knowledge, attitudes, and competencies; (2) to increase participants' self-confidence and commitment to learning or their involvement in the planned activity or process; (3) to improve communication between facilitator and participants; (4) to determine what should be undertaken next; and (5) to establish or alter the pace of the learning or other activity. Planners of religious education seek regular feedback concerning the materials, methods and strategies, pacing, and setting of the educational activities that they have planned. Such feedback allows religious educators to make prompt adjustments in current programs and provides them with considerable data they can use as they continue in the planning process to revise current programs and to develop new ones.

Informal evaluation, in effect, makes participants in the planning process, as well as in the programs that the planning process develops, key contributors to the ongoing planning process of the religious organization. Informal evaluation is carried out through observation, personal assessment by the religious educator after each planning or activity session, and questions to colleagues and participants. Some of the questions that the religious educator might keep in mind, include: Are participants following the materials? Are they participating in the activities? Is there any apparent confusion regarding the directions or explanation given by the leader? Do the participants appear to be comfortable? Are the heating (or air conditioning) and lighting adequate? Asking these types of questions and responding promptly in an appropriate manner keeps planners and facilitators of religious activities in touch with the participants and demonstrates to the participants the active interest and concern of the planners and facilitators.

Formal Evaluation

Formal evaluation, whether formative or summative, is a "micro" process that is carried out according to a definite plan.[33] In contrast to informal evaluation, it is an undertaking whose planning is included from the beginning in the program planning process and whose construction and implementation are accomplished in a comprehensive and systematic manner. There are a number of functional and useful models

---

33. Anderson and Ball, *Profession and Practice,* pp. 43–109; Beder, "Program Evaluation and Follow Up," pp. 264–81; Brinkerhoff et al., *Program Evaluation*; Herman, *Program Evaluation Kit*; Knowles, *The Modern Practice of Adult Education;* Kowalski, *Organiazation and Planning of Adult Education,* pp. 153–59.

that planners and facilitators of religious education programs can follow. Several are included in the works cited throughout this section; some that may prove particularly suited for evaluating the planning process in religious organizations are discussed toward the end of this chapter.

The objectives-based evaluation model presented here has proven quite serviceable both for religious educators who are just becoming acquainted with the evaluation process as well as for those more experienced with conducting evaluations. Once the planners have decided the purposes and timing of the formal evaluation, they must then determine what data needs to be collected and the best methods and strategies for collecting that data. The actual process of formal evaluation, which is outlined in figure 1 and is discussed in some detail below, involves (1) focusing the evaluation, (2) designing the evaluation and collecting the data, and (3) drawing evaluative conclusions based on the analysis of the data collected.[34]

The purpose of objectives-based evaluation is to collect and analyze data on the outcomes produced by the persons (participants, planners, facilitators, staff, boards, and committees, and so forth) or processes involved in the planning of religious programs. If the formal evaluation process works or is working, what data or evidence are present (stated in terms of objectives)? What happens/will happen/will have happened if/when the program is successful?

Focusing the Evaluation

The first major step in the process of planning formal evaluation, already discussed at some length earlier in this chapter, is to focus the evaluation. Failure to ask the critical questions, What needs to be evaluated? and Why? contributes to the uncritical practice of using standardized, non-specific questionnaires (called, sometimes pejoratively, "happiness" or "smiley-face" forms) that ask generic questions about how participants

---

34. As on previous occasions (see Ferro, "Evaluating Young Adult Religious Education" and "Evaluating the Family Religious Education Program") the author feels a personal and moral obligation to express a deep sense of gratitude to his former faculty colleagues at Ball State University, James H. McElhinney and George S. Wood Jr. The objectives-based evaluation model presented in this chapter bears the marks of McElhinney and Wood's tutelage and mentorship and is based on material originally developed by them and used by this author in teaching college courses and segments of courses on program evaluation.

Figure 7.1
Objectives-Based Evaluation: An Outline

   I. Focusing the evaluation: formulating evaluative questions

     A. Why? What is the purpose (What are the purposes) of this evaluation?

     B. What should be evaluated in order to achieve this purpose?

     C. When? What are the most appropriate times to gather the information that will help the religious educator accomplish the stated purpose of the evaluation?

     D. What specific parts or aspects of the religious education program and/or planning process need to be targeted?

       1. Identifying objectives

       2. Determining indicators (criteria)

  II. Designing the evaluation and collecting the data

     A. Developing/selecting data collection instruments

     B. Using the instruments to collect data

       1. Interviews

       2. Surveys and questionnaires

       3. Observation

 III. Analyzing the data and drawing evaluative conclusions

     A. Analyzing the data

       1. Recording/reporting the data

       2. Interpreting the findings

     B. Reporting findings and making evaluative decisions

       1. Written report

       2. Decision-making process

felt about the process or program. While information gathered in this fashion can be useful, the data thus collected is very limited-and limiting.

Focusing involves asking certain questions: Who needs to know? What do they need to know? Why do they need to know? What questions must the evaluation address in order to achieve its purposes?[35] Knowles calls this step "formulating evaluative questions," with the questions falling into two categories: those having to do with operational objectives

---

35. Beder, "Program Evaluation and Follow Up," pp. 264–69; Brinkerhoff et al., *Program Evaluation,* pp. 7–34; Dirks, "Evaluation," p. 233.

and those dealing with educational objectives. Operational objectives are concerned with organizational climate and structure, assessment of needs and interests, definition of purposes and objectives, program design, program operation, and program evaluation; "educational objectives always define [the] behavioral changes an educational experience is designed to help participants achieve."[36] Religious educators focusing primarily on evaluating the planning process will be most concerned with operational objectives.

Evaluation, then, can and must look at the process as well as the outcomes.[37] Therefore, planning the evaluation must be part of the religious education program development phase. Because questions in the evaluation design will focus on various aspects of the planning process, data collection instruments and procedures must be in place and ready for use when that part of the process takes place. Opportunities to evaluate various steps of the religious education planning process will be missed if planners and facilitators wait until the program is over before designing and attempting an evaluation. Focusing the evaluation culminates in two specific activities: identifying objectives and determining indicators and criteria.

Identifying Objectives

As Knowles suggests, the objectives that have been developed during the program planning and development process can also serve as the basis for the evaluation.[38] An objective consists of three elements. First, the objective names the person who will be doing what will be measured, making that person the subject of the statement. Second, an active verb states the desired action to be accomplished by that person. Third, the object of the statement identifies what is to be accomplished. Sometimes a fourth element is added: a time frame or deadline.[39] The

---

36. Knowles, *Modern Practice*, pp. 205–8.

37. Winifred DeLoayza, Rene Grosser, and Elly Bulkin, *A Source Book for Evaluating Special Projects* (Altamont, N. Y. : Interorganizational Relations, 1988), pp. 4–10.

38. Knowles, *Modern Practice*, pp. 205–10; see Ferro, "Setting Up a Young Adult Religious Education Program," pp. 357–58.

39. The process and format for writing objectives is discussed by Gary J. Dean and Trenton R. Ferro, *AKC Judges Institute Instructional Design and Teaching Manual* (New York: American Kennel Club, 1991), pp. 12–13, 27–32; DeLoayza, Grosser, and Bulkin, *A Source Book for Evaluating Special Projects,* pp. 11–14; and Trenton R. Ferro and Gary J. Dean, "General Principles and Procedures," in *Handbook of Young Adult Religious*

objective is written in the form, Who will do what (by when)." When writing objectives, religious education planners must strive to develop statements that actually can be tested in some way.

Determining Indicators (Criteria)

Clear, precise, and well-written objectives allow for the development of indicators or criteria for collecting and analyzing data. The subject of the Indicators is the same person who is the subject of the objective that the indicators measure. These indicators, which also may be called criteria, provide the basis for answering the question, How can stakeholders (all persons and groups involved in, and affected by, the religious education program) ascertain whether the persons or processes have accomplished their intended outcome(s)? Elias calls the objectives, criteria, and standards, the "values" that indicate the "expected reactions and attitudes of participants, learning outcomes, behavioral outcomes and tangible results."[40] They are statements of concrete evidence that will be used to test how well the religious education planning process objectives have been met. If the process has desired outcomes, then these outcomes should be capable of a clear statement and should produce data that can be collected. Examples of objectives and indicators are presented in figure 2.

Designing the Evaluation and Collecting the Data

This second step is composed of two interrelated parts: (1) developing and/or selecting appropriate data collection instruments and (2) using those instruments in the actual data collection process. This is another place where many evaluations break down. When there is a lack of group planning, the right questions are not asked and consequently the right methods of data collection are not used.

The development and selection of data collection instruments hinge directly on the objectives and indicators that have been identified for the evaluation. There are three primary ways to collect data: (1) talk with people (interviews), (2) have people respond in writing (questionnaires and surveys), and (3) observe or watch people. At least one data

Education, ed. Harley Atkinson (Birmingham, Ala.: Religious Education Press, 1995), pp. 179–81.
    40. Elias, *Foundations and Practice of Adult Religious Education,* p. 276

Figure 7.2
Writing Objectives and Indicators

MODEL: (1) Who (2) will do (3) what (4) by when?

EXAMPLE A:

Objective: (1) The program planner (2) will select (3) an appropriate text for the marriage enrichment program.

Indicator: (1) The program planner (2) will request (3) samples from at least three religious publishers (4) by the end of next week.

Indicator: (1) The program planner (2) will recommend (3) her first choice (4) at the next meeting of the planning committee.

EXAMPLE B:

Objective: (1) The religious educator (2) will develop (3) three activities for youth (4) by the next board meeting.

Indicator: (1) The religious educator (2) will present (3) a written plan for an activity for the elementary grades.

Indicator: (1) The religious educator (2) will present (3) a written plan for an activity for the junior high grades.

Indicator: (1) The religious educator (2) will present (3) a written plan for an activity for the senior high grades.

collection item should be included in the collection instrument(s) for each indicator or criterion; ideally, since several types of data collection should be undertaken, several data collection items of different types should be developed for each indicator or criterion.

This use of multiple and varied data collection items for each indicator or criterion is called "*triangulation*."[41] Steele describes the strength of this procedure: "Information about the same program secured through two or more independent means often provides better understanding and sounder conclusions than one large study. In the same fashion, viewing a program or its results from several perspectives . . . gives

---

41. Michael Quinn Patton, *How to Use Qualitative Methods in Evaluation* (Newbury Park, Calif. : Sage, 1987), pp. 60–61, 161–62; Royse, *Program Evaluation*, pp. 25–27, 89, also calls this approach *convergent analysis*.

a better understanding of the value of the program."[42] Figure 3, which illustrates the relationships among objectives, indicators (criteria), data collection instruments, and data collection items, also demonstrates how to plan for triangulation.

The Three Methods for Collecting Data

Because there are three primary data collection procedures, there are consequently three major types of data collection instruments: interview protocols, surveys and questionnaires, and observation schedules. Each of these procedures will be discussed in turn and advice will be given on planning and constructing each type of data collection instrument.

Interviews. The strength of the interview is that it allows respondents the opportunity to construct their own responses. Interviews also allow the religious educator to pick up on verbal and visual cues and to pursue these cues as additional avenues of information. In addition, a symbiotic relationship can develop; the interviewer and respondent are "in this thing together." Consequently, the source of the data has a freedom in responding which is not available through the use of questionnaires and observations.

On the other hand, interviews require a great deal of time. An entire group of participants can respond to a questionnaire in less time than it takes to conduct one interview. Furthermore, data collected from interviews cannot be reported easily and quickly. Considerable "massaging" of raw interview data (demanding greater skill on the part of the evaluator) is required in order to combine responses from several sources and "reduce" them to reportable form. Nevertheless, religious educators who wish to be thorough and comprehensive—to triangulate their findings—will select indicators or criteria for which they will collect data by interview.

Before actually conducting interviews, evaluators[43] need to develop an interview protocol, which is simply a guide, a list of questions to be

---

42. Sara M. Steele, "The Evaluation of Adult and Continuing Education," in *Handbook of Adult and Continuing Education* ed. Sharan B. Merriam and Phyllis M. Cunningham, (San Francisco: Jossey-Bass, 1989), p. 270.

43. The terms "evaluator" and "evaluators" are used throughout this section to recognize the possibility that many more members of the religious organization than the religious educators themselves may be—and ought to be—involved in the evaluation process.

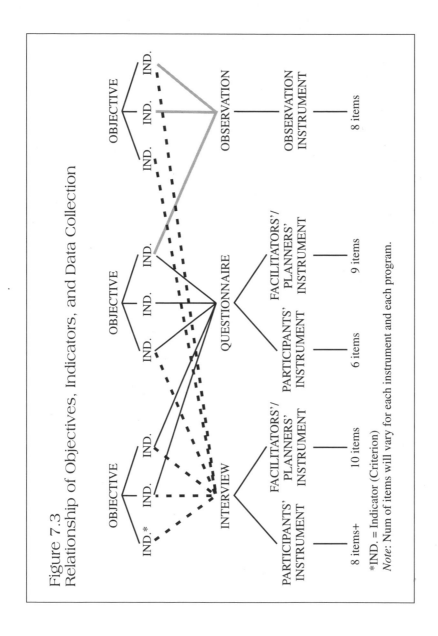

Figure 7.3
Relationship of Objectives, Indicators, and Data Collection

asked of each respondent. The protocol is developed and the interview is conducted using a five-step procedure:

1. The evaluators select the indicators or criteria for which they wish to collect data by interview.
2. Evaluators develop clear, specific, and precise questions that will elicit the type of data required by each indicator or criterion. These questions should be phrased in such a way that respondents are required to respond with their own thoughts, feelings, and reactions. Since questions can be intimate and personal, great care needs to be taken in deciding what questions to ask (they should seek only information that is pertinent to the established indicators and objectives) and how to ask them. Evaluators avoid questions that can be answered simply Yes or no. They generally do not use interviews to ask for demographic or factual information that can be gained just as easily through the use of a questionnaire.
3. Evaluators sequence the questions in a way that allows for a comfortable yet informative interview. Questions that respondents are expected to answer quickly and readily are placed first; those calling for greater thoughtfulness—or which may be more sensitive—come later. In this way a certain rapport or trust is established before respondents are asked to "bare their souls." Evaluators also sequence the questions so that each flows as naturally as possible from the previous question and response.
4. Evaluators conduct the interview. If interviewer and respondent know each other, establishing a comfortable climate is usually not difficult. If they do not know each other, some time and effort must be devoted to establishing such a climate. The interview is conducted in a place where the respondent feels at ease (for example, at the respondent's home, in a restaurant, at the program site, or in some other place of the respondent's choosing). Some casual conversation that allows the two to get acquainted precedes the actual use of the protocol. The job of the evaluator is to get the respondent talking; the purpose of the protocol is to provide "prods" when the discussion lags. The evaluator does not interrupt the respondent in order to follow the sequence of the protocol; the evaluator is concerned only that all the questions have been covered, even if out of order. While the respondent is talking, the evaluator takes notes or, if the respondent agrees, records the conversation.

5. As soon as possible after the interview, evaluators need to attend to
   several particulars. They transcribe the interview (if it was recorded
   on tape), review their notes to add any observations or materials that
   they did not have time to record during the interview, and prepare a
   summary that highlights specific responses to each of the questions
   asked. The more time that passes between the interview and these
   activities, the greater the likelihood that important information will
   be lost.

Surveys and questionnaires. Many strengths and weaknesses of surveys and questionnaires are opposite those of interviews. These prepared
forms on which participants record their responses allow for the collection of data from a much larger group. These forms are also useful for the
collection of factual and demographic data. On the other hand, except
when open-ended questions are used, responses usually are limited to the
specific questions that are asked. Furthermore, evaluators do not have the
opportunity to follow up on enticing comments or to ask for clarification
of responses. Consequently, great care must be taken in the construction
of questions so that items are perfectly clear to the respondents and they
elicit the types of responses desired by the evaluators.

The preparation process for developing surveys and questionnaires
begins in a fashion similar to planning interviews. Evaluators select the
indicators or criteria for which they wish to collect data by interview.
Evaluators develop clear, specific, and precise questions that will elicit
the type of data which can be used to evaluate each indicator and the
objective under which each indicator falls. At this point evaluators must
also decide what types of questions they want to ask. Dean and Ferro
describe and illustrate five types of questions: fill in the blank, scales,
multiple choice, checklist, and open-ended.[44] Each type is described in
the text below. Examples of each type of question are included in the
tables following the description of each type.[45]

44. Dean and Ferro, *AKC Judges Institute Instructional Design and Teaching Manual,*
pp. 19, 21–26.

45. Other authors provide different schemes and examples. See, for example, Bradley
C. Courtenay and Margaret E. Holt, "Evaluating Program Impact," in *Materials and
Methods in Adult and Continuing Education: International—Illiteracy* , ed. Chester
Klevins, (Los Angeles: Klevens, 1987), pp. 168–74; Patricia Cranton, *Planning In-
struction for Adult Learners* (Toronto: Wall & Thompson, 1989), pp. 182–94; Knowles,
Modern Practice, pp. 210–15; Kosecoff and Fink, *Evaluation Basics,* pp. 111–76; Patton,

Fill-in-the-blank items are used primarily to gather descriptive information about participants. This information can be collected beforehand to help religious education planners and facilitators better plan and prepare a prospective program, or it can be collected during or after a program to determine the level of a participant's involvement.

Figure 7.4
Fill-in-the-Blank Items

Examples of questions that might be asked before class, workshop, or program begins:

I have been a member of this religious group for _____ (state actual number) years.

I have attended _____ previous programs/classes.

My favorite books/portions of Scripture are [here several blanks might be provided]: _____

I am most interested in the following types of programs [several spaces might be provided]: _____, _____, _____, _____.

Examples of questions that might be asked during or following a program:

I have attended _____ (state number) sessions.

I have tried _____ (state number) activities suggested during the workshop at home.

I have tried the following suggested activities at home [several spaces might be provided]: _____, _____, _____, _____, _____.

How to Use Qualitative Methods in Evaluation, pp. 139–226; and Royse, *Program Evaluation,* pp. 115–49

Rating scale items allow participants to express their personal reactions to a particular statement or their views about a specific position. Rating scale items are especially useful for eliciting attitudes and values. There are several ways to structure such items. One is to use a *Likert scale*, a line or continuum that offers a sequence of choices, from one pole to another, in response to a particular statement. Respondents circle the number that best corresponds to their position or feelings. The poles, and the positions in between the poles, need to reflect the type of statements being made. Sets of contrasts might be strongly disagree——strongly agree, low——high, very weak——very strong, dislike——like, strongly disapprove——strongly approve, and so forth.

In a *modified Likert scale* the responses are placed in a list rather than on a scale, and respondents place an X or a check mark before their desired choice. *Rank order* provides a list that allows participants to indicate the relative importance they place on, or their preference for, each of the items on the list by ranking them in a sequence.

Multiple-choice items can be used to check participants' knowledge or understanding of a topic or to have them select from among options.

Checklists allow participants to identify what items are important to them, what items they know, or what items they prefer. The usefulness of this type of item is that the respondents can make as many choices as they want.

Open-ended questions allow respondents to write out an answer to a question. Respondents are not limited to selecting only those responses that have been provided or anticipated by the planners, facilitators, or evaluators. The difficulty with using open-ended questions is that they take longer to complete and many people do not want to take the time to write out their responses. In order to be most effective and to elicit the type of information desired by evaluators, open-ended questions must be written in such a way that participants cannot respond merely with a yes or a no. Rather, questions are written that allow respondents to state their beliefs, ideas, knowledge, or feelings about a particular topic. When developing the actual questionnaire, evaluators need to leave sufficient space for participants to give a developed response.

3. After evaluators have developed the questionnaire, which will usually contain several types of questions, they determine the best time for its administration. When seeking information to assist in the process of planning the program, planners will look well in advance of the scheduled program for a time and place when the target group of

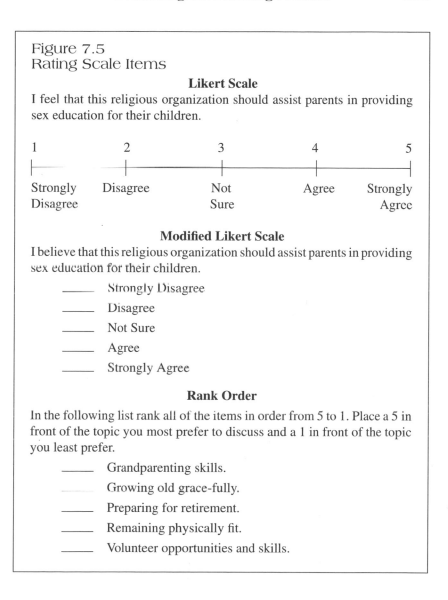

Figure 7.5
Rating Scale Items

Likert Scale

I feel that this religious organization should assist parents in providing sex education for their children.

1	2	3	4	5
Strongly Disagree	Disagree	Not Sure	Agree	Strongly Agree

Modified Likert Scale

I believe that this religious organization should assist parents in providing sex education for their children.

_____ Strongly Disagree

_____ Disagree

_____ Not Sure

_____ Agree

_____ Strongly Agree

Rank Order

In the following list rank all of the items in order from 5 to 1. Place a 5 in front of the topic you most prefer to discuss and a 1 in front of the topic you least prefer.

_____ Grandparenting skills.

_____ Growing old grace-fully.

_____ Preparing for retirement.

_____ Remaining physically fit.

_____ Volunteer opportunities and skills.

participants will be gathered or can be gathered. If the questionnaire seeks the reactions of participants during the actual implementation of the program, then a time when the participants are gathered for one of the program meetings can be used. The evaluation should not be the very last activity, even for collecting summative data. Possibly it can be administered when the group reassembles following the last

Figure 7.6
Multiple Choice Items

If you plan to participate in the marriage enrichment program, which time
frame would best fit your schedule? (Circle the appropriate letter.)

    a. A weekend retreat (Friday evening through Sunday afternoon)
    b. Three consecutive Saturdays (9:00 a.m. to 4:00 p.m.)
    c. The first Saturday of three consecutive months
    d. Six consecutive Wednesday evenings (7:00 to 10:00 p.m.)
    e. Six consecutive Sunday evenings (7:00 to 10:00 p.m.)

Which of the following do you consider to be the most important trait for
a married couple? (Circle the appropriate letter.)

    a. Faithfulness
    b. Honesty
    c. Open communication
    d. Reliability

Figure 7.7
Check Lists

Place an *X* by the skills and services you would be willing to provide to
community volunteer and nonprofit organizations and agencies.

_____ Cook	_____ Babysitter
_____ Companion	_____ Counselor
_____ Office help	_____ Yard work
_____ Phone hot line	_____ Fund-raising

break in the program, or it can be the first activity of the final morning
or evening if the program is spread over several days or weeks. By
allowing sufficient time for completing the evaluation, planners and
facilitators communicate nonverbally the importance placed both on the
data-gathering process and on the information respondents are being
asked to provide. Requesting participants to complete the instrument

---

Figure 7.8
Open-ended Questions

How can this religious organization best help you grow and develop spiritually, mentally, emotionally, socially, and physically?

Please descript your "picture" of the ideal after-school religious education program.

Note: Leave ample space for responses to open-ended questions. Either provide lines (double-spaced) on which to write or leave a large amount of white space.

as they are gathering their belongings and putting on their coats elicits hurried and inadequate responses.

4. The data gathered by means of the questionnaires should be tallied as soon after administration as possible. By looking at the results promptly, evaluators can also use their fresh memories of the program or activity to help them better understand, interpret, and use the responses provided by the participants.

Observation. As the name suggests, this mode of data collection allows evaluators to actually view a group in action. The observers are not dependent on reports of others which, of course, can be tainted, distorted, or skewed if those reporting are not skilled in observation or if they have their own agendas. On the other hand, observations can require considerable time in order to gather sufficient data, and they do call for some skill on the part of observers.[46]

---

46. Readers interested in going beyond this brief introduction are encouraged to consult Marlene E. Henerson, Lynn Lyons Morris, and Carol Taylor Fitz-Gibbon, *How to Measure Attitudes* (Newbury Park, Calif.: 1987); Herman, *Program Evaluation Kit*;

Before actually conducting an observation, evaluators need to develop an observation guide or instrument. This instrument includes definitive statements itemizing specific behaviors that are to be observed and noted (an example is included in fig. 9). Observation is not a process of just watching everything that is going on. Rather, it is a disciplined activity requiring evaluators to carefully and systematically look for certain actions or modes of conduct described in the observation items and to disregard extraneous activity.

The development of the observation guide and the observation itself based upon its use follows a four-step process. First, the evaluators select those criteria or indicators for which they wish to collect data by observation. Second, evaluators develop a clear set of definitive statements describing as precisely as possible the action or condition to be observed and the context in which that condition or behavior is to occur. The item should also indicate if the frequency of the condition or behavior is to be recorded. Most observed behaviors are not dichotomous; rather, they occur to a degree or with relative frequency. When constructing items to be observed, a good practice is to utilize a recording continuum not unlike the Likert scale. The ends of the continuum should be marked with the absolute presence or absence (that is, never——always) of the behavior or with terms or quantification symbols that are as universally understood as possible. When a continuum is used, it is often desirable that points along the continuum be marked and that the observer record only at the marked points so that data from more than one observer or observation can be combined. A serviceable observation schedule lists only as many continua as are needed to collect the desired data and as are reasonable for the length of time of the observation. The schedule must be managed easily by the observer. An observation continuum is illustrated in figure 9.

Third, evaluators conduct the observation. Proper arrangements are made in advance with facilitators so that they are at ease during the observation. Providing the facilitators with a copy of the observation guide in advance helps with this process because they then know what the evaluators intend to observe. Further, coaching the facilitators to conduct business as normal establishes an observation setting that produces

---

Danny L. Jorgenson, *Participant Observation: A Methodology for Human Studies* (Newbury Park: Sage, 1989); and James P. Spradley, *Participant Observation* (Fort Worth, Tex., : Holt, Rinehart & Winston, 1980).

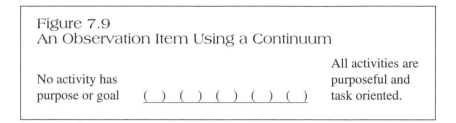

Figure 7.9
An Observation Item Using a Continuum

No activity has   All activities are
purpose or goal   ( ) ( ) ( ) ( ) ( )   purposeful and
                                                       task oriented.

useable data. Evaluators make themselves as unobtrusive as possible so that their presence does not distract from or alter the normal sequence and scope of activities, behaviors, and conditions that normally transpire in the program setting. If the evaluators are already participants in the group, their presence will not be problematic.

Evaluators mark the items on the observation instrument as soon as they feel they have enough exposure to make an accurate observation. They should not depend on memory. If at any time they observe a behavior that would contribute to the content of an item but is not built into the guide, they write a note on the guide explaining the contributing behavior.

Fourth, the data gathered by observation should be tallied as soon as possible after the observation has taken place. By looking at the results promptly, evaluators have fresh memories of the program or activity to help them understand, interpret, and use the observations that have been recorded.

Analyzing Data and Drawing Evaluative Conclusions

Once all the data have been gathered according to these guidelines, religious educators are ready for the third step of the process: the preparation of a report. This report consists of several parts. First, it explains why the evaluation was undertaken, describes the evaluation design and data collection methods, and presents the data collected.

Second, the religious educators present an analysis of the data. The analysis, in turn, is a two-step procedure. The initial step is to *describe* the data by asking and answering questions like: What do the data say? What do the data tell us? The data are organized so that they make sense and so that both the evaluators and those with whom they will share the data can understand them. *Interpretation* follows: What do the data mean? How do we interpret the data? What sense can we make of it all?

This analysis and interpretation brings the religious educators and their colleagues full circle—they have come back to the purposes of the evaluation. After the stakeholders have had a chance to review the written report, they meet with the religious educators. With the findings in hand, evaluators and stakeholders agree on answers to the evaluative questions that focused the evaluation process and prompted the collection of the data. This important activity is the "value" part of evaluation-it is time to make judgments and decisions. The group determines the course, or various courses, of action for the organization and the religious educators; the group also decides what to change or alter, what to augment, what to stop, what to begin. These decisions lay the foundation for new religious education program planning endeavors. In the process new questions may arise that will provide, in addition, the basis for a new evaluation cycle or sequence.

THE CONTEXT OF EVALUATING
THE PLANNING PROCESS

Change and Tradition

Change is a part of life; it is natural; it is to be expected. Change in communities drives the local religious community and the religious educator responsible for its programming to evaluate programs. Religious communities are not exempt from change, nor are the surrounding communities— the immediate neighborhood, the geographical region, the state, the nation, and the world. Such evaluation of the planning process is absolutely necessary. The religious educator must determine whether current programs are meeting the needs of those whom the religious community has identified as its primary area of responsibility. The DREs must decide how current programs may be modified to better accomplish their purposes, to determine if some programs must be terminated because they no longer are serving their purposes, and to identify areas that may require new programming.

However, many parishioners resist changes both in society and in congregational programming. That resistance is evident in what some punster has called the "seven last words of the church": "We've never done it that way before!" Never mind the fact that today's tradition was yesterday's change. Every tradition had a beginning. Somewhere beyond the current collective memory some previous religious educators conducted an "evaluation" of the religious organization's current situation and determined that something needed to be done. Consequently, a new program was planned, developed, and initiated. That program took root, other people bought into the idea, and the program became part of that organization's life. It became "tradition," that is, it has been handed down from generation to generation and has become a comfortable, often meaningful, part of people's lives.

What accounts for the desire to hold on to "tradition"? There are some sound reasons for resistance to change. First, people want to find something steady to cling to when everything around them seems to be shifting, a safe haven from the storms of life, an island of stability amid seas of change. This is the concept expressed in the line from a Christian hymn, "On Christ, the solid rock, I stand; All other ground is sinking sand."[47] Second, the program (for example, summer camp, youth outings, huge dinners, social evenings, vacation church school, etc.) made a major impact in their own lives and thus is filled with personal meaning. Yet, interest and participation in the program overall may be waning. The energy and cost involved in the program may no longer be justified rationally. Resources currently used for this program could be more usefully directed elsewhere; nevertheless, that program still meets the needs of a particular group, which is dwindling in numbers . Third, because the program has been so meaningful to them, the resisters want others—especially their children and grandchildren—to have the same experiences and consequent fond memories that they themselves had and have. It does not matter that others may not be interested in the program. Emotions, not reason, frequently control the reaction process.

Power and Authority

How can the religious educator deal with this common barrier to programmatic and evaluative decisions? First, the DRE develops an understanding of why such phenomena occur (some of the reasons have just been discussed). Then the DRE develops and uses strategies that recognize and even build on the reasons for resistance.

Membership in a church, synagogue, parish, or other religious organization is a voluntary activity and commitment. Participation in

---

47. Edward Mote, "My Hope Is Built on Nothing Less," in *Lutheran Book of Worship*, ed. Inter-Lutheran Commission on Worship, (Minneapolis: Augsburg, 1978), no. 293.

the religious, educational, and social life of that organization is also a voluntary activity. People who participate by choice and commitment develop a sense not only of belonging but of ownership. They tend to resist changes when they have not had sufficient opportunities for input and involvement—especially if they disagree with the decision. Organizational leaders and religious education planners can achieve neither agreement with nor acquiescence to change through control, regulation, or force.

Resistance is a natural part of the human experience; it is the attempt to gain some control over one's own life. When "others" are perceived as making changes that affect oneself or when outside forces are perceived as invading one's own territory, then the natural response is to protect oneself and one's own. This is human instinct at work. It is the "fight or flight" reaction that takes over when a person's basic needs and security are threatened.

A major step for a religious organization to take in planning and evaluating programs (that is, to effect change) is to involve in the process those who are or might be affected by decisions to add, drop, and/or change programs. Ways need to be found to allow and encourage these stakeholders to exercise the power they already possess. They have a vested interest; they are affected by programmatic decisions. As a matter of fact, the future success of the planning and evaluation process depends on the involvement of these members. Making them part of the process helps them better understand the choices and dilemmas faced by the religious educator. These stakeholders now become allies in the process rather than foes. They may even become ardent supporters of the changes that are agreed upon mutually and often become key players in the successful implementation of that change.

OTHER MODELS FOR EVALUATING
THE PLANNING PROCESS

Elias[48] points out that historically and traditionally, religious educators have not given much attention to evaluation. While some have advocated strongly for evaluating programs, most religious educators have devoted their attention to other aspects of the process of planning, delivering, and

---

48. Elias, *Foundations and Practice of Adult Religious Education,* pp. 270–72.

implementing programs. However, evaluation is closely connected with accountability because educational programs are frequently developed and implemented with limited resources. As resources become more restricted, greater attention will and must be given to the evaluation process. The process itself, according to Elias, involves the *development of values* (his term for objectives, criteria, standards, yardsticks) and using various *methods* to collect evaluative data, including interviews, questionnaires, checklists, controlled observations, and testing.[49]

Jerold Apps, following Steele, depicts three elements as necessary for program planning: criteria, evidence, and judgment. "An educational program is judged against criteria. The judgment is based on evidence collected about the extent to which the program met the criteria."[50] Apps suggests that a series of check sheets can be developed for collecting the needed evidence: "Some . . . are useful in determining how the present program is going, some can help you get information about what participants are learning, and some are most useful in providing clues for future programs."[51]

James DeBoy states that evaluation must be planned before the program, that is, during the planning process. Evaluation, then, is deciding the actual means by which the religious educator will determine if objectives have been met In fact, the setting of good objectives is crucial not only for the success of the planning process and the actual delivery of the program. They are also "especially important if effective evaluation is to be possible."[52] According to DeBoy, "part of the planning process should include the design of a method by which the program will be evaluated according to the stated, specific goals."[53] Since evaluation takes place throughout the planning process, the evaluation methodology also must be decided during the planning process. Each aspect of the evaluation must be considered, including submission of the program for approval, actual delivery and implementation, and the conclusion. Those who are to be included in the evaluation of the planning process

---

49. Ibid., pp. 273–77.

50. Jerold W. Apps, *How to Improve Adult Education in Your Church* (Minneapolis : Augsburg, 1972), p. 84; see Sara M. Steele, "Program Evaluation—A Broader Definition," *Journal of Extension* 8 (Summer 1970): 7.

51. Apps, *How to Improve Adult Education in Your Church*, p. 84.

52. James J. DeBoy Jr., *Getting Started in Adult Religious Education: A Practical Guide* (New York: Paulist, 1979), p. 93.

53. Ibid., p. 95.

include the religious educator *and* participants and by all involved. The program objectives serve as the major criteria against which to evaluate the program. By keeping careful records, the religious educator will collect sufficient, even abundant, data or evidence for making judgments about the program.

Finally, Reginald Wickett emphasizes the ongoing nature of evaluation: "It should be stated at the very beginning that evaluation is something which occurs throughout the process of an educational activity."[54] After reviewing briefly some of the topics discussed earlier in this chapter, he discusses "intervention points" during which the religious educator can undertake meaningful evaluations: "There are three periods of time when evaluation should be considered; the period when the course is being planned, the period when the course is running, and the period after the course has been completed. Valuable information may be acquired during each period depending upon the nature of the learning activity."[55]

Wickett then identifies categories (formative and/or summative, informal and/or formal) and methods of evaluation that are appropriate during each of these periods. He too emphasizes the importance of including the participants in the evaluation process.

CONCLUSION

Conducting evaluations requires much planning and thoughtfulness in order to solicit, gather, and interpret the information that forms the basis for making decisions about program components, procedures, and results. The prospect of undertaking an evaluation of the planning process may appear daunting. However, as when learning any skill, planners must take their first plunge. With each repetition they will learn, both from their mistakes and from their successes, and they will become increasingly proficient in the process.

---

54. R. E. Y. Wickett, *Models of Adult Religious Education Practice* (Birmingham, Ala., : Religious Education Press, 1991), p. 68.
55. Ibid., pp. 68–69.

PART 3

IMPLEMENTING PLANNING

8

INVITING OWNERSHIP BEYOND
THE PLANNING TEAM

Elizabeth Francis Caldwell

An essential part of the planning process in religious education is involving people beyond the planning team in giving commitment to the design and taking ownership of it. The implementation process of planning in religious education can be illustrated by Scripture and a case study.

A Scripture that illustrates a wider audience is found in three of the Gospels. As Jesus is teaching among the people, parents came forward with their children.[1] Jesus' disciples had been with him as he moved out from this devoted group of followers to share his message with a wider audience. The crowd was growing, and on this occasion people came to Jesus bringing their children to meet him and perhaps to receive a blessing. Oddly, the disciples sought to prohibit this interaction.

When Jesus saw what was happening, the Gospel writer Mark records, "he was indignant and said to them, 'Let the little children come to me; do not stop them; for it is to such as these that the kingdom of God belongs. Truly I tell you, whoever does not receive the kingdom of God as a little child will never enter it.' And he took them up in his arms, laid his hands on them, and blessed them."[2]

---

1. Mark 10:13–16 NRSV
2. Mark 10:13–16 NRSV

In spite of the disciples' actions, Jesus was able to get his message across to the people among whom he was teaching. It was essential that Jesus' hearers take ownership of this message as Jesus moved toward the final days of his ministry.

This biblical story serves as a helpful reminder of the importance of a planning team's involving larger groups in owning and implementing an educational design or program. The leader in this case, Jesus, obviously thought that his leadership team—the disciples—understood the approach they would be taking when they met with others outside the group. The gospel accounts give evidence that Jesus' assumption was wrong.

CONSIDERING A CASE STUDY

Two pastors in the same neighborhood and denomination, each serving one congregation, began a conversation about a new way to respond to the religious education needs in their area. The minister of the larger congregation initiated this concept by inviting the neighboring pastor to discuss both religious education needs in the area and potential staffing to meet those needs.

As a result of that initial conversation, three congregations located within a ten-mile radius of each other were invited to send congregational representatives and their ministers to a meeting to discuss the possibility of working together to coordinate programs of religious education. The decision to consider a new area religious education concept grew out of an idea suggested by one of the four pastors of these three churches.

The history of the congregations in staffing religious education varied. The church with five hundred members included the pastor who initiated this concept. It employed a church religious education director, who had recently resigned. The church staff also included an associate pastor.

The ministers and two or three members from each of the three congregations met to discuss the concept of responding to area needs for religious education. This area planning group established basic affirmations about who they were. The first affirmation stated that each congregation had a historically strong commitment to religious education for persons of all ages. Though only the largest congregation had employed a professional religious educator, the other two congregations had active religious education committees responsible for religious education programming.

This multicongregational planning team also affirmed that while each congregation's religious committee was doing a good job of maintaining the church school and ministry with youth, each congregation could benefit from the leadership of a professional educator. The reality for the two smaller churches was that they did not have the money to hire a full-time professional religious educator on their own. The larger congregation did not have this problem. The multicongregational planning team floated an idea: what if we banded together to hire one person to work with all three of our congregations?

Questions arose immediately. How do we begin to plan for such an idea? Is there anyone else using this model? If we developed such a proposal, how would our respective congregations respond?

Representatives of the three congregations decided to meet on a regular basis to continue their planning. Over a period of two years the following priorities became clear:

1. Study the feasibility of working together to hire an educational consultant who would provide professional leadership in religious education for all three congregations. This feasibility plan would include a proposal for a job description and a budget.
2. Work to secure a planning consultant to help with the design phase of the planning process.
3. Identify a time line for the development of a proposal for responding to the area needs of religious education and present this proposal to all three congregations.
4. Affirm the intention of this plan by asking the congregations to own the work of the multicongregational religious education planning group. Establish a joint coordinating committee composed of three representatives from each congregation.
5. Communicate with the three congregations in regard to the goals and the progress of the area religious education planning group. This communication would be both verbal (reporting at meetings of committees and governing bodies) and written (articles in congregational newsletters).
6. Affirm the connectional nature of this multicongregational religious education planning process by planning and implementing common

religious education events for church school teachers and leaders of the congregation.

In a sense, the multicongregational religious education planning group, which became the Joint Coordinating Committee, conceived of a two-tier approach to their model. The planning group knew that communicating their proposal was essential for understanding, acceptance, and commitment. The Joint Coordinating Committee spent the necessary time proceeding slowly in talking through their design as they moved toward articulating a job description for an educational consultant. As the committee worked, they were in conversation with their respective congregations. At the same time they decided to demonstrate how this concept of area religious education could work in practice.

Cooperative teacher training events were offered for religious education teachers and leaders from all three congregations. Workshop leaders for each age group (preschool, elementary, youth, and adult) were recruited from among experienced local church teachers and experts in towns nearby. When each congregational religious education committee worked in the spring to invite teachers to teach particular age groups in the church school, each could promise that teacher training would be available in the fall to help the teaching staff get started.

Common training events for church officers were also planned and offered on a yearly basis, rotating the location among the three churches. These actual experiences of the three congregations working together helped to make real the dreams and visions of the Joint Coordinating Committee.

At each step in the process, the congregations were kept informed about the process of the Joint Coordinating Committee. One challenge was to keep the communication link open between the congregations and the Joint Coordinating Committee. A clear communication link was essential so that questions could be raised and answered, concerns could be addressed, ownership could be extended beyond that of the original area planning group.

The Joint Coordinating Committee proceeded with their planning and hired a consultant to work with them on thinking through the job description, budget, and the roles and relationships necessary in this full-time professional religious education position. After completing their work on the job description, the committee knew it was essential to inform the congregations about this proposal.

The committee planned a series of congregational dinners—one for each congregation—for the purpose of explaining the multicongregational educational consultant concept and the need for a full-time professional in religious education. The committee explained the job description, asked for questions, and sought support for this venture, which they believed was breaking new ground in models of religious education. Once approval of the job description had been secured from each of the congregational governing bodies, the committee began advertising the position and seeking applicants.

MOVING FROM PLANNING TO IMPLEMENTING

The evolution of a planning group is always a fascinating process to observe. Some groups move easily through the stages and see their visions accomplished. Other groups never get beyond the planning stage to implement a design.[3] What is the difference between the two?

Understanding how leadership and membership differ gives insight into the implementation phase of planning. There are certain social processes identifiable in the evolution of leadership. Evelyn Eaton Whitehead suggests that "leadership refers to the exercise of initiative and influence in the achievement of a group's goals."[4] She goes on to say that in their attempt to understand the characteristics of the processes of leadership, social scientists have traditionally focused on a particular characteristic or personality style possessed by a leader. After decades of observing the group life involved in planning, social scientists came to understand that leadership styles were less easily identified with a person than with the function of a group. Leadership came to be understood as a process rather than an attribute. Social scientists once

---

3. There are numerous models for program development. One procedural model that identifies the phases of planning from diagnosis through evaluation is found in Donald G. Emler's *Revisioning the DRE* (Birmingham, Ala.: Religious Education Press, 1989), p. 104.

4. Evelyn Eaton Whitehead, "Leadership and Power: A View from the Social Sciences," in *Alternative Futures for Worship: Leadership Ministry in Community*, vol. 6 (Collegeville, Minn.: Liturgical, 1987), p. 46.

considered leadership as something a person has, an attribute, rather than a process, meaning something that is going on among a group of people. "Leadership is not just what one person in a group has; it is something that people in a group do together."[5]

For Whitehead leadership is a process, a "social transaction: it is what goes on in a group to enable members to mobilize their power to achieve their common goals."[6] This theoretical understanding of leadership shifts the focus from the particular qualities possessed by one individual to the way the group functions as a whole.

It is possible that some groups never move beyond the planning stage because of an inability to enable each other to function together. If implementation of an religious education design is to occur, particular attention must be paid to four issues of group interaction: inclusion, power, intimacy, and effectiveness.[7]

Inclusion

Planning groups are composed of individuals who agree to work together toward a common goal. A planning group begins with formation and inclusion.[8] Early in the planning process the group seeks to determine its identity as a group. How did it come to be formed? Why were some persons included and others excluded? In what ways will the

---

Figure 8.1
Differences in Planning Teams

Think for a few minutes about planning groups in which you have been a participant. Recall a group that was able to work together to accomplish its goals. Now recall a group that never seemed to get beyond the planning stage. Step back and look at these groups objectively, and describe the differences between them.

---

5. Whitehead, "Leadership and Power," p. 47.
6. Ibid.
7. These four factors are identified by Whitehead, "Leadership and Power."
8. Jon R. Katzenbach and Douglas K. Smith, *The Wisdom of Teams* (New York: HarperBusiness, 1993), pp. 43–49. Complementary skills and a small number of persons are suggested to ensure a functioning team.

individuals evolve as a group? Will the group be able to work together? Why was the group formed? What commonalties and differences are characteristic of this group?[9] Issues of inclusion and identity continue to be addressed at each stage of the planning process, particularly as some members drop out and others are added.

Power

As a group moves along in the planning process, the issue of power becomes more obvious.[10] Some persons emerge as strong and powerful while others struggle with personal power issues: What do I have to contribute? Where is my power? What influence do I have in this group? If I speak, will my suggestions be heard? Whitehead notes that as power issues emerge, conflict becomes a reality. Such conflict, she believes, is a positive sign that the group is working toward a new phase in its life together, a phase that must be addressed with intentionality.

Intimacy

Groups working on a common goal also deal with issues of intimacy. How close will we become? How self-revealing will I be with this group? What expectations do individuals bring to this process? What personal investments do individuals make to this group process and what needs does each bring?

Effectiveness

In addition to issues of closeness and function, a planning group is also concerned with the task—the effectiveness of their process of working together toward a common goal.[11] Effectiveness relates to both personal

---

9. A group may begin to identify itself based on who they are not. This is an early warning to the leader that the group is attempting to identify itself "over against" another group. For further reading, see James D. Whitehead and Evelyn Easton Whitehead, *The Emerging Laity: Returning Leadership to the Community of Faith* (New York: Doubleday, 1988), pp. 105–34.

10. Power is "a process occurring *within* a group; it is a relationship. To 'locate' power in this way, in the group's interaction, radically influences the role and status of leaders." Whitehead and Whitehead, *Emerging Laity*, pp. 35–49. For further reading see Ronald A. Heifetz, *Leadership without Easy Answers* (Cambridge: Harvard University Press, 1994), pp. 254–55.

11. Leadership and "effective group behavior" are discussed in *Learning to Work in Groups,* by Matthew B. Miles (New York: Teachers College, Columbia University, 1959), and in "Effective Group Behavior," pp. 11–26, 215–16.

goals and contributions to the planning task as well as the way the group functions as a whole.[12]

As a group moves from planning to implementing a religious education design, communications must be clear and direct and should be focused in two directions: within the group and from the group to the congregation. Intentional focus on the four issues of group interaction help to ensure that clear communication within the group is a priority.

In reflecting on the case study discussed earlier, we can trace a group's ability to envision. Once the vision was clear, the group moved to conceptualizing a model and then to involving ownership of the model by larger groups, and finally to the realization of the original vision. What made it possible for one person's vision to be shaped, owned, and enlarged by a group?

The role of individuals and their particular visions and commitments to a common goal are key in moving a plan from paper to reality. James Fenhagen discusses enablement as a process that "demands a particular type of vision."[13] He believes that three functions are essential to the process of internalizing a vision: support, energy, and education.

Fenhagen believes that intentional thinking about the functions of leadership and membership over the course of designing a program is essential to a viable theory of planning. A person involved in planning must feel supported. As groups work together toward a common goal, they need to feel support from the larger system providing accountability and recognition. They also need a continuing understanding of how

---

Figure 8.2
Participating in a Planning Team

Consider planning groups in which you have been a participant or for whom you have served as a leader. What enabled or what prevented your participation? Who or what enabled your continued participation and contribution to this group?

---

12. David Arthur Bickimer, *Leadership in Religious Education* (Birmingham, Ala.: Religious Education Press, 1990), pp. 61–65.

13. James C. Fenhagen, *Mutual Ministry: New Vitality for the Local Church* (New York: Seabury, 1977), p. 106.

their part in planning for a program relates to the larger purposes of the congregation.[14] How does what we are doing in this process relate to our faith—our common calling as Jews, Protestants, or Roman Catholics?

Energizing is a second important function of enabling others. "We energize when we make it possible for others to draw creative energy from us—when in a very real sense we serve as life givers."[15] Energizing takes place in worship, in times and places when people connect by helping others to communicate, in caring for another through the touch of a phone call or a conversation, and, most critically, through listening.

A third function is educational, an intentional focus on skills and resources needed to accomplish a goal. Fenhagen describes this function in terms of trust and a sense of being open to exploring new possibilities. The educational function is also concerned with resources needed for the task—both material resources and resources that individuals bring to the group planning process.

For Fenhagen, enabling or involving others is a theoretical approach to planning that requires that a group to be involved in a continuous cycle of information gathering, evaluating, and goal setting. Enabling a group begins by knowing where people are in terms of their needs. Knowing where a group has been and where they desire to go are additional critical issues involved in enabling a community.[16]

The Hebrew Bible contains many stories of people responding to God's call for leadership. Wise rulers, judges, and prophets were selected by God to speak God's word to God's people. Women and men were chosen for various reasons: background, experience, age, personality, leadership potential. God spoke to these people and God's message of covenant love (ḥesed) and peace (shalom) was in turn shared by them with every widening circles of people.

So too in planning for religious education, the ownership of program ideas needs to be shared by the entire congregation if understanding, commitment, and participation are to be achieved.[17] Introducing of a new program design to a congregation requires careful thought. A small

---

14. Enlarging accountability in the planning process is discussed in Whitehead and Whitehead, *Emerging Laity* pp. 170–71.

15. Fenhagen, *Mutual Ministry,* p. 108.

16. Ibid., p. 109.

17. Planning in religious education includes a cooperative effort that seeks conversation with an enlarged group. John L. Elias states that the determination of objectives includes the involvement of others such as administrators, learners, teachers. See John L.

group that has worked together closely over a period of time has come to know and trust each other. Group members have invested themselves in each other, in their planning process, and in the religious education design they are proposing. The process of moving from planning to implementing requires an important middle step—communicating the design to a larger group.

Think about this issue in relation to a concrete example. Many parishes struggle with the place and role of children and youth in worship. Are young people truly welcome on Sunday morning or a Friday evening at a Shabbat or are they only tolerated? A religious education planning group working to recommend the inclusion of children and youth in the participation and leadership of congregational worship will need to be clear about the history of the present religious education practice, the rationale for change, and the expected outcomes of the proposed new practice.

In a sense, in presenting a religious education design to the congregation, the planning group must help the whole parish understand the thinking, insights, judgments, and vision involved in the program being introduced. The religious education planning committee opens a window to the larger group, letting people see not only what is being proposed but the decisions that lead up to the proposal.

Central to the success of the planning model described in the case study earlier in this chapter was communication, ownership, and intelligent, committed leadership—people with a vision.[18] Clear communications are essential to obtaining support for the design or program, as well as promoting ownership of it both within the planning group and among the congregation.

MOVING FROM IMPLEMENTING TO MAINTAINING

Once a group has moved from planning a religious education design to implementing it, there are several issues to be addressed: What if

Elias, *The Foundations and Practice of Adult Religious Education* (Malabar, Fla.: Krieger, 1982), pp. 224–26.

18. Communication and vision result in a shared purpose. For more extensive reading in the area of visioning, see Burt Nanus, *Visionary Leadership* (San Francisco: Jossey-Bass, 1992), pp. 133–56.

stagnation occurs? What if the design is not implemented in the time frame or process as it was originally conceived by the religious education planning group? What if the parish leadership changes? What are some ways to enable smooth transitions as members and leaders of the original religious education planning group change over a period of time? What role does the original planning group take in maintaining the educational design?

Two key words for planners to remember are flexibility and fluidity. Congregational planning processes eventually encounter resistance, which is commonly expressed in two familiar sayings: We've never done it this way! and We've always done it this way.

All that would have been required for the process described in the case study to come to a screeching halt would have been a chorus of voices saying,

> It won't work!
> We can afford our own full-time religious educator; why do we need to share one?
> It's not feasible to think that one person can split her or his time among three congregations.
> It has never been done before; what if it fails?
> We'll never find a person who will be willing to take this job.
> We can't afford it!

Religious education planning committees need to be prepared to face the doubters with thoughtful and calm responses. They also need to be flexible in their ability to respond to suggestions. As implementation of religious education programs or designs begins, changes and adaptations can still be made. The planning group needs to practice awareness of the participants and the leadership of the planning process as it plans, implements, and maintains the religious education programs.

Occasionally a delay or a breakdown occurs in the transition from planning to implementation to maintenance of a new religious education program. The group's carefully planned goals and time line languish as members of the original planning group resign or rotate off the committee and new members must be recruited and oriented to the task. Such interruptions are normal aspects of the planning processes and must not be allowed to disrupt it completely.

> ### Figure 8.3
> ### Issues of Transition
>
> *Take a few moments and consider your own experience of problems that occur toward the end of the process as a design is implemented and maintained. Describe the problems. Could they have been foreseen? What did you learn from them? How did you handle issues of transition of membership and leadership?*

Letty M. Russell speaks of a "space of hospitality to make connections to one another in community."[19] Though Russell is describing a classroom, her words also apply to a planning group. For Russell, a classroom becomes the learner's home regardless of how hierarchical and rigid it may be architecturally. The learners connects with one another through their respective traditions. The learners become partners in learning with the world, taking risks through the learner's questions so that growth may occur. [20] Russell seems to be advocating reflective processes, the kind that invite questions and encourage critical thinking. They affirm the connections between the work of small groups and the larger purposes of the congregation as well as the congregation's role in the community and the world. Notice also how she equates classroom with home, where connections, risk, and questions are involved in the growth process.

A religious education planning committee that works together in moving through the planning process from conception to implementation has learned a great deal from and with each other. Invited to envision a new religious education model or design, a group risks growth and change. The congregation also experiences growth and change. The circle of learners, the planning group, works to expand their circle of participants during the entire planning process.

Consider the concept of expanding the circle of leadership as you think about transitions within the planning group. Over a period of two to three years, it is not unlikely that membership and leadership will change. Religious education planning groups can anticipate such transitions by

---

19. Letty M. Russell, *The Church in the Round: Feminist Interpretation of the Church* (Westminster/John Knox, 1993), p. 199.

20. Ibid.

asking persons to serve in classes, each having a term.[21] For example, each class rotates yearly so that rotation on the area planning group or in the religious education planning committee occurs smoothly.

Members from the three congregations described in the case study served set terms, so that no two members from the same congregation rotated off at the same time. This process helped to insure ownership and involvement by each congregation. In addition, leadership of the Joint Coordinating Committee rotated among the three churches. A chairperson was elected for a two-year term and rotated among lay leaders and the clergy. Prior to his or her first meeting, a new member was oriented to the work of the committee.

There are at least two ways to conceptualize a model of religious education leadership that moves a planning group from implementation to maintenance. One is a boardroom, specifically, a corporate boardroom. It is tastefully decorated and has a conference table long enough to seat eighteen people, lovely wood chairs, and artwork. (Some congregations have duplicated these boardrooms in their buildings.) Usually the leader sits at one end of the table and conducts the meetings from that vantage point.

Consider another model of leadership. It takes place at a round kitchen table where, as Russell says, "we get down to the sweaty tasks of daily living . . . [because the] round tables draw us into a partnership of sharing and reflection."[22] As a planning group moves to the practical side of implementing its vision, members must be ready to roll up their sleeves and take their places around the kitchen table, less concerned with rank and order and more concerned with the partnership of learning that takes place in the midst of change.[23] As Russell suggests, the round table, with its emphasis on "the daily work of women who care for

---

21. For specific ways to anticipate the changes of members and/or team leaders see Katzenbach and Smith, *Wisdom of Teams,* pp. 162–67. One of the benefits of a new team member is the "returning to the basics" in conversation about team mission and task. This often becomes a way for the full team to clarify direction.

22. Russell, *Church in the Round,* p. 75.

23. The term "round table has become a symbol of hospitality and a metaphor for gathering for sharing and dialogue. It speaks concretely of our experiences in coming together and connecting at home, at work, and at worship; it also points to the reality that often persons are excluded from the tables of life, both through denial of shared food and resources and through denial of shared naming and decision making for their community, nation, or world. . . . the round table is a sign of the coming unity of humanity." For further information on the "round table" see Russell, *Church in the Round*, pp. 12, 17–19.

homes and families, preparing the dough for the future of their children and sometimes breaking the bread not only at home but in the assembled church community,"[24] is a more useful image than the long, rectangular table in the boardroom.

MOVING FROM MAINTENANCE TO VISIONING

Religious organizations have relied heavily on management theories of planning and organizational behavior even as curriculum writers have paid thoughtful attention to developmental theorists and models of teaching and learning. But there is another dimension that completes this congregational approach to planning in religious education. We look at the goals of our planning through the eyes of faithful people. We bring a foundation of theological and religious education along with a faithful way of living as we come together to do our work. Whether the religious education committee is planning a vacation Bible school sponsored by a cluster of churches, or working across faith traditions to produce a cookbook with proceeds going to homeless shelters, or planning a "sharing Shabbat" for families on Saturday mornings, it does so because it names God and rightfully claims to be God's people seeking to live more faithfully in the world.

Spirit or ethos is another way to name this foundation that supports communities as they work together in the planning process. When an organization is filled with vitality, energy, and enormous vision they are said to be inspired. Other organizations may operate with less spirit. "One of the basic functions of leadership is to stimulate and focus the organization's spirit."[25] James Ritscher discusses the challenge of spiritual leadership by suggesting that the dull and tarnished spirit that some organizations have makes them likely to be blown every which way by any prevailing wind that comes along. If leaders do not rise to the challenge of enspiriting their organizations, there will be no spirit at the heart of their organization, no real, vital nature. Ritscher is clear that all organizations do have a spirit. "Only an organization that is well grounded in its spiritual nature has the will and the strength to

24. Russell, *Church in the Round*, p. 76.
25. James A. Ritscher, "Spiritual Leadership," in *Transforming Leadership: From Vision to Results*, ed. John D. Adams (Alexandria, Va.: Miles River, 1986), p. 61.

survive."[26] Ritscher is clear that spirit in an organization does make a difference.

In working with a religious education planning group, a leader should be able to make a fairly quick assessment of both the spirit of the group and their ability to envision, to plan, and to implement. But, such capabilities may be lacking, or they may be "dull and tarnished," to use Ritscher's phrase.[27]

Leadership and spirituality are essential to the survival of the organization. Ritscher uses the term "enspiriting an organization" to describe the work of the leader.[28] Karen Wilhelm Buckley and Joan Steffy discuss the unseen as part of leadership. They identify intuition and alignment as essential leadership components. By intuition they mean "the behind-the-scenes processing of information and images that occur incessantly, although we neglect to pay attention to it."[29] Buckley and Steffy believe that while "intuition guides actions," "alignment focuses energy." Alignment refers to organizational harmony.

> *Alignment of vision and action opens the system to feedback and input of critical information. Too often in organizations, the invisible signals of internal or external distress are ignored or invalidated. The capacity to receive internal and external feedback and input and to respond in aligned actions becomes particularly important during times of profound change when what was known no longer is, and what is to be has not yet emerged.*[30]

In times of change, leaders work to ensure that alignment is taking place within the organization. Such alignment creates a climate that includes "trust, high-quality interaction and open interpersonal communications."[31]

Equally essential to the process of planning for religious education is paying attention to the spiritual side of the congregation. The concept of

---

26. Ritscher, "Spiritual Leadership," p. 61.
27. Ibid., p. 62.
28. Ibid., p. 61.
29. Karen Wilhelm Buckley and Joan Steffy, "The Invisible Side of Leadership," in *Transforming Leadership: From Vision to Results*, ed. John D. Adams (Alexandria, Va.: Miles River, 1986), p. 235.
30. Buckley and Steffy, "Invisible Side of Leadership," p. 235.
31. Ibid.

spirituality goes far beyond a superficial ego-oriented view. Spirituality is an experience of the *depth* of life that has to do with the heart.[32]

At some point along the way, as the religious education planning committee moves from planning to implementing and involving larger groups in owning the process and the program, it is possible that problems may arise. Someone works to block the process, someone else raises criticisms that the planning group has not heard before, and so on. This is the time to remember what Ritscher is saying about spirit. A religious education planning group that is aware of its spiritual nature can find strength when questions arise. Remembering also the larger purposes that inform its planning supports the planning group in their work during times of reassessment.

Richard R. Broholm identifies four concerns that should be recognized in the planning process. The first is converting reaction into creative action. When a planning group presents a program plan to a congregation, the group opens itself to questions, positive and negative assessments, and suggestions for change. Planning groups that are able to turn their reactive responses into positive strategies for creative change are better able to move beyond potential roadblocks. Broholm's second concern is converting fatalism into hope. Imagining a more hopeful situation involves the ability to see possibilities in the present reality. Third is enabling a collaborative rather than a competitive style. When faced with potential roadblocks, a religious education planning group can be pulled apart by individual, competing strategies for change. Broholm suggests that a collaborative approach to a common vision is a more productive style of working and planning.

Broholm's fourth concern is encouraging a "systems" rather than a "problem-solving" approach to change. Broholm suggests that when a group isolates a problem and fails to recognize the larger system in which it exists, it unintenitonally creates an issue that is far more serious issue than the original problem.[33]

If a religious education planning group keeps these four concerns in mind as it continues with implementation and oversight of a religious education design, it will be able to make creative responses to most of

---

32. Ibid., p. 61.

33. Richard R. Broholm, "Envisioning and Equipping the Saints for Change," in *The Laity in Ministry: The Whole People of God for the Whole World* ed. George Peck and John S. Hollman (Valley Forge, Pa.: Judson, 1984), p. 134.

the problems that may arise. It is also important to remember the concept of spirit. James Ritscher discussed the leader's role in "enspiriting the organization." If Russell's model of a round kitchen table is taken seriously, then the role of "enspiritor" could come from anyone in the planning group.

The implementation phase of a religious education design needs creative visioning and spirit as the group moves toward completion of the planning process. A wise leader knows that such creativity and spirit is potentially present in each person and works to enable that to emerge.

SETTING THE ROUND TABLE:
SOME CONCLUDING REFLECTIONS

It seems appropriate at this point to make some concluding comments on the case study and the ending of the story. The case study mentioned earlier in this chapter provides a concrete example of a religious education committee moving through the implementation phase of the planning process. Particular attention has been given to involving ownership beyond the planning team.

Some time ago I received a call from the chair of the Joint Coordinating Committee, asking if I would be interested in interviewing for the job of religious educator for the area. The Joint Coordinating Committee considered this position to be a groundbreaking opportunity. The committee members could find no one else trying such an educational model. They were excited about their design and wanted to find an educator who would join them on this unique venture.

I agreed to interview for the job, and eventually served as their educational consultant for eleven years. Triennial evaluations were built into the job description. One feature of these evaluations was an outside consultant who would evaluate both the onsite educational consultant and the work of the Joint Coordinating Committee. Over the years, as a result of evaluations and learnings, the job description changed slightly in response to the reality of the work with the three congregations. Membership and leadership changed, rotating among the three congregations. There were always persons who were willing to serve and to commit to this vision of religious education.

The Joint Coordinating Committee met monthly for the first three years, then quarterly. Reports of my work were shared with the three congregations. Budgeting was done by the committee and presented to each congregation for their pro-rata share of the expenses.

The work of the religious education committee shifted over the years. They had begun with a hope and a vision of partnership and steward-ship of time, energy, and resources. The committee's job shifted into maintenance and supervision once the consultant was hired. Keeping the three congregations informed about the work of the committee and my work was always a priority. For the multicongregational religious education ministry approach to continue, it was critical to keep a flow in the coordination and sharing of information.

Gradually other congregations heard about this model and requested information on it. Finally, the denomination took an interest in this religious education model. A booklet entitled *Clustering for Educational Ministry* was made available to those interested in considering a cluster approach to religious education. Articles on this religious education model appeared in denominational magazines. The Joint Coordinating Committee saw the dream and vision that had originally empowered the work of the planning committee stay alive. They were proud of their work and were glad that others were interested in what they were learning and had accomplished.

I became excited about the possibilities of this position when I heard the original planning committee's enthusiasm. They were able to com-municate their dream! I sincerely believed that this concept would work and that it had great potential for growth.

When I joined the Joint Coordinating Committee, they had been working together for three years. Some team members were tired and ready to rotate off. Some members considered their work to be completed once the consultant was hired. The implementation process saw new members coming on board. It was never difficult to find persons willing to serve because the congregations knew that this committee was well organized. New members of this planning group found opportunities to make personal contributions to creative planning in religious education.

As I began to work with the Joint Coordinating Committee in the planning and implementation of educational programs for leaders in the congregations, we experimented with varieties of designs and methods. Members of the Joint Coordinating Committee both trusted my judgment and felt comfortable with trying new models of religious education. They continued to live and plan as an "enspiriting organization" in the same ways they had at the beginning of the planning process. Implementing and maintaining this area wide model of religious education was never perceived as dull and ordinary. In many ways we continued to be inspired by the vision of the original planning group and continued to be challenged by the job to which we were all committed.

The unity of theory and practice is essential in the process of planning. A congregational model of religious education planning is designed, developed, and delivered though conversation and listening to congregational views. As a planning group moves from visioning through implementation, it faces the additional challenge of enabling a larger group to understand, own, and commit to a new religious education program. As Fenhagen points out, a theoretical approach to planning that uses an enabling model must be attentive to communication between planners and those who will implement a program of religious education.

Returning to Russell's image of a round kitchen table, she describes such a table as a place where growth and change occur. A person making bread kneads the dough at the table, preparing it for the moment when it will rest and slowly change form as it rises. Once the dough is in the oven, the baker watches it change shape once more as the heat of the oven turns the bread a golden brown.

Religious education planners also have a vision for the end product. They are enspirited by each other, challenged by their plan, and eager to see the plan take shape in their midst. Like the baker who places the risen dough in the oven so it can be baked into bread, planners offer their programs to larger groups expecting some changes. Even in the latter steps of implementation and maintenance, changes do happen.

Planners who sit at the round table welcome and encourage the insights and suggestions that arise as religious education programs move into the reality of congregational experience. A round table of equality is a place where all are welcomed equally and each is held accountable, where dialogue is encouraged, and where visions are shared. Such a table invites the kind of environment that enables religious education plans to move from paper to reality.

9

IMAGINING RELIGIOUS EDUCATION PLANNING ANEW

Nancy T. Foltz

MIDRASH CAN ALSO BE UNDERSTOOD AS A PROCESS OR ACTIVITY, RATHER THAN AN OUTCOME. IT DENOTES THE PROCESS OF ENCOUNTERING A TEXT, CHALLENGING IT WITH AN EVER-NEW SET OF QUESTIONS AND STRUGGLING TO EXTRACT FROM IT EQUALLY NEW ANSWERS.[1]

Professionals in religious education have been trying for decades to maintain stability.[2] We have been attempting to drive chaos back from our congregational planning doors. But times have changed and religious education planners are encountering challenges and questions that require new processes and activities. Chaos is a part of our world, our community, our congregation. Not only do the old answers not work in planning but the old questions are blocking our pathway to the future.

For example, when parish leaders spend most of their time, energy and finances working on building needs, it may be time to raise the

---

1. Neil Gillman, *Sacred Fragments: Recovering Theology for the Modern Jew* (Philadelphia: Jewish Publication Society, 1990), p. xxvi.
2. Margaret J. Wheatley, *Leadership and the New Science* (San Francisco: Berrett-Koehler, 1992), pp. 1–23. Margaret J. Wheatley and Myron Kellner-Rogers, *a simpler way* (San Francisco: Berrett-Koehler, 1996), pp. 11–19. Ralph D. Stacey, *Complexity and Creativity in Organization* (San Francisco: Berrett-Koehler, 1996), pp. 13–18. Ralph D. Stacey, *Managing the Unknowable: Strategic Boundaries between Order and Chaos in Organizations* (San Francisco: Jossey-Bass, 1992), pp. 29–36. Henry Mintzberg, *The Rise and Fall of Strategic Planning* (New York: Free Press, 1994), pp. 183–188.

question, What is it that God would have us be and do? Would our parish have a ministry without a building as we know it? It is a time of making midrash. A time to face the question anew: How do we rethink the planning process in religious education?

Relinquishing what has been cherished and abandoning held interpretations about planning in religious education takes courage. As Einstein is often quoted as saying, "No problem can be solved from the same consciousness that created it."[3]

It is time to stop talking about whether or not a parish is interested in change. Change is not an option. Change surrounds us. Discontinuity is experienced daily. What once was no longer is. For example, attendance at synagogue or parish events used to be fairly predictable. Today, attendance levels can vary dramatically for no apparent reason. Today, instead of initiating change, parishes attempt to anticipate change and to plan in accordance with the forecast of change.

Parish leaders have experience of change. Congregations have abundant experience with change. Leaders need to have confidence in their ability to lead the change effort. They can build up their confidence by considering questions such as, What in the life of a congregation is the most concrete evidence of the capacity to change? Where are the most recent, vivid significant changes occurring?

During a morning service the members of the Smithfield United Church dedicated the Smithfield United Church of Christ Pittsburgh Pastoral Institute Counseling Center, which was planned to be located in the church. The pastor intoned fifteen changes made by the congregation over the past fifty years, including the move from its previous location a block away to the present new building, the opening of a shelter for homeless women, the ecumenical help week, the recent church merger. Such a litany of change boosts a congregation's confidence in their capacity to plan change efforts.

Another way to identify a congregation's capacity to plan change is to write a scenario beginning with the question, If our parish continues on our current path, where will it be in five years? The question planners must ask is, What results from the ability to plan effectively? Past successes in planning efforts need to be remembered as new planning efforts are considered. Rethinking processes, redesigning educational

---

3. Wheatley, *Leadership and the New Science*, p. 5. There is an excellent video on this book available from CRM video by the same name.

efforts, and redefining the definition of what is and is not included in religious education is a significant first step in the planning process.

> *Every midrash, then, is a temporary consolidation, a plateau, the outcome of a struggle to rethink a tradition that has become, at least to some Jews, irrelevant. It is then inherently transitory, itself easily becoming anachronistic, lingering until we are shocked out of our complacency when our children tell us that we no longer 'speak' to them.*[4]

Some churches greet worshipers with a sense of hospitality, a warmth, a genuine welcoming. Someone has a hand extended in welcome, people in the pews smile and speak, there is a comfortableness that is unmistakable. Somewhere behind this welcoming scene, though, people have planned; people have paid attention to the details. Once an environment is suffused with "an attitude," "a force," "a presence," the atmosphere becomes contagious. Think about an exceptional place, a memorable experience that lingers in the memory because it stood out, it drew and grew energy.

Physicist K. C. Cole describes "fields" as a concept that was used to overcome the main objection to Newton's notions of gravity. In his study on particles and fields Cole found that "fields" spread the influence of particles out into space.[5] Cole uses the historical analogy of annexations that spread the influence of a country. Another example of a "field" is diplomatic exchange between two countries or a fire that spreads to another place. There are force-carrying particles that create a field out in space. Cole speaks of "a force field" as a mental and mathematical tool used to visualize how a force operates. Cole's research found that force fields exist *on their own*, separate from the particles that create them.[6]

Margaret Wheatley calls this dimension an "invisible field." Fields are invisible spaces where something perceptible is going on, which usually can be named. Invisible fields are unseen connections that influence behavior. [7]

---

4. Gillman, *Sacred Fragments*, p. xxvi.

5. K. C. Cole, *Sympathetic Vibrations: Reflections on Physics as a Way of Life* (New York: Bantam, 1985), pp. 97–98.

6. Ibid., p. 98.

7. Wheatley, *Leadership and the New Science*, pp. 12–13.

Working in a newly reorganized parish, I listened as the nine people on the parish staff spoke about their concerns for members of the parish. After spending several hours with the staff members, I saw that they were unified in their desire to serve the parish. They respected one another and shared a clear intent to be available to parishioners. Staff members understood the need to listen to members of the congregation who were grieving their losses in a reorganized parish. Four months ago eight individual ethnic parishes existed. Now there was one parish. Previous among parish staff was an invisible field of trust and respect. Care and concern graced staff conversations. Effective planning emerges as a staff responds to the invisible fields.[8]

One person may exude incredible energy upon walking into a room. Soon the whole environment is energized and a sense of anticipation heightens. Or someone contributes to a conversation and suddenly the room seems to enlarge. The idea of having staff members verbalize "a new agreement" when dealing with conflicts is taken and three other people add to it. Soon the whole group has agreed to participate in the new agreement. Invisible fields are contagious and they are unmistakably present in congregational life.

The contrary is also true. Negative invisible fields exist. These are environments that people want to escape. One planning team began to work on the issue of clergy accountability. Once the idea of "making clergy accountable " was sent up, a heaviness hung in the air and people became uncomfortable. There was an invisible field of uncomfortable-ness. When someone begins to offer negative, low-trust examples in a meeting or a conversation, an edge creeps into someone else's language, and soon a dark, heavy cloud lowers the room's ceiling. Then the walls come in. Finally the conversation, the ideas, the vision shrink along with the room. These negative air particles are also contagious and they linger in our experience.

Defining planning in religious education is like describing batting in a quilt. The batting may not be visible to the eye, but the body that the quilt covers feels the warmth and texture. Just as batting is the invisible

---

8. Ronald A. Heifetz, *Leadership without Easy Answers* (Cambridge: Harvard University Press, 1995), pp. 104–10. Heifetz states that building trust begins with knowing what generates it. Consistent values and problem-solving skills are major components of building trust.

stuff of a quilt, so planning in religious education is the invisible stuff of congregational warmth. The previous chapters in this book have focused on what is visible—the parts of planning that can be touched. But how can these "invisible fields" be located?

Lifting some of the threads of the religious education planning quilt exposes the inside of the quilt. Invisible fields are not magical or mysterious, but they are difficult to access, illusive to articulate, and most definitely impossible to create or change alone. Invisible field planning requires a collective, collegial attentiveness and agreement on what exists in this congregational space and what religious education planners and the congregation want to exist in this space.

Invisible fields are spaces in which there is a definite environment. The field can be positive or negative. They do exist within congregations. We can feel their presence and see their impact on planning in religious education. These fields can help religious education professionals know why specific environments need to be created, changed, or enlarged. For the purposes of examining planning in religious education, the focus is to identify those positive invisible fields.

Space is never empty. Space is filled with something. In invisible fields, space is filed with messages. Planners send messages. Congregations send messages. Staffs send messages. These messages are released into the air waves of a congregation and community, and they create a field. A field is a collection of ideas that together have the potential to bring energy into form. When the messages change, the fields change. Individuals shape invisible fields through activity.[9]

In a congregation, space is filled with conversations and actions. When leaders infuse congregational space with messages that are supportive and forgiving, positive energy is generated within that space. When leaders fill congregational space with messages that are inconsistent and conflicting, negative energy is generated. Planning in spaces filled with high energy is a very different experience from planning in spaces filled with negative energy. Paying attention to the invisible field of energy is critical when planning. For example, in one congregational planning session thirty leaders were seated at eight separate tables. During the session the small groups at the tables began to murmur about "why the senior staff of five couldn't get along." Outbursts and rude exchanges

---

9. Wheatley, *Leadership and the New Science*, pp. 55–56.

between staff were audible in the halls of the church, and members were concerned. Staff were neglecting to "put equipment away" and "were leaving the microphones on." These negative particles were infusing the invisible environment and creating an atmosphere that was heavy and difficult for a planning session that was supposed to address the future of the congregation.

These invisible fields are dynamic. As messages are given, expanded upon, clarified, and discussed, the energy space changes. Planners affect this invisible field of energy space and are affected by it. The collective and individual energy of planners impacts and shapes invisible fields.[10]

What if congregational space were filled with energetic, imaginative "invisible fields"? There would be an end to contradictory messages, and an end to the "jumble of behaviors and people going off in different directions, with no clear or identifiable pattern."[11] There would be an end to the waiting until most of the congregation is ready to change to begin planning efforts.[12] Instead of the waiting there would be an active engagement with the environment and the messages in the invisible field.

For example, when the purpose of the congregation is unclear, religious education may include vacation Bible school and Sunday school. When all the teachers in the Sunday school have been teaching since they graduated from high school, chances are there is a message in the environment about recruiting, training and keeping teachers. When services are held on only one day of the week, when there is probably a message being given. Scanning our congregational environment for invisible fields may offer clues to leadership needs for a new model of planning in religious education.

EXAMINING FOR INVISIBLE FIELDS WHEN PLANNING IN RELIGIOUS EDUCATION

How can invisible fields be examined? The first time a planner begins the task of planning there are skills and behaviors that need to be addressed. How much time will the planning require, who will participate, why was this planning effort initiated in the first place? Many questions add to the

---

10. Ibid., pp. 56–57.
11. Ibid., p. 57.
12. Ibid., pp. 49–53.

understanding of why at this particular time a planning effort in religious education needs to be undertaken. During the planning process, other learnings and needs emerge: Do members of the planning team listen to people in the congregation? Are members of the planning team beginning to trust one another? How are decisions being made? Is the team making progress in managing conflicts? For a planner, understanding these dimensions is different from knowing how to manage a planning process of steps, time lines, and budgets. These elements can constitute an invisible field of trapped or released energy for a planning team.

This chapter will explore five invisible fields for religious education planners: (1) chaos as a desirable state, (2) planning as an expression of resilience, (3) diagnostic question formation as the beginning of listening, (4) creativity and imagination as awakeners of the soul, and (5) transition as a pathway to change. Each of these elements is present in the congregational environment to some degree. The challenge for planners of religious education is to excel in releasing trapped energy hidden in invisible congregational space.

Chaos as a Desirable State

Most religious education planners want stability in their religious education planning process, not chaos.[13] This desire to hold programs, events, and people stable is a planner's nemesis because the desire for stability reflects a hollow hope rather than a realistic practicality.[14] Stability suggests that the parish environment include programs that work, events that people enjoy, along with positive attitudes and behaviors in congregational life and in the community. Conflicts would be nonexistent, problems would never reach the stained glass windows, and the future of religious education would take care of itself. Life would be idyllic in such a parish.

The reality for most planners is that chaos exists. The footprints of chaos can be seen in statistics that show serious numerical decline in mainline denominations. People are changing jobs, marriage partners, homes, and countries with more frequency than ever before. What we value, believe, and live out is being challenged, our sense of right and wrong is being questioned, and the opportunities for congregational life are more open than ever before. It is nonsense to deny the presence of

---

13. Mintzberg, *Rise and Fall of Strategic Planning*, pp. 184–86.
14. Ibid.

chaos and the need to develop planners who acknowledge, anticipate, and respond to chaotic times.

Edward Lorenz, a research meteorologist working in the field of weather forecasting, came across the phenomenon that is known as "chaos." Behavior that appears to be random and unpredictable proceeds with precise and "often easily expressed rules."[15] Newtonian laws of nature that suggested order, sequence, and stability were challenged to include nonlinear systems that are more like walking through a maze with walls that rearrange themselves continuously.[16] Chaos for Wheatley is "the final state in a system's movement away from order."[17] There is in fact order without predictability. There are also boundaries within chaos, which Lorenz refers to as "windows of order inside chaos."[18] A basic understanding of chaos offers some hope for reducing the fear of chaos in congregational life that is encouraged through planning endeavors.

What if leaders decided as a congregation to embrace chaos instead of striving for stability and equilibrium? Planners in religious education have participated in chaos for a long time. What if chaos were welcomed, acknowledged, and studied? What if leaders and planning processes were developed with the knowledge that chaos is part of the fabric of our world? In fact, what if chaos leadership skill sets were developed?

The scientists who were the first chaos theorists shared certain sensibilities. Instead of looking for regularities, they kept an eye out for new patterns. They had a "taste for randomness and complexity, for jagged edges and sudden leaps." They believed that they were looking for the whole.[19]

First experiences with chaos led scientists to transform their way of thinking. Changed assumptions and thought processes, an openness to observation, to possibilities and to new patterns emerged as a result of their experience with chaos.

Disorder exists.[20] Disorder has a valuable role in planning. Ignoring disorder usually does not eliminate the behaviors that accompany it. Planners desire regularity. Planners develop skills expecting cycles,

---

15. Edward Lorenz, *The Essence of Chaos* (Seattle: University of Washington, 1995), pp. ix–xii.
16. Ibid., p. 24.
17. Wheatley, *Leadership and the New Science*, p. 122.
18. James Gleick, *Chaos: Making a New Science* (New York: Penguin, 1987), p. 74.
19. Ibid., p. 5.
20. Gleick, *Chaos,* p. 68.

events, patterns to repeat. The skill needed is the ability to discover the irregularity in behavior and to generate a realistic possibility for working with the disorder. A baker who does not know about oven temperatures is not a good baker. When chaos heats up congregational life religious education planners need to lean into the chaos, the disorder, to extract and release energy and possibilities.

Effective planning in religious education includes the ability to manage contradiction and tension in congregational life. The very desire for stability affects the way planners think about instability.[21] In religious education planning has worked toward creating stability or equilibrium rather than developing leadership skills that identify the causes of the chaos or disequilibrium.

Closed systems maintain equilibrium. Open systems thrive on nonequilibrium. In closed systems there is a "laziness law" that is observable as a system closes down. There is no energy left to give. The internal life can produce nothing. Life is truly going downhill. On the other hand, open systems stay energetic and viable by maintaining a state of nonequilibrium. By keeping their system off balance organisms can change and grow. "They participate in an active exchange with their world, using what is there for their own renewal. Every organism in nature including us, behaves in this way."[22]

The state of chaos in congregational life includes an understanding of open systems. If planners in religious education need some sense of security when planning in open systems, perhaps there is comfort in the knowledge that there are boundaries within chaos. In fact, chaos and order exist in tandem. Although stability is never guaranteed, there is confirmation that "chaos always conforms to a boundary."[23] A planning challenge is to figure out the new emerging patterns that are clues to new ways of responding to open systems in religious education. The Newtonian model, a seventeenth-century physics theory, operates with images that govern the universe. This theory separates things into parts and believes that influence occurs as a direct result of force. This theory produces a characteristic mind-set: old rules hold true and if the old rules were still obeyed the good old days would return to the parish. The new science model is based on principles extracted from quantum

---

21. Stacey, *Managing the Unknowable,* pp. 44–48.
22. Wheatley, *Leadership and the New Science,* pp. 76–78.
23. Ibid.

physics, chaos theory, and evolutionary biology. If energies were placed in the development of leadership ready to respond in such environments, what might emerge? Comparing leadership characteristics for religious education planners of a Newtonian model with leadership characteristics of the new science model begins this attempt at uncovering an invisible field.

Figure 9.1
Leadership Characteristics for Religious Education Planners

New Science Model	**Newtonian Model**
CHAOS	
• is a process of becoming	• is a state of being
• has open systems, nonequilibrium	• has closed systems
• expects irregularity	• expects regularity
THE CHALLENGE IS	
• to create a field—a rich partnership congregational space by clarifying, discussing, modeling, and filling space with consistent messages we care about	• to experience contradicting and conflicting messages, creating dissonance and behaviors that mirror contradictions and a loss of partnership
• to integrate planning as a whole religious education endeavor	• to separate planning into numerous efforts of religious education

Planning as an Expression of Resilience

The reality of many congregations is that communities are changing, membership is dwindling, budgets are tighter, and programs attract fewer people than they did a decade ago. These are warning signals. While religious educators were preparing for the parish to repeat its annual programs, "change" moved into the congregational neighborhood.

Conditions dominated by change call for resilient planners. Resistant planners are dangerous to the future of religious education because they keep the congregation embedded in the historical and traditional ways of congregational life. If new traditions are to be created, religious education planners must risk beginning on a new page, writing a new script, imagining what no parish has done before. Resilient planners will lean into the congregational resistance factor and will work in the midst of it.[24]

Resilience leadership characteristics includes an ability, a passion, and a desire to plan in times of ambiguity, turbulence, and discontinuous change. Resilience includes viewing congregations as self-renewing systems.[25]

Chaotic times demand planners who are resilient. Leadership for this time and place is about the capacity for resilience rather than the ability to create stability. Change, flexibility, and imagination are greatly needed in the leadership of religious education. Instead of holding onto the tradition and as-we-have-always-done-it attitudes, we need to do spring housecleaning, to see the essence of who we are as religious planners. Some things need to be dragged out to the curb. We need to enlarge our recreation space and reduce our storage space.

There are times in the life of a congregation when planners stand at a crossroads between death and transformation. Scientists call this the bifurcation point.[26] Religious education planners have reached this bifurcation point, the point at which the system has the highest potential for creating a future.[27] When the parish is living in a neighborhood that is in transition and there is incredible resistance to change, planners know the bifurcation point has been reached. In fact, those who study chaotic dynamics "discovered that disorderly behavior of simple systems acted as a creative process."[28] Religious education planners who live through this bifurcation point pull forth energies that form new dimensions of congregational life. A new way of being in the community emerges, a new vision is claimed, and from that moment on, congregational life is forever changed. Without the resilience factor planning becomes static and lifeless.

The resilience dimension in planning is one reason why step-by-step planning processes must be used with caution. There are always some unknowns that are contextually unique to a given region and affect the

---

24. Stacey, *Managing the Unknowable,* pp. 198–203.
25. Wheatley, *Leadership and the New Science,* p. 88.
26. Ibid., p. 96.
27. Ibid.
28. Gleick, *Chaos,* p. 43.

way a plan is implemented. It is not always possible to anticipate each and every new wrinkle.

Resilience is defined as "tending to regain strength or high spirits after weakness," "bouncing or springing back into shape, position . . . after being stretched, recovering strength quickly, buoyant."[29] Perhaps the word is not quite adequate to describe what it is like to plan in today's church. Resilience suggests never going back to the original position or shape. When resilience occurs during a time of change, a different shape emerges. There is no return to the original shape or position. Developing the quality of buoyancy, which is the "the power to keep something afloat, resilience of spirit,"[30] appears to be a viable challenge for religious education planners.

What if planning in religious education were seen as an expression of resilience? What if religious education leadership were expected to be dynamic rather than static? What if parishes anticipated change as a way of creating new pathways? What if planners had a voracious appetite for ambiguity because it challenged parishes to see new connections and dynamics? What if religious educators assumed that each planning session involved some rethinking and flexibility, since most environments deliver more chaos than stability to our doorstep? What if religious leaders were encouraged to risk? What would planning in religious education look like as a result of religious education leaders' responses to these and similar questions?

If ambiguity, chaos, and a lack of clarity as an environment can be lived in rather than resisted, religious education planners will be able to discern multiple future pathways and the congregation will in fact be in a self-renewing mode. Most congregations have the capacity to be a self-renewing organization. Maybe, when chaos reaches its peak and the internal, natural way of organizing is threatened, the system erupts. Science tells us that this is the way an organization calls attention to itself as a way of creating a point of bifurcation, which is a time of decision making. Although the possibility of transformation exists at this point, the usual practice of religious congregations is to stabilize the congregation, whatever that may mean. Instead of creating

---

29. *Webster's Third New International Dictionary,* s.v. "resilience" (Chicago: Lakeside, 1966), p. 1932.
30. Ibid., p. 189.

stability, planners may well be closing off the potential that exists for the congregation to open up to the future.

These concepts about self-renewing systems, chaos theory, and bifurcation points are new territory for most of us. If each person is to be more than a cog in a large machine, planners in religious education need to create and imagine an image other than parts and pieces of a machine. Wheatley suggests that these new concepts are like clouds: they appear in the sky, they move about and at times transform into various shapes. Clouds are self-organizing in that they can form a hurricane, a rain front, or a thunderstorm. Organizations are capable of such transformation and are self-organizing in their environments. "And we would do well to take clouds more seriously. They are spectacular examples of strange and unpredictable systems, structured in ways we never imagined possible. After all, how do you hold a hundred tons of water in the air with no visible means of support? You build a cloud."[31]

Diagnostic Question Formation as the Beginning of Listening

Questions are often more valuable to religious education planners than answers. Diagnostic questions elicit the assumptions that underlie congregational life. The skill of diagnostic question formation is predicated on the planner's ability to listen to the needs of the people in our congregations and communities.[32]

Each year I teach several planning seminars for leaders in profit and not-for-profit organizations. One module of the planning seminar is called "Spin the Blahs." Persons pair off into groups of twos with one member playing the role of a medical doctor and the other a patient who has come into the office with a case of the blahs. The patient decides what ailment he or she has and the doctor begins the conversation with diagnostic questions. The patient is asked to answer each question without giving more information than the doctor requested. In this exercise, it is easy to hear the patterns of questions and easy to see who understands how to formulate a question that requires more than a yes or no response.

---

31. Cole, *Sympathetic Vibrations:*, pp. 97–104.
32. Stephen D. Brookfield, *Developing Critical Thinkers* (San Francisco: Jossey-Bass, 1987), pp. 92–97.

Figure 9.2
Resilience

New Science Model   **Newtonian Model**

RESILIENCE

- recovers strength after being   - maintains the previous state
  stretched

- assumes that chaos will   - assumes that the planner will
  necessitate a flexible response   work to stabilize the
  in which the planner   organization
  anticipates change

THE CHALLENGE IS

- to anticipate a bifurcation point   - to reach the bifurcation point
  and see the potential   and respond out of fear rather
  transformation possibilities in   than imagination
  the situation

- to see parish life and planning   - to block the self-renewing
  as having a self-renewing   capacity of planning in parish
  capability   life

- to expand the appetite for   - to deny the reality of
  ambiguity, looking for patterns   information and trends that are
  to guide the planners   ambiguous

- to revel in resilience and to   - to resist the need for resilience,
  learn ways of developing   ignoring anything that is
  leaders who possess this   unclear
  quality

- to develop the quality of   - to keep the present course
  buoyancy in planners; to mark   regardless of danger signs
  the channel for the future

- to experience the following as   - to experience the following as
  components of a self renewing   opposites which conflict:
  system:

      change   stability
      newness   continuity
      autonomy   control[33]

33. Wheatley, *Leadership and the New Science*, pp. 75–99. I developed this figure from the work of Wheatley.

The skill of diagnostic question formation takes time and effort to develop. The intent is to identify the heart of an issue or need. This skill is inseparably linked with the capacity to listen. The voice is less important than the ear. Planning in religious education needs leaders who are proficient in diagnostic question formation and have the capacity to hear the response. This is an invisible field in that there are numerous informal opportunities for religious leaders to ask questions and listen to responses.

Creativity and Imagination as Awakeners of the Soul

Religious education planners are awakeners of imagination. We are the ones who will participate in the creating and imagining of the new.[34] What if we increased our capacity for creativity? What if our energies were directed toward planning ways to awaken the soul? Some of the basic skills of creativity include: (1) rejecting standardized ways of problem solving, (2) being interested in a wide range of related and divergent fields, (3) seeking multiple perspectives on a problem, (4) viewing the world in relative and contextual ways instead of universal and absolute ways, (5) using trial-and-error methods for experimenting with approaches, (6) orienting to the future and embracing change as a valuable potential, (7) being self-confident and trusting one's own judgment.[35] The creative process is essential to the critical thought process. One stimulates the other. Until the mental processes are shaken from the deep slumber of same-old, the imaginative possibilities will be unavailable.

The point is not necessarily to conceive of the new by ourselves but to develop ways of encouraging planners to think imaginatively and creatively. Letting go of programs, events, or approaches that have lost their usefulness is part of the creative change dynamic.

What is it that keeps planners stuck in old patterns and outdated programs? Perhaps it is an inability to recognize that old practices have a paralyzing effect on congregational life. Old practices worked once upon a time; however, they are insufficient to carry the parish into the future. Futurist Joel Barker suggests that each organization has a set

---

34. Ibid., pp. 114–32. Senge, *Fifth Discipline*, pp. 150–55. Sharon Parks, *The Critical Years: The Young Adult Search for a Faith to Live By* (San Francisco: Harper & Row, 1986), pp. 113–14. In the chapter on imagination Parks discusses Immanuel Kant, Samuel Taylor Coleridge, and imagination as "the composing activity of the mind."

35. Brookfield, *Developing Critical Thinkers,* pp. 115–16.

of rules. These rules or paradigms set the behaviors and practices for the group. These rules create boundaries in the way the organization works. Unfortunately, planners and congregations become paralyzed by these paradigms.[36] But the paradigms become outdated. The rules become obsolete before religious education planners are ready to give them up. Instead of constantly scanning the horizon for new ways of doing planning in religious education, planners are content to reproduce last year's ministry with a few minor changes.

Congregations that were effective forty years ago are dying today. Numbers are diminishing, leaders are weary, and the congregation has yet to discover anything new that it can offer. This is where creativity and imagination come in. Engaging our brains in new ways takes energy. "The brain is a rigid information-sorter that needs a little side-pushing to put the imagination in gear."[37] Children's painting adorn walls and refrigerator doors. Each new creation draws kudos from everyone. As children grow up they find few opportunities to display what was going on inside. What forms are there that reflect what is going on in the soul? Planning in religious education must reach the soul level. Creativity is one way to stimulate the conversation of the soul.[38]

Planners in religious education need a new to be introduced to the creative thought process. It is a discipline of the mind to encourage planning teams to distinguish generating ideas from judging ideas because most of the time ideas are presented and are judged immediately. The McNellis Creative Planning Company calls the separation of these two functions pure form thinking.[39] When participants know that their

---

36. Joel Barker, *Future Edge* (New York: William Morrow, 1992), pp. 84–92.

37. Edward DeBono is considering Indianapolis as the international headquarters for his World Center of New Thinking. In an article "Worldwide 'Think Tank' May Locate Here" *The Indianapolis Star*, 10 December 1994, p. B3, DeBono describes his plans for Fort Harrison.

38. Thomas Moore, *Care of the Soul: A Guide for Cultivating Depth and Sacredness in Everyday Life* (New York: HarperCollins, 1992), p. 302.

39. The McNellis Company specializes in teaching leaders an approach to planning called "compression planning." In my opinion, this approach to planning is by far superior to any approach I have seen for creating and imagining as well as for gaining ownership to implement what is generated. The excellence in this approach can be attributed to creating and maintaining an environment that encourages creativity, and realistic thinking without sacrificing either. Every planning session includes a skilled facilitator who encourages contributions from all participants while maintaining a clear focus for each planning session. The approach also teaches the pure form environment which is necessary for both lateral and vertical thought processing. The McNellis

ideas will be allowed a space without being judged, their participation and imaginative contributions increase. The converse is also true. When ideas are judged with no allowance for developing them, most bright people withhold their ideas. If a person's ideas are continually met with responses like "we tried that," "there isn't money in the budget," or "it's too complicated," idea generation will cease.

DeBono suggests that both the vertical and the lateral thought processes are needed to generate new ideas or to bring forth new resolutions to old problems. Vertical thinking is accessed when the most probable, most likely, and most reasonable pathway is desired. Being right is important at each step or phase of the plan. When something new is desired, lateral thinking is used. The lateral thinker creates multiple ways or approaches, knowing that there may be something emerging or there may not be. The probability of uncovering a clear pathway using the lateral thought process is less likely than when using the vertical thought process. However, imaginative potential increases with use of the lateral thought process. In fact, anything that is uncovered using lateral thought processes may appear fresh and new.[40] It is unlikely that anyone could have identified the new idea if the group had not used such a low-probability route.

DeBono suggests that digging a new hole is not accomplished by digging deeper in the same space. Most experts in a particular field are found at the bottom of very deep holes.[41] Lateral thinking encourages planners to dig in new places. For example, lateral planners could find people who know little to nothing about some event or program and ask how they would approach the plan. Generating a variety of options or looking at the plan from numerous perspectives uses different thought processes. When new planning skills are used to develop creativity, new possibilities for religious education will emerge in the planning process. Both skills—generating new ideas using vertical thinking and developing ideas using lateral thinking—are needed by religious education planners.

The leader of a group of planners in an urban ministry asked the group to think from the minds and lives of different people in order to shift

---

Company can be contacted by calling 800-569-6015. They instruct planners from for profit and not-for-profit organizations.

40. Edward DeBono, *New Think: Unlock the Awesome Creative Powers of Your Mind* (New York: Avon, 1967), pp. 11–16.

41. Ibid., p. 14.

their perspective. If Mother Teresa of Calcutta were to slide her chair up to this planning table, how would she contribute? The group decided that she would not be stopped because she did not have a building to work from. Her ministry would go into the streets. Often what seems initially to be madness offers new perspectives and options.

Developing techniques that encourage both vertical and lateral thought processes are a way to release potential stored-up creativity.[42] Since most adults need permission of some kind to think in new ways, it is critical to negotiate with the planning team how the team will work in receiving and judging ideas. I work with a planning company that encourages creativity. We place small very lightweight yellow balls on the planning table. The group negotiates how to use the balls to keep the environment pure. When a group member passes judgment of an idea, any one in the planning session is free to playfully pass, toss, or throw a yellow ball. Negotiating the use of artifacts to keep environments pure is critical in teamworking agreements.

Create artifacts to name behaviors that must end in order for new contributions to the planning process to be made. It was Buckminster

---

Figure 9.3
Vertical Thinking/Lateral Thinking

Vertical Thinking		Lateral Thinking
• develops	IDEAS	• generates
• stacked	BLOCKS	• scattered for patterns
• high	PROBABILITY	• low
• most likely	PATHWAYS	• new patterns of flow
• subscribes to reason	RULES	• diverges from reason (madness/chaos)
• in control of	MIND	• at the service of
• straight ahead	THINKING	• sideways
• same hole deeper	DIGGING	• trying again elsewhere
• necessary at every stage	TO BE RIGHT	• emphasis for conclusion[43]

---

42. Ibid., pp. 175–85.

43. Ibid., pp. 19–34. The figure is not in DeBono's book, but I developed it from his chapter. This is an excellent resource for explaining creativity and how simple exercises can assist in enlarging and changing perceptions.

Fuller who suggested creating an artifact to support a change in group behavior. The use of lightweight yellow balls is a direct effort to create a desirable environment in which ideas are considered and expanded rather than diminished and eliminated.

DeBono tells the story of a man who owned a cat. Having to let the cat in and out became annoying, so the man cut a hole in the door that allowed the cat to come and go at will. When the cat had four kittens, the man cut four more holes in the door.[44] Too often planning is merely a response to what we have always done. Approaching the present situation or future needs in new and imaginative ways means we stop before we repeat historically what we have always done.

How can we begin to rethink, to imagine anew? DeBono suggests four techniques that capitalize on lateral thinking.[45]

1. Predetermine the number of pathways. Since any event, or program, problem can be approached in more than one way, begin by determining how many ways will be examined. Explore multiple ways, since using only one way automatically shuts down the creative possibilities. Two possible ways set up polar opposites which invites people to take sides or to limit their thinking. Three or more options give planners lateral leaping potential. To lateral leap is to give the imagination space to live and create what at present is not spoken or thought. For example, if the planning team is generating possible directions for the congregation's religious education outreach, the planner could suggest, "Can we agree to generating a minimum of twenty ideas? Then we can group the like ideas together and select three that fit our finances, overall ministry vision, and community need."

2. Turn things upside down. Reverse the major issues. Deliberately turn the things upside down by consciously reversing some relationship or issue. If the purpose of the planning session is to resolve a problem, try examining the opposite of what is traditionally considered. For example, if the same planning team from the previous example were present the planner could suggest, "What ideas can we generate to impact the community? What if instead of sitting here wondering we each spent two hours this week asking the community what they need from us as a congregation? What are other ways we could bring the community into the parish? Another example of turning ideas upside down might include a conversation on making it simple for people to volunteer in the

---

44. Ibid., p. 46.
45. Ibid., pp. 95–110.

church. The planner might ask, "What makes it difficult? What if instead of tight criteria and expectations for participation the congregation had no criteria? What if an international volunteer dimension were added to our criteria, the new volunteer plan stating that within a five-year period 5 percent of the congregation would have volunteered in some other part of the world? Or what if instead of trying to buy the adjoining property to expand church space, planners considered using available spaces in different parts of the community?

3. Analogy. "If our mission statement were water how would we experience our mission?" Try converting an abstract situation into a concrete situation through analogy. Note how the preceding question makes a mission statement come alive. "If we wrapped every member of the congregation and community in our mission, what would they look like?" How would behaviors change if we were each wrapped in our mission? How would life be different for us as a parish? The Scriptures are full of such conversations. Scripture compares people to flowers of the field and branches on a tree.

4. Shift of emphasis. This technique shifts the emphasis from one part of a problem to another. In any given problem to be resolved there are multiple parts. Planning creative resolutions often requires an intentional delineation of the major parts of the problem. Shifting from the area receiving the most amount of energy and attention to some less volatile area can eliminate a planning block.[46] Perhaps the issue is not that new people are not coming to our church. What if the question were: What memorable ways could we use to locate new people for religious education opportunities? Recruiting new people is not the church's emphasis. What is done as a response to new people coming to church is the emphasis. What if personal interviews were conducted with the last ten new people who came to our parish—with five persons who did not stay and with five persons who did stay?

Transition as a Pathway to Change
Transition is getting to and getting on the pathway; change is the experience of being on the new path and walking it.[47] Any religious educator with experience in major change knows that the change must

---

46. Ibid., pp. 108–09.
47. William Bridges, *Managing Transitions: Making the Most of Change* (Reading, Mass.: Addison-Wesley, 1991), p. 3.

be secured in the plan and a clear plan of transition must be thought through. Otherwise, the change will bring no demonstrable difference.

Knowing how to manage the change is one issue. Understanding and developing a plan for the transition is the phase of planning that is least understood. "Faced with the choice between changing one's mind and proving that there is no need to do so, almost everybody gets busy on the proof."[48] Some of the basic differences between managing transition and managing change are displayed in Figure 4.[49]

In the implementation phase of planning a team identified four behaviors they wished to change in the way they worked together. Their plan was to attract a new audience and to provide worship experiences designed for this twenty- or thirty-year-old audience's particular needs. The several major planning issues to be addressed were (1) to describe the new behaviors needed by staff and (2) to identify the ways staff could mark the ending of the old and the beginning of the new.

Several questions can be used to begin the conversation when change

---

Figure 9.4
Comparison of Transition and Change

Transition Is	***Change Is***
• "the psychological process people go through to come to terms with the new situation"	• situational—the new pastor, the new member, the new building
• internal	• external
• focus on "the ending that you will have to make to leave the old situation behind"	• "focus on the outcome that the change will produce"
• "the first task of transition management is to convince people to leave home"	• "the first task of change management is to understand the destination and how to get there"

---

48. Ibid., p. ix. This is a quote from John Kenneth Galbraith, American economist.

49. Ibid., pp. 3–32. CRM has an excellent video on change. I have used it with strategic planning teams when they begin to define their vision. The title of the video is "Taking Charge of Change."

and transition are a part of the work to be implemented. Figure 5 displays some of the most critical questions:

Figure 9.5
Change and Transition Questions

MANAGING CHANGE QUESTIONS

What is over?

Why do we believe these changes will make a significant difference?

What has to happen to ensure that these changes take effect?

MANAGING TRANSITION QUESTIONS

How can we support and encourage those who are ready for the change?

What are ways we can resource and support those who are resistant to this change?

What are ways we can mark the ending of the old?

What are our current losses? (these are directly related to this new change)

What are our old wounds? (these may have occurred years ago; but this time of change becomes a resurrection moment for what has never been reconciled)

What are our continuities? (these are resources that served us well in the past; we intend to use them in our future)

What are rituals that can assist us in welcoming the new?

How can we visualize what we are moving toward?

How can we keep the end in sight?

What are ways to separate "old issues" from those related to this transition?[50]

It is complicated to begin the change process. Change issues get tangled up. Old issues and hurts attach themselves to the new issues. Often the resistance that is felt during the transition from the old to the new is not related to this specific change at all. In fact, the resistance

---

50. Some of these questions come from William Bridges's *Managing Transitions* and others are ones that have emerged as a result of my planning with teams over the past thirty years.

is from an old wound or hurt that was never articulated, never cared for, and never resolved. One team member turned to another during such a conversation and said, "This is an old wound, but it has bothered me for three years. I need to say it and be done with it. Then I can go on." In congregations old wounds are often experiences related to past changes that were dictated rather than negotiated with the congregation. Old wounds are related to some violation of the way people felt they should be treated in a faith community. Resistance needs to be clarified. Is the resistance elicited by the present transition or is it connected to an old wound?

Bridges reminds us that rituals and symbols are ways to mark endings. They give a clear message that something is over and something is coming. But creating a pathway to the new requires more than words.

When the religious Order of Mercy became a world order, it sponsored a gathering with representatives from around the world. The symbols, rituals, and liturgies that were used were designed for this historic occasion. The final celebration marked an ending and a beginning. The auditorium was divided by a huge paper drape hanging from the ceiling and concealing half the space. Women religious from each hemisphere had drawn visions of what life would be like when the order became worldwide. These pictorial images made up the wall of paper. Half of the sisters were ushered into the auditorium through a door at one end of the space and the other half came in from the opposite direction. Neither group was aware of the other group beyond the paper divider. At an appointed time each group began to sing. Hearing the voices on the other side of the paper divider became a confirmation that there was more than one hemisphere. Sisters sang and moved toward the divider. They broke their way through the paper divider to reach one another. Two hemispheres were now one in a world order. This moving ritual was recorded and videotaped. It is an example of marking an ending and a beginning in one ritual.

The Spanish conquistador Cortes landed with his men at Veracruz. He realized that his men were highly ambivalent about what they were about to do. In fact, some called the task hopeless. They faced a continent full of adversaries and most wanted to go home. Cortes burned the ships.[51]

---

51. William Bridges, *Managing Transitions*, p. 29.

SUMMARY

Planning in religious education cannot afford an attitude of "it's good enough." Just like the rabbi who appears at the beginning of chapter 1, we need to be awakened to other possibilities. Planners in religious education are in a time of making midrash, a time of encountering, challenging, formulating, struggling to extract the new set of questions. Many wonder what is at stake as planners of religious education step into the abyss of the unknown in terms of the untried and the new. The transformation of planning in religious education as we know it and the renewal of our souls is at stake. The Trappist monk Thomas Merton cautioned against settling for too little. He suggested that no opportunity to transform the work, the home, or oneself should be wasted. Transformation time reclaims "the depths and complexity of our being and the magnificence of our home, the earth. Let us begin. Who will make those first leaps of faith?"[52]

Planning in religious education is an act of faith.[53] The planning process in religious education is pregnant with potential to reform, to transform and to reclaim a contribution to the meaning of life. Persons are searching for ways of knowing God that enhance, inform, and transform our world. People hunger for nourishment for their souls. The soul of planning is that invisible part of planning without which there is no hope. It is time for the invisible to be named and lived!

---

52. Kim McMillen, "The Workplace as Spiritual Haven," in *When the Canary Stops Singing*, ed. Pat Barrentine (San Francisco: Berrett-Koehler, 1993), p. 116.
53. Wheatley and Kellner-Rogers, *a simpler way*, p. 74.

PROFILES OF CONTRIBUTORS

BRADLEY SHAVIT ARTSON currently serves as rabbi of Congregation Eilat, Mission Viejo, California. He holds degrees from Harvard University and the Jewish Theological Seminary of America. His publications include *It's a Mitzvah: Jewish Living Step by Step* (Behrman House and the Rabbinical Assembly, 1995) and several articles. He serves on the advisory board of Shomrei Adamah: Guardians of the Earth.

ELIZABETH FRANCIS CALDWELL is professor of educational ministry at McCormick Theological Seminary in Chicago, where she has been on the faculty since 1984. She is an ordained minister of the word and sacrament of the Presbyterian Church (U.S.A.). She has published extensively, including the co-authored *Prayers of the Bible for a Faithful Journey*, Horizon's Bible Study for Presbyterian Women, 1993.

PAUL M. DIETTERICH currently serves as executive director of the Center for Parish Development, a church-related, ecumenical research and development agency. Dietterich serves as adjunct professor in several seminaries in the United States, Canada, and the Netherlands. He is the editor of *The Center Letter*, a monthly research publication concerned with church transformation. Among his publications are the *Leadership Skills for Church Transformation* series and *Clergy Growth and Church Vitalization*, written with Russell Wilson in 1979.

TRENTON R. FERRO is associate professor and graduate coordinator of the master of arts program and community education at Indiana University of Pennsylvania. He earned his doctorate in adult continuing education at Northern Illinois University, DeKalb, and has been teaching adult education at the university graduate level since 1986. He co-chaired the adult religious education unit of the American Association for Adult and Continuing Education and is currently vice president of the Religious Education Association.

NANCY T. FOLTZ holds a Ph.D. in adult education from the University of Pittsburgh and is an adjunct professor at Pittsburgh Theological Seminary. She is the principal of a consulting and planning firm and has held a variety of leadership positions in religious education. She is contributing editor of the *Handbook of Adult Religious Education*, (Religious Education Press, 1986), and *Caring for the Small Church*,

275

1994, as well as other books and articles. Foltz is a lead planning specialist with the McNellis Creative Planning Company and is the director of the Oberlin, Ohio, Leading Groups Institute.

ESTELLE ROUNTREE McCARTHY is a certified educator and has served the Presbyterian Church at national, regional, and local levels. McCarthy was associate professor of Christian education, Presbyterian School of Christian Education, Richmond, Va. McCarthy has devoted much of her professional life to engaging more effective, faithful teams.

GILBERT R. RENDLE is a senior consultant with The Alban Institute in Washington, D.C. Rendle, an ordained United Methodist clergyman, received his Ph.D. from Temple University in organizational development and group processes. He has served as consultant to congregations in areas of planning, program development, and conflict management. Rendle has pastored congregations and was the director of the Office of Resourcing, the Eastern Pennsylvania Conference of the United Methodist Church.

MARK N. STAITMAN is rabbi of Rodef Shalom Congregation, Pittsburgh, Pennsylvania. He has led the congregation in a transformational process, the Learning Congregation Project, which builds community and investment in the congregation through the shared value of lifelong Jewish learning. He hold degrees from the California State University, Hebrew Union College—Jewish Institute of Religion, and Pittsburgh Theological Seminary. He is the author of many publications, including chapters in *The Pittsburgh Platform in Retrospect* and *Principles of Anesthesia in Pediatric Organ Transplantation*. He is the chairman of the National Conference on Soviet Jewry and is a member of the Conference of Presidents of Major American Jewish Organizations.

DOUGLAS ALAN WALRATH is the Lowry Professor of Practical Theology, Emeritus, at Bangor Theological Seminary in Bangor, Maine. He is a church strategy consultant and serves as consultant to boards, agencies, regional judicatories, and local congregations of various denominations. His book *Making It Work: Effective Administration in the Small Church* (Valley Forge, Pa.: Judson Press, 1994), is one of many publications he has authored. Currently Walrath is researching and writing on the changing image of clergy in American cultures as reflected in American novels published during the past two hundred years.

INDEX OF NAMES

INDEX OF SUBJECTS

collecting, 145–155
  areas of, 146
  inferential learning techniques,
    152–153
  interviews, 148–151
  nominal group techniques,
    151–152
  records, congregational, 147
  surveys, 147–148
  theology and, 153–154
nature of, 131–132, 133–135
  goals and, 131–132
  marketing, 133–134
  selling, contrasted to, 133–134
necessity of, 131
paradigm shift in, 163
purposes of, 135–136
rationale for, 131–133
shared vision model, 157–160
  antidote to data-driven, 158–159
  nature of, 158–159
  steps in, 158
  three variables in, 157–158
  usefulness of, 157–158
size of congregation, 160–162
  influential variable in, 160
  planning style, 160–162
ways of approaching, 136–142
  opportunity model, 139–142
    church leaders and, 142
    competency model, as, 140–142
    preparation for, professional,
      141–142
    steps involved in uing, 140
  problem model, 136–139
    crisis, as distinct from, 136–137
    force field analysis and, 138–139
    playing detective in, 137–138
    problem solving and, 139
New Science model, 260
Newtonian model, 259–260
Nominal group techniques, data collection
  and, 151–152
Normative thinking, 74–75

O.D., *see* Organizational Development
Objectives, contrasted to goals, 108
  see also Performance Objectives
Operational Planning, *see* Strategic and
  Operational Planning

Opportunity Model for Needs
  Assessment, *see* Competency
  Model for Needs Assessment
Organizational Development ((.D.),
  181–192
  characteristics of, 183
  contributions of, 185
  function of, 182
  historical background of, 181
  ministry and, 191–192
  nature of, 181–182
  recent developments in, 185–188
    Deming method, 186
    Senge method, 186–187
  reflections, 189–192
  suggestions for planning teams,
    188–189
  work teams and, 183–185
    human relations movement and,
      183
    learning roles and, 183
Ownership, 135, 231–249
  beyond planning team, 231–235
    apostles vs. Jesus, 231–232
    case study, illustrative, 232–235
      congregational history, role of,
        232
      joint coordinating committee,
        234–235
      priorities, setting, 233–234
      professional education and, 233
  sense of, 135

Paradigm, operating, 122
Patchwork mentality, 29
Performance objectives, 110–111, 120,
  172, 197, 208–213, 239
  decisions, planning and, 120
  enablement, as, 239
  evaluation, as used in, 197, 208–213
    criteria, determination of, 211
    designing, 211–212
    focus, as aid to, 208–209
    identification of, 211–212
    outline of, 209
    process and product, 210
    triangulation, 212–213
    writing, 212
  managing change and, 52
  practical behaviors and, 110–111

discerning, 106
imagination and, 106
individuals and, 238
inspired by, 249
lack of, 168
making real, 234
nature of, 51, 106
people with, 240
performance objectives and, 52

shared, 188
statement, 150

Whims, 111
Work in progress, person as, 82–83
Worldview, 64, 81, 122, 153

Yom Kippur, 82, 87

Z model, needs assessment and, 145

m7081-LL
20